MACHINE GUNS
IN
NARRAGANSETT BAY

MACHINE GUNS IN NARRAGANSETT BAY

THE COAST GUARD'S WAR ON RUMRUNNERS

CHRISTIAN MCBURNEY

THE
History
PRESS

Published by The History Press
Charleston, SC
www.historypress.com

First published 2023

Manufactured in the United States

ISBN 9781467149686

Library of Congress Control Number: 2023932167

Notice: The information in this book is true and complete to the best of our knowledge. It is offered without guarantee on the part of the author or The History Press. The author and The History Press disclaim all liability in connection with the use of this book.

CONTENTS

ACKNOWLEDGEMENTS

Unlike my other books, I did not seek or receive much help from others for this book. But no project of this scope can be accomplished alone. John Taft of Newport was most helpful. He is leading an effort to produce a film documentary about the extraordinary *Black Duck* affair, the story of which appears prominently in this book. His expertise and knowledge of rumrunning in Rhode Island were a tremendous help. From his collection, Taft generously provided to me some useful copies of Coast Guard documents, as well as leads on relevant photographs and books. He also did close reads of two draft manuscripts and provided useful comments and corrections.

I also thank Dennis Conrad, retired from the Naval History and Heritage Command, for reviewing a manuscript of this book. It is the sixth manuscript of mine that he has reviewed that has been published as a book, for which I am very grateful.

Any mistakes remaining in this book are my own.

I extend my thanks to Mark Gall and Susan Kosiba, who performed helpful research obtaining some relevant articles from the *Providence Journal*.

I thank the librarians at the National Archives in Washington, D.C., who assisted me in researching Coast Guard records, in both Buildings 1 and 2.

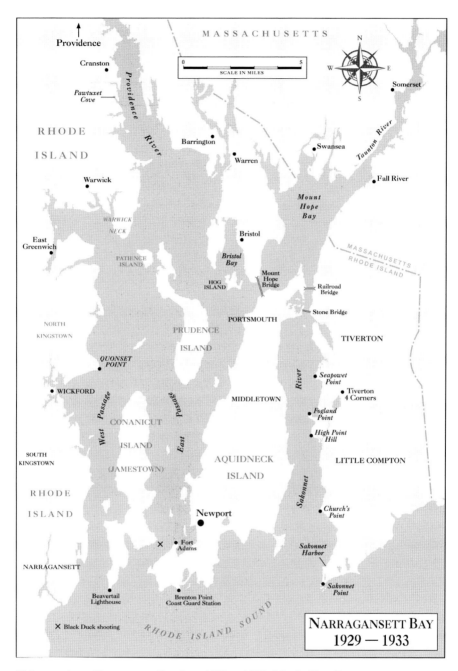

This map shows Narragansett Bay from 1929 to 1933. *Map by Tracy Dungan.*

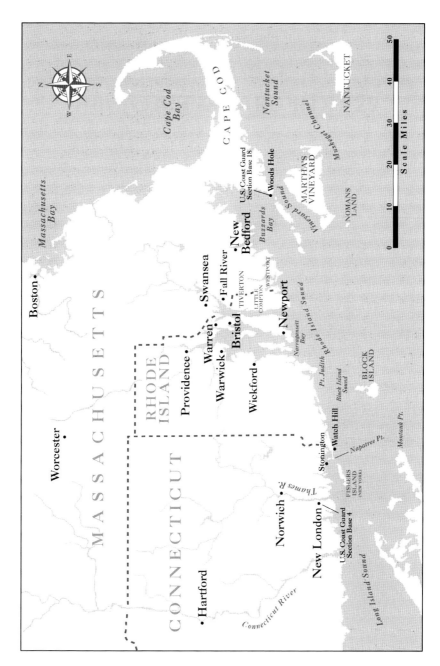

This map shows southeastern New England from 1929 to 1933, from Woods Hole, Massachusetts (where Coast Guard Section Base 18 was located), to Narragansett Bay and to New London, Connecticut (where Section Base 4 was located). *Map by Tracy Dungan.*

INTRODUCTION

During World War I and World War II, numerous army and navy fortifications and artillery pieces surrounded Narragansett Bay, but no shots were ever fired in anger. By contrast, from 1929 to 1933, during Prohibition, Coast Guard vessels fired thousands of machine gun and one-pound cannon rounds…at fellow Americans. The intended targets were crew members on rumrunners who, using speedy powerboats, had picked up illegal liquor from supply ships stationed at "Rum Row"—an area beyond the twelve-mile zone off the coast of southern New England and Long Island. The rumrunners, operating at night or in foggy conditions, would cruise up Narragansett Bay to assigned drop off points to unload their liquor. Because buying and selling alcohol was illegal under Prohibition laws then in force, the profits from a successful voyage could be enormous.

The Coast Guard became the lead federal government agency fighting the "Rum War" at sea. Coast Guard patrol boats insisted on inspecting vessels suspected of carrying illicit liquor, and if they did not stop after being signaled, they were targeted with live ammunition from large-caliber weapons—machine guns or one-pounder cannons.

Sometimes the extraordinary one-sided "battles" were witnessed by Rhode Islanders from the shore. For example, in October 1930, a veteran of World War I, from his house at Watch Hill, told a *Providence Journal* reporter about the Coast Guard's attack on the rumrunner *Helen* off nearby Napatree Beach: "I could see the flash of the one-pounder and I think they [the Coast Guard patrol boats] must have fired it 50 times. Searchlights were flashing along the beach and the reports of the one-pounder and the rat-tat-tat of machine-guns sounded like a battle….I told my wife and daughter to get away from the window."[1]

The Coast Guard was in a difficult position. It had the duty of enforcing federal laws at sea within the waters of the United States, and it did not want lawbreakers to escape simply because they used speedboats. If the Coast Guard had been dealing primarily with speedboats that were illegally importing harmful drugs such as heroin or opium, then having their patrol boats fire machine guns at the fleeing speedboats would not have been particularly controversial. But that was not what was happening during the Prohibition years from 1920 to 1933. Drinking alcohol recreationally remained wildly popular among wide swaths of the population in the United States, particularly in northeastern states, including Rhode Island. Even many public officials—governors, mayors, attorneys general—drank bootleg liquor. Moreover, the crews on the rumrunners typically were not hardened criminals. Many of them were former struggling fishermen or ordinary young laborers, otherwise good people who during the desperate years of the Great Depression saw rumrunning as a chance for making a quick buck. Thus, having Coast Guard vessels fire their machine guns at rumrunners became a controversial practice.

This book will examine the incidents in which Coast Guard vessels fired large-caliber weapons—Lewis machine guns and Hotchkiss one-pounder cannons—at and into fleeing rumrunners in Narragansett Bay and in or near other Rhode Island waters from 1929 to 1933. The source material is primarily contemporary Coast Guard records and newspaper articles.

In the incidents covered in the following pages, three crew members on rumrunners were killed by machine gun fire; one drowned after his boat was machine gunned, caught fire and exploded; another fell off his boat and drowned in mysterious circumstances after his boat was chased and fired upon; two others suffered serious, life-threatening bullet wounds; and eight more received minor or moderate bullet wounds. It is a wonder that more men were not killed and wounded. A total of twenty-nine shooting incidents in which the Coast Guard fired large-caliber guns at rumrunners, striking the craft or probably striking the craft (a few boats escaped so the information on them cannot be confirmed), occurred in or near Rhode Island waters. In several of them, hundreds of machine gun bullets were fired. (See the appendix for a summary of the shooting incidents.)

One Coast Guard officer and his patrol boat will be mentioned more than any others in these pages: Boatswain Alexander C. Cornell and *CG-290*. While in command of this vessel, Cornell ordered the firing of a machine gun at the fleeing *Black Duck*, resulting in the killing of three crew members and the wounding of its captain. Cornell, usually commanding *CG-290*, opened up his machine gun in Rhode Island waters on five other rumrunners: *High Strung*, *Helen*, *Idle Hour*, *Mitzi* and *Yvette June*. In the incident involving the last vessel, the machine gun bullets and one-pounder shells fired by Cornell's patrol boat caused *Yvette June* to explode, killing a crew member. Thus, one aggressive Coast Guard officer was responsible for the most violent and deadly episodes in Narragansett Bay. Still, his superiors at New London's Section Base 4 praised his tenacity in bringing rumrunners to heel and enforcing the laws. Other Coast Guard officers began to imitate Cornell, such as Elsworth Lathan based in Newport; Cecil MacLeod based in Woods Hole, Massachusetts; and Theodore Losch stationed at New London, Connecticut.

In one sense, the Coast Guard officers and crews ordered to enforce Prohibition were not to blame. The Coast Guard was part of the Treasury Department. Most of any blame was due to Coast Guard and Treasury Department policies that authorized Coast Guardsmen to employ large-caliber weapons to shoot at fleeing vessels trying to avoid inspection. When those strict "law and order" policies intersected with the wildly unpopular Prohibition law and the demand for illicit liquor, accidents leading to tragedies inevitably occurred.

On three occasions, in federal district court in Providence, federal judges lambasted the Coast Guard for shooting at fleeing rumrunners. On one of those occasions in March 1932, U.S. District Court judge Ira Lloyd Letts, at the trial of the Rhode Island rumrunner *Eaglet*, called Coast Guard patrol boats firing 470 machine gun bullets at *Eaglet* "a rather sad commentary on the administration of law in this country."[2]

This book will also show that many Coast Guard patrol boat commanders failed to follow the federal statutory requirement for a gun to be fired as a signal, and the Coast Guard policy requiring three blank one-pounder shells be fired as signals, before any machine gun bullets or live one-pounder shells could be fired at a fleeing vessel. In addition, noncompliance with these rules rarely had any consequences. The Coast Guard also had rules requiring Coast Guardsmen firing weapons to be careful not to endanger the lives of innocent persons onshore, but the rules were so vague as to be almost useless guidance.

Another interesting aspect of the incidents described in the following pages is that Coast Guard patrol boat commanders and their superiors were, too frequently, not truthful when it came to explaining the circumstances to the public surrounding the shooting of live ammunition from large-caliber guns at rumrunners.

Chapter 1

PROHIBITION COMES
TO RHODE ISLAND

How did this situation happen, with the channels of Narragansett Bay turning into a virtual war zone on moonless nights from 1929 to 1933? How did it come to pass that three crewmen of the rumrunner *Black Duck* were shot to death by Coast Guardsmen off Jamestown on December 29, 1929?

The story begins with the passage of Prohibition in the United States by the enactment of the Eighteenth Amendment of the U.S. Constitution in 1919. In Britain, Lord Curzon described Prohibition as "Puritanism run mad," while Winston Churchill called it "an affront to the whole history of mankind."[3]

The temperance movement had been strong in America since the 1880s. By the early 1900s, a few states and numerous localities using local option rules, mostly in the South and Midwest, were dry.[4]

Various movements and trends came together to make the prohibition movement a remarkable success on the national level. For one, the period leading up to the passage of the Eighteenth Amendment was a time of excessive drinking. Dank saloons dotted the street corners of many cities. Middle-class and upper-crust reformers resented working-class men squandering their money on local saloons and depriving their families of needed funds. There was also a related belief that excessive drink led to more crime and family abuse and separation, as well as automobile and work accidents. Reformers further believed that by reducing crime and social ills, prohibition would in turn reduce the tax burden created by prisons and poorhouses and improve health and hygiene.

While America had a drinking problem, the do-gooders addressed the problem with a sledgehammer, as opposed to an approach directed at the core issues. Rather than more targeted approaches, such as limiting the number of saloons and their hours and locations, prohibitionists sought a total ban on the recreational use of alcohol.

Temperance was also a way for the rural population in the United States, still significant in the first part of the twentieth century, to assert control over growing urban influence. Moreover, many conservative Protestant denominations, which carried considerable sway in the halls of the U.S. Congress, viewed drinking liquor as sinful and were deeply concerned about the influx of immigrants and hyphenated Americans, many of whom were Catholics. Many conservative Protestants associated Catholicism—unfairly—with excess drinking.

The "dry" forces, remarkably well organized, developed a powerful lobby in the political arena. Those supporting prohibition were not necessarily a majority in a particular state, but in close elections, regardless of party affiliation, by throwing their weight to "dry" candidates, they were consistently able to defeat "wet" candidates. Politicians feared the power of the "dry" lobby—conservative Protestants tended to vote in large numbers in elections. Many women, exercising their right to vote at the state and local levels often for the first time, supported prohibition.

The tipping point in the national dry campaign was World War I. After America declared war on Germany in April 1917, resentment against German American beer makers and Irish American drinkers ran high, as they were viewed as favoring Germany. The German "hun" became the despised enemy, and Ireland was in the midst of its own bloody war for independence against America's ally, Great Britain. Thus, two important pressure groups opposing prohibition were placed on the defensive and remained relatively quiet.

Prohibitionists and temperance organizations managed to convince Congress to approve a ban on alcohol with more than a 2.75 percent alcohol content. The purported reasons were to save grain for the war effort and to protect America's soldiers and sailors, but Congress actually passed the bill *after* the armistice had been declared. Soldiers told that they were fighting for world freedom in Europe returned home after June 30, 1919, to discover that their freedom to have an alcoholic drink had been curtailed.

With momentum on their side, dry activists pushed for a prohibition amendment to the U.S. Constitution. In August 1917, the U.S. Senate voted 65 to 20 in favor of the proposed Eighteenth Amendment. On December 17, 1917, the House of Representatives followed suit, by a vote of 282 to 128.

Two-thirds of the states were needed to ratify the amendment for it to become part of the U.S. Constitution. On January 16, 1919, the Eighteenth Amendment became law after the 36th state legislature, Nebraska, ratified it. The amendment was to take effect exactly one year later.

Most of the amendments to the U.S. Constitution after the Civil War expanded individual rights. The Eighteenth Amendment was just the second one to restrict individual liberties. (The first one was that Americans could not enslave one another.)

The Rhode Island General Assembly never ratified the Eighteenth Amendment. The resolution to ratify the amendment was introduced in the state senate on January 22, 1918. On March 12, a motion to indefinitely postpone consideration of the amendment prevailed by a vote of 20 to 18.[5]

The matter was not reintroduced during the 1918 legislative session, making Rhode Island one of only two states of the then forty-eight states to fail to ratify the Eighteenth Amendment (Alaska and Hawaii were not yet states). Neighboring Connecticut was the other holdout. This was not a coincidence, given that Rhode Island and Connecticut had the two largest percentages of Catholics in the nation, about 76 percent and 67 percent, respectively.[6]

The 20–18 vote in the state senate was close, but that was because the Rhode Island Senate remained, as it had for more than a century, absurdly dominated by the rural towns of the state at the expense of Providence, Pawtucket and other urban areas. Each Rhode Island town, regardless of its population, was entitled to a senator.[7] Thus, for example, in 1925, rural towns with just 8 percent of the state's total population held twenty-two of the thirty-nine state senate seats.[8]

No referendum on prohibition was held in Rhode Island prior to 1920, but if there had been, it likely would have lost resoundingly. The state had a high percentage of immigrants, second- and third-generation hyphenated Americans, and Catholics—groups that generally opposed prohibition. In 1915, fully two-thirds of Providence's total population of 247,660 residents were of foreign parentage.[9] Irish Americans, French Canadian Americans, Italian Americans and Portuguese Americans were mostly Catholics. They did not want to be lectured to by Protestant moralists claiming to be helping them improve their lives.

Something of a referendum was held in the Italian American–dominated ninth ward of Providence, mostly comprising Federal Hill. In December 1918, voters were asked whether or not the municipality should be authorized to grant liquor licenses. The referendum passed with 76.1 percent of the vote.[10] Italian Americans wanted to continue their tradition of drinking wine during meals.

Still, prohibition was not without some support in Rhode Island. Rural areas, many Protestant churchgoers and some middle-class reformers in the state supported the Eighteenth Amendment. The state had a history of supporting local option laws and had even passed a state prohibition amendment in 1886—although the dry experiment was overturned overwhelmingly three years later.[11]

At the national level, Congress had to pass a federal statute to implement the Eighteenth Amendment and provide for its enforcement. The National Prohibition Act, better known as the Volstead Act, passed in October 1919.

The Volstead Act banned importing, exporting, transporting, distributing, selling and manufacturing intoxicating liquor in the United States that had an alcohol content of more than .05 percent. First offenders could suffer fines of up to $1,000 and six months in jail, with penalties increasing for subsequent violations.

The Volstead Act had some major loopholes. The consumption of alcohol at home and the mere possession of alcohol were not prohibited. Thus, Americans could stockpile liquor in their basements for future use.

Alcohol was also approved for industrial, medicinal and sacramental purposes. Catholics used sacramental wine in church masses under the direction of priests. (The Romano Winery in North Kingstown would benefit from this exemption.) Sacramental wine was commonly used in Jewish religious observations at home, thereby resulting in substantial wine circulating in Jewish communities. Each American household was permitted annually an allocation of ten gallons of sacramental wine for religious purposes.[12]

On January 17, 1920, the United States went dry, shutting down the country's fifth-largest industry. In Rhode Island, the Narragansett Brewing Company—the purveyor of ales, lagers and porters—had been founded by six German Americans at Cranston. By 1914, it had become New England's largest beer brewery. Overnight, its brewing facilities were rendered practically worthless, with no compensation offered by the federal government. The company struggled along making and delivering soda and ice—as well as a malt beverage that tasted like and had a similar kick to a porter beer that it was licensed to sell for medicinal purposes.[13]

Liquor seized by law enforcement early in the Prohibition years. *Library of Congress.*

From the beginning, the dry laws were flagrantly violated throughout the country. Bootleggers smuggled alcohol from Canada, stole it from government warehouses or produced their own. Rumrunners in small boats brought to U.S. shores foreign-made liquor carried in supply ships stationed off the United States. Saloons were replaced by illegal speakeasies, which were hidden in basements and office buildings and typically admitted only those with membership cards.

Three federal government agencies tried to enforce the new Prohibition laws. On land, the newly formed Prohibition Unit (later called the Bureau of Prohibition) had the authority to enforce the law. But with just 1,550 federal agents initially and a small budget, it could hardly stem the flow of huge quantities of alcohol being smuggled into the country, manufactured in local stills and served in local speakeasies. Two other federal agencies were also employed against smuggling alcohol into the country, as they historically had the role of preventing smugglers generally: the Coast Guard and the Customs Service.

Rumrunners bringing in liquor from the sea unloaded from "outside" vessels were viewed in some circles as performing a valuable public service. By making available alcohol to the public, rumrunners generally fostered the public's freedom to continue to drink. Without the work of rumrunners in particular, access to good-quality and safe brand-name whiskey, gin and rum manufactured overseas by credible outfits would have been limited. The bootleg alcohol, locally manufactured in secret stills, was usually of poor quality and could sometimes endanger the health—or even the life—of the drinker. Even if the rumrunners' product was sometimes watered, at least the alcohol was made by professional distillers.

Because of this quality, bottles of whiskey and other liquor brought in by the rum boats were much pricier than bootleg beer or gin. Accordingly, often only wealthy elites, including politicians who professed to uphold Prohibition, could afford the imported product on a regular basis.

Rhode Island had all the hallmarks of flagrant avoidance of Prohibition. Its population was heavily Catholic, filled with recent immigrants and second- and third-generation immigrant families and was largely urban. Most of them wanted no one to interfere with their personal drinking habits.

Those looking to profit from continued demand for alcohol quickly came to a startling realization. Narragansett Bay, with its scores of coves and estuaries where small boats could be used to "drop" cargos of illegal liquor at night, was a natural place for smuggling in alcohol. The smuggling operations that arose would serve not only drinkers in Rhode Island but also those in Boston, the rest of New England and even New York City.

Commercial fishing remained an important industry in Rhode Island and the rest of southeastern New England. With their small boat experience and skills, fisherman were ideal candidates to man the rumrunners that were needed. They were highly motivated by the incredible earning potential from rumrunning. Before Prohibition, many commercial fisherman sometimes experienced difficulty keeping their families fed with consistent meals. Coast Guardsmen called fishermen who became rumrunners "bottle fishermen." They were hardly the hardened criminals law enforcement sometimes tried to make them out to be.

The investors and crew members of rumrunners could be compared to the merchants of New England who evaded British-imposed taxes on sugar, molasses and rum in colonial times. Merchants such as John Hancock of Boston and John Brown of Providence did not lose prestige by becoming well known for evading the tax laws. They argued that it was wrong for Britain to impose taxation without the thirteen colonies being represented in Parliament. In many circles, investors and crew members of rumrunners did not lose prestige either by their rumrunning activities. The difference from colonial times was that during Prohibition, fellow Americans had enacted the Eighteenth Amendment and Congress had passed laws to enforce it.

In the early years of Prohibition, Rhode Island was one of the few states in the country not to have passed its own state enforcement law. As a result, its state and local police forces were significantly hampered in enforcing the federal Volstead Act. Meanwhile, just five federal Prohibition agents from the new federal Prohibition Unit were initially assigned to Rhode Island, an absurdly small number given the hundreds of miles of state beaches, coves and other coastal lands that were ideal for landing liquor by sea.

A 1922 newspaper report supporting the dry laws focused on three New England states—Massachusetts, Connecticut and Rhode Island—as being the biggest violators of the National Prohibition Act. The report turned to Rhode Island:

> It is Rhode Island which is the wet spot of New England, this being due, as has been noted previously, to failure of the State Legislature to enact an enforcement law that would bring into play the local police forces.
>
> "The wets," says the correspondent in Providence, "are actively pushing the liquor business. They are kept busy supplying every corner of the State with plenty of 'booze,' proceeding with absolute assurance that they will be able to escape arrest. Everyone knows that it is easy to get and drink liquor without much effort. Near beer saloons do a thriving business and hundreds of stills are said to exist. The liquor saloon has been abolished in Rhode Island, but prohibition enforcement is a joke."
>
> While some social conditions have improved since prohibition, the correspondent notes, the actual amount of crime is about what it previously was. He also writes:
>
> "Superintendent Gilmartin of the Police Department says that there are as many if not more arrests for drunkenness now than there ever were before. Sixty percent of the arrests made in Providence for intoxication were of men who were attempting to drive automobiles under the influence of liquor." [14]

It was reported that when a large national men's association was considering where to hold its convention in 1922, a Rhode Islander piped up and said that while he could not guarantee any cash subsidy for having the next convention in Rhode Island, he did say, "Off our coast is the finest rum fleet in America." That sealed the decision—the convention came to Providence. [15]

In May 1922, as a result of outside pressure, and the fact that its legislature continued to be disproportionately represented by rural towns, Rhode Island finally enacted its own state legislation to mirror the National Prohibition

Boston policemen seize illegal casks of liquor during Prohibition. *Boston Public Library, Leslie Jones Collection.*

Act. Now its state police and town police forces could more effectively help federal Prohibition agents, customs agents and Coast Guardsmen enforce the law.

Even so, Rhode Island continued to be regarded as one of the wettest states in the Union, if not the wettest on a per capita basis. The first time a person was arrested in Rhode Island for the violation of the National Prohibition Act did not occur until 1924.[16]

In April 1924, the National Convention of the Women's National Committee for Law Enforcement, a citizen pro-dry group, met in a hotel in Washington, D.C., to consider the enforcement of the prohibition laws in each state. Louise (Aborn) Peck of Providence, formerly an organizer for the women's suffrage movement, announced that Rhode Island "stands among those [states] in which the 18th Amendment is least enforced." She continued:

> *For this there are many reasons; among them are its great wealth, its large foreign population, the great number of pleasure seekers who spend their summers on its shores, and Narragansett Bay with many beaches where*

is easily landed the bootlegger's supplies for inland states. We have not been aided, as was expected, by the Federal authorities. Many Prohibition officials have been political appointees. All Prohibition officers should be placed under the Civil Service Act, and all liquor confiscated should at once be destroyed and not placed in warehouses to cause bribery, robbery and even murder.[17]

Peck was right to mention the social scale of Prohibition violators, ranging from Newport elite's to recent immigrant families. The former wife of the secretary of the treasury, the fabulously wealthy Andrew Mellon, asked him how to move a case of bootleg scotch from Newport to her winter home in the South.[18]

Those Rhode Islanders who refused to abide by the Eighteenth Amendment were following a long tradition of Rhode Island showing an independent streak. In colonial times, Rhode Island was the first of the thirteen colonies to renounce its allegiance to King George III (on May 4, 1776), and it was the last of the former thirteen colonies to ratify the U.S. Constitution and join the new United States (on May 28, 1790).

Chapter 2

1924

RUMRUNNERS ENJOY SUCCESS
(BUT NOT *VEREIGN* AND *HERRESHOFF*)

For many, in the early years of Prohibition, it was a source of national embarrassment that the Coast Guard had allowed the "outside" supply ships on Rum Row, and their "contact" boats based on the mainland, to operate virtually unfettered. Most of the outside ships hailed from two French-owned islands in Canada, St. Pierre and Miquelon, as well as Great Britain and Bermuda. Newspaper articles detailed how Rum Row operated and how easy it was to run rum illegally.

There were several Rum Rows on the Atlantic coast. The largest ones served New York and New Jersey and extended from Montauk Point, Long Island, to Atlantic City, New Jersey. The one off southeastern New England, serving Rhode Island "contact" boats and those from other southeastern New England ports in Connecticut and Massachusetts, typically extended from south of Nomans Land off Martha's Vineyard to south of Block Island.[19]

The *New York World* newspaper, in its March 8, 1923 edition, ran a story about Rum Row that was subsequently republished in more than one hundred newspapers nationwide. It began with a description of Rum Row, as discovered by newspapermen who were taken on a boat from Newport to Block Island and from there to Rum Row.[20] The article began:

> Out in the Atlantic Ocean, ten miles beyond the three-mile limit and between Block Island, off the Rhode Island coast at the extremity of Long Island Sound, and Nomans Land, there has been lying for the last three weeks a liquor-bearing armada of fourteen or sixteen vessels which has been flooding New York and New England with 20,000 cases of liquor weekly.

More than half the vessels in this fleet are part of the international system of two rival New York syndicates. Both of these organizations ship their liquor directly from England and Scotland in tramp steamships to St. Pierre [and] Miquelon. Here it is transshipped to three-masted Gloucester fishing smacks, carrying 2,000 cases each, which make up the armada off Block Island.

These schooners are operated by a skipper and crews of nine or ten deep-sea fishermen, strong, hardy and courageous. They are all armed with automatic pistols and sawed-off shotguns, although an ordinary strong man, even armed with a club, would hesitate to attack one of these fishermen who had only his bare fists for defense.

The article described the relationship between the investors onshore, the rumrunners and the mother ships:

The signals are arranged between the captain of the vessel and its agent on shore. These financial men, as they are called, make their headquarters in one of the newest and largest hotels of Providence, R.I. Here the purchaser makes his payment and receives a note calling for so much liquor and also gets the station of the vessel and its code.

The purchase is not quite as simple a matter as this, of course. Even if you know that Mr. Smith stopping at the hotel is an agent for one of these vessels you can't call him on the telephone and make a deal. Mr. Smith will instruct the prospective buyer to come to a certain room, and to come alone except for his bank roll.

When you arrive you will find that Mr. Smith is not alone, but has his gunman with him, and seeing this, you will not, if you are wise, argue with him or attempt to carry on the interview after the agent has announced it is closed. That is, not unless you happen to be a gunman yourself.

Not but what the prices will make you feel like arguing. The vessels are mostly laden with Lewis Hunter rye at $54 a case; Peter Dawson Scotch whiskey at $45 a case, and White Horse Scotch at $45 a case. They occasionally have some wines and champagnes, and the Transatlantic always will bring these on order.

Prior to the passage of nationwide Prohibition, the Coast Guard was already burdened performing its traditional tasks of manning lighthouses and saving distressed ships, sailors and passengers at sea. In 1921, for example, the Coast Guard assisted 14,000 persons, 1,600 of whom were in peril.

A speedboat outpaces a small, slower Coast Guard patrol boat in the Atlantic Ocean, 1927. *National Archives.*

The Coast Guard lacked adequate funding, vessels and manpower to assume the additional, mammoth task of enforcing U.S. customs and Prohibition laws at sea, whether on the East Coast, West Coast, Gulf of Mexico or the Great Lakes. In addition, many Coast Guard vessels were small and sturdy, designed to stay at sea in all types of weather, but could not go faster than ten or twelve miles per hour. They were not designed to chase speedboats.

In 1924, President Calvin Coolidge and Congress increased the Coast Guard's budget by almost $14 million. The new appropriations were used to refurbish twenty destroyers loaned by the U.S. Navy to the Coast Guard and to construct more than two hundred cutters and hundreds more other smaller and faster patrol boats.

With the additional funds, the Coast Guard also increased its manpower to man the new ships. Between 1924 and 1926, Coast Guard personnel jumped from six thousand to ten thousand. Needless to say, the thousands of new recruits did not have the training or experience of the veteran service personnel.

The backbone of the fleet became the cutters, 75-foot patrol boats, also called "75s." They could go about eighteen miles per hour and carry a Hotchkiss one-pounder cannon at the bow and a Lewis machine gain on an aft deck. They were typically manned by six to eight men.

Smaller patrol boats, ranging from thirty-five to thirty-eight feet—called "36-footers," "cabin picket boats" or just "picket boats"—were equipped with eight-cylinder gasoline engines that could go even faster than the 75s. But they were more lightly armed, with one or two Lewis machine guns and Coast Guardsmen carrying Springfield rifles.[21] They typically had a crew of three or four men.

According to Rear Admiral Frederick C. Billard, the Coast Guard's new commandant in 1924, the destroyers would be used to track the movements of the Rum Fleet off the shorelines of New York, New Jersey and southern New England. Meanwhile, the battleship gray 75-foot cutters would be used to operate against the smaller rumrunners returning from Rum Row to the coastline after picking up their cargos from the larger "outside" vessels. The picket boats would operate mainly in the bays, coves and inlets, near the landing zones of the rumrunners. A Coast Guard captain gloated, "It's going to be pretty hard for a rumrunner to slip through a [three-tiered] sieve like that."[22]

Beyond dividing the field of battle into the three zones, Billard and senior Coast Guard commanders refused to say more. "We are at war and cannot divulge our plans," was the response from Coast Guard headquarters.[23]

The same boatyards that constructed speedboats for the rumrunners often received contracts to build the Coast Guard's new vessels. For example, Crowninshield Shipyard at Somerset, Massachusetts, received a contract to build ten 75-foot cutters, and Nock's Shipyard at East Greenwich received a contract to build five 36-foot picket boats.[24] The picket boats were equipped with 180-horsepower Speedway motors, which could power the craft to a speed of more than twenty-five miles per hour. The first one, built at East Greenwich, *CG-2202*, was tested at the Watch Hill Coast Guard Station.[25] As will be seen in upcoming pages, these two shipyards built and repaired rumrunners too.

The State Department in 1924 began negotiating international maritime agreements with Great Britain and other countries, extending U.S. territorial waters from three miles offshore to "an hour's steaming distance." This standard was taken generally to mean about twelve miles off the U.S. coast.[26] This made the work of contact boats more daunting. They faced greater difficulties finding their outside vessels, and they had increased exposure on the longer return journey when they were loaded with liquor and unable to move as quickly.

With the additional resources, by 1924 the Coast Guard was able to become more aggressive—and successful—in challenging outside vessels. Initially, the Coast Guard focused on trying to put Rum Row in the Northeast out of business. A favorite tactic was for a Coast Guard cutter to station itself next to an outside vessel on Rum Row and remain in the area. This discouraged contact boats from taking off liquor from the outside vessel, which eventually had to sail to an entirely new area, thus disrupting the onshore operations of the rumrunners. But the Coast Guard lacked the ships to shadow every outside vessel. And crew members did not like being at sea for long stretches without liberty, making it hard for the Coast Guard to retain enlistees.

In March 1925, there were some forty-seven rum ships off the Atlantic coast. After the Coast Guard in May began its first major "offensive" following its buildup, Rum Row was reduced to just ten mother ships. But the Coast Guard still lacked the resources to maintain the intensity of the effort. Outside vessels slowly returned to Rum Row.[27] Still, each year, the Coast Guard, through dint of experience and increased forces, improved its capability of harassing the mother ships on Rum Row, as well as catching and seizing rumrunners returning from them to the U.S. coastline.

In 1924, two incidents occurred in which Coast Guard vessels fired guns with live ammunition at rumrunners operating from Rhode Island.

The first boat steaming from a Rhode Island port was the unlucky *Vereign*. In the early morning of June 5, 1924, the large and formerly luxurious yacht, 130 feet long and with a 12-foot beam, steamed out of Newport. With three funnel stacks and a low raking oil burner, the turbine-powered steam yacht was said to be able to attain a speed of thirty-nine knots per hour. It was at one time declared to be the fastest yacht in existence. That was not the case anymore, but it was still plenty fast.

Vereign had cost its first owner, Gail Borden, the head of Borden Milk Company, $200,000 when it was built by Charles L. Seabury & Company at Morris Heights, New York. Its original name, *Little Sovereign*, was shortened twice, first to *Sovereign* and finally to the even shorter *Vereign*. Upon Borden's death, his estate sold it to the U.S. Navy near the end of World War I on June 14, 1918. For ten months, it was used by the U.S. Navy for patrol duty on the New York coast. In 1919, it was sold to a private party. Now it was a rumrunner operating out of Newport.[28]

After leaving Newport and reaching Rum Row, *Vereign* took aboard an impressive cargo of 1,200 cases of champagne, whiskey and alcohol, later valued at $100,000. But the heavy load also meant the yacht's speed would be cut dramatically in the event of a chase by a Coast Guard vessel.

As *Vereign* headed to the Connecticut shore for its drop off destination, it was spotted eight miles southeast of Block Island by the Coast Guard cutter *Seminole*. This vessel was one of the older, slower cutters that had difficulty keeping up with rumrunners, but it was armed with a long-range one-pound cannon.

As the rumrunner tried to speed away, weaving in a zigzag course, the *Seminole*'s captain, Philip H. Scott, ordered his cutter's one-pounder fired at the fleeing vessel. A blank shot was first fired as a warning across *Vereign*'s bow. When the *Vereign* reacted by going even faster, Captain Scott ordered his crew to fire solid shot. Four solid shots were fired but failed to find the mark.

The luxury yacht *Sovereign* before its days as a rumrunner. *Naval History and Heritage Command.*

Captain Scott then ordered his gun crew to fire explosive shells. The first shell exploded over the vessel's pilothouse. The next shot pierced the window of the pilothouse and exploded inside, disabling the vessel, which hove to immediately. The thirteen-man crew, most hailing from New York, surrendered themselves and the boat.

Lieutenant Rae B. Hall, sent to board the stricken vessel, discovered that John Stack of Brooklyn, New York, the supercargo and one of the investors in the voyage, had been severely injured after the last exploding shell tore away a portion of his right thigh and removed a thumb. The *Vereign*'s captain and another member of the crew had minor shrapnel injuries. Bonds for the captain and Stack were said to have been provided by an outfit in Detroit, Michigan, indicating where the bulk of the ultimate investors were likely located.[29]

John Stack was taken to a hospital in New London. It was reported that as a result of his severe leg wound, Stack would require at least a two-month stay at the hospital. Whether he recovered is not known.[30]

The first time the Coast Guard employed firepower against a fleeing rumrunner in Narragansett Bay may have occurred on the night of November 11–12, 1924. The target was *Herreshoff*, named after the famed yacht-building family from Bristol (but the family did not own the vessel). In this incident, Coast Guardsmen used high-powered rifles and not machine guns. Machine guns were not yet common on Coast Guard patrol boats. When the case came to trial, the firing of guns in Narragansett Bay drew a harsh rebuke from a federal U.S. District judge sitting in Providence.

The story of *Herreshoff*'s capture began when the Coast Guard officer in charge of the Brenton Point Coast Guard Station at the southern tip of Newport received a telephone call from a local informant he had relied on in the past. On occasion, a wily informant, after building up trust with the Coast Guard, would try to send the Coast Guard vessels to the wrong place, leaving an opening for the rumrunner. In this case, the informer claimed to have knowledge that a rumrunner would be bringing in a load of liquor up the Sakonnet River (the easternmost channel in Narragansett Bay) the night of November 11.

The Coast Guard officer in command of picket boat *CG-2204* at Brenton Point suspected that his informer was trying to trick him. That night, the Coast Guard officer motored toward the Sakonnet River. But then, about halfway, he turned his boat around, shut off his running lights and headed back toward the West Passage of Narragansett Bay (the westernmost channel in Narragansett Bay). Waiting in silence in the passage, the crew soon heard in the distance the sound of a powerful motorboat.

CG-2204 gave chase, but then the speedboat turned and headed east for the Sakonnet River. Soon something else strange became apparent: the speedboat was moving too fast and high in the water. Coast Guardsmen determined that it must not have a load of liquor on board and instead was a decoy. The Coast Guard vessel doubled back to the West Passage, in time to spot a second speedboat roaring up the West Passage. This one too was riding too light and thus was also ignored as a decoy.

The Coast Guard commander ordered *CG-2204* to patrol the west side of the West Passage. His decision was soon rewarded. At about 9:30 p.m., he saw in the distance the outline of the 70-foot gas screw yacht *Herreshoff*, a known rumrunner, moving slowly against the shoreline. When its crew found out that it had been discovered and saw a Coast Guard picket boat headed its way, *Herreshoff* veered into the channel and opened its engines. An ensign on the Coast Guard vessel fired a rifle across *Herreshoff*'s bow, to no effect, except to make the steam yacht run even faster.

The Coast Guard commander ordered his sailors carrying high-powered rifles to open fire. Soon bullets banged into the armor plate protecting the pilothouse of the fleeing rumrunner and sprayed into cases of liquor stored on the deck. A crew member on *Herreshoff* turned on its bright searchlight, hoping to temporarily blind the Coast Guard helmsman, but a rifle shot soon disabled the searchlight.

Herreshoff kept its distance from the pursuing picket boat, but after a chase of some twenty miles up Narragansett Bay toward Providence, it was running out of room. Just beyond the Rhode Island Yacht Club, the crew members of the rumrunner ran their boat close to the shoreline, scrambled into shallow water and escaped into the night.

The Coast Guard captain chose not to order his men to fire on the shore for fear of hitting innocent bystanders. But the Coast Guardsmen did seize the rumrunner and its cargo of about four hundred cases of whiskey and champagne. Upon investigation, it was discovered that from ten to fifteen bullets had pierced the quarter-inch steel cover of *Herreshoff*'s pilothouse.[31]

Coast Guard officials must have been concerned about Rhode Islanders hearing and learning about Coast Guardsmen firing high-powered rifles in Narragansett Bay. A justification for the firing was needed. Newspaper reports, most likely following the Coast Guard's lead, informed readers

Coast Guardsmen armed with rifles approach a suspected rumrunner about March 1927, before machine guns were commonly used. Rifles were employed against *Herreshoff* in Narragansett Bay in 1924. *Library of Congress.*

that the crew aboard *Herreshoff* had attempted four times to ram *CG-2204* and, when ordered to heave to, responded with pistol fire aimed at the Coast Guardsmen.[32]

Court cases often expose false claims and reveal the truth, as court submissions and testimony must be made under oath of telling the truth. Not telling the truth could result in the liar spending time in jail.

On June 24, 1925, the wood-paneled federal district courthouse in Providence took on a bustling air. Prosecutors from the Providence U.S. Attorney's Office prepared to make their case to convince the court to grant their request to declare *Herreshoff* as forfeited. The U.S. District Court judge, James Morton, heard evidence that *Herreshoff* had been "riddled with bullet holes."[33]

Herreshoff was defended by an attorney hired by the unidentified investors who owned the boat. The attorney made a weak attempt to argue that the seizure was improper under a technicality, but Judge Morton was not convinced and ordered the boat's forfeiture.

Judge Morton did not, however, let this case pass without a warning to the Coast Guard. During the hearing, a Coast Guard official, under cross-examination, admitted that the crew of *Herreshoff* had not fired on *CG-2204* or tried to ram it. The Coast Guard's information about the circumstances of the rumrunner's capture, used to justify the gunplay in newspapers, was exposed as lies.

Judge Morton further railed from the bench, declaring that the "promiscuous firing by government men on boats that are being chased cannot be tolerated by the government unless the government men first are attacked." He added, as a warning, "Had the shooting incident in connection with the *Herreshoff* occurred in Massachusetts waters under similar circumstances, and any of the occupants had been killed, then the government officers would be charged with murder."[34]

The Coast Guard apparently heeded Judge Morton's warnings, at least for a time. Coast Guard vessels operating in Narragansett Bay apparently did not again fire live rounds of ammunition at a fleeing rumrunner until 1929. From 1929 to 1933, however, as the following pages attest, it became commonplace for Coast Guard vessels to fire Lewis machine guns or one-pounder cannons, or both, at rumrunners in Narragansett Bay.

Chapter 3

RUMRUNNING IN 1929

THE SPEEDBOATS AND TACTICS

Rumrunning syndicates operating from Rhode Island and the rest of southern New England were well organized by 1929. Typically, they purchased or hired an "outside" vessel (also called a "mother ship") that was loaded with thousands of cases and sacks of liquor from Miquelon or St. Pierre, two remote French-owned islands that sit about sixteen miles off the coast of Newfoundland in Canada. Occasionally, an outside vessel came directly from Great Britain or British-controlled Bermuda. The outside vessels would be stationed beyond the twelve-mile zone, where they could not be interdicted by U.S. Coast Guard vessels. The outside vessels that worked with contact boats from southeastern New England used the Rum Row extending from Nomans Land off Martha's Vineyard to south of Block Island.

On assigned nights, the syndicate would send rumrunners from the coast to meet the outside vessel stationed on Rum Row. There the outside vessels unloaded contraband liquor onto the speedboat. For ease of handling at sea, most of the bottled liquor was in burlap sacks, which had replaced heavier and bulkier wooden cases. Then the speedboat would rush to the coastline, looking for the designated cove where the sacks would be unloaded onto a wharf or a beach. From there, waiting trucks would be loaded with the liquor. Sometimes touring cars that had been tinkered with to create hidden cargo spaces for liquor were used—the cars were faster, and state policemen would be less likely to suspect them of carrying illegal liquor.

Ideally, the syndicate preferred the vehicles to be driven directly to illegal liquor wholesalers or retailers. Sometimes, they instead had to drive to local hideouts where the valuable cargo would be stashed until it could be sold and distributed.

Coast Guard boats could harass the outside vessels beyond the twelve-mile zone, but they could not arrest the rumrunners unless they saw them being loaded with illicit contraband. Thus, the Coast Guard also focused its operations on trying to intercept the returning speedboats. After 1924, when the Coast Guard's budget was increased substantially, the Coast Guard began to experience some success.

By the late 1920s, rumrunning syndicates had developed professional, business-like skills to evade capture. Most crucially, they had developed fast speedboats. At the beginning of Prohibition, many of the rum boats used to bring in the liquor from offshore were slow fishing boats and motorized yachts. But after the Coast Guard significantly upgraded the vessels it used to try to interdict rumrunners in 1924 and 1925, and with the longer distances needed to reach the outside vessels, rumrunners realized that they had to use faster boats.

Suddenly, dozens of streamlined speedboats were manufactured at boatbuilding yards in southern New England, such as Crowninshield Shipyard at Somerset and Nock's Shipyard at East Greenwich. They were driven by powerful marine engines. Often two or three or even four engines were installed on a single speedboat. Sterling engines were popular with rumrunners at first.

Liberty engines converted to marine use became even more prized by rumrunners. Liberty engines had been used by the U.S. military as airplane engines during World War I. After war's end, with a huge surplus of the engines, the U.S. military sold them at auctions. Rumrunners purchased them in droves, often for cheap prices.

By 1925, the new speedboats were in use. One newspaper reporter who investigated the rumrunning industry that year wrote:

> [M]ost of them are about 36 feet in length and with a capacity of 200 cases of whiskey. The slowest of the craft, with 800-horsepower engines, can "do" 35 miles an hour without a cargo, and better than 30 when fully loaded. The fastest, most of them with twin Liberty motors, with a combined horsepower of 1160, travel as fast as 40 miles an hour.[35]

Coast Guard officers wanted Congress to pass a law outlawing the sale of Liberty engines, but nothing was ever done about it.[36]

By 1929, Packard engines had become another preferred motor. Rumrunners took note when the world's fastest boat, *Miss American VII*, built and driven by millionaire sportsman Gar Wood of Detroit, broke the speed record by going 93.12 miles per hour, using two 1,100-horsepower Packard Motor Car Company engines.[37]

The weight of the speedboats was also closely monitored. According to one investigative newspaper reporter, "Every cleat and sheet of copper that goes into these boats is weighed with the nicety of a jeweler's scale. Each boat must weigh so much and no more, barely enough to counterbalance the engine, which is huge for these small craft."[38]

On the other hand, the rumrunners were not solely about speed. They also had to have deep enough drafts so that they could carry a decent-sized load of liquor from the outside vessel to the shore. Thus, strong engines were needed to keep the speed when a rumrunner was weighed down by a large load of liquor. The same newspaper reporter added, "The boats are built for seaworthiness when loaded. It would not be so bad to capsize empty, but no boat builder would risk 200 cases in a tricky craft."[39]

Still, even loaded with illicit cargo, speedboats were often faster than their counterparts operated by the Coast Guard. The speed of Coast Guard vessels had improved since 1924 and subsequent years, but they were still no match for the new, speedy rumrunners. A speedboat captain could typically leave a pursuing craft far in its wake and disappear into the night. But this was not always the case if the rumrunner got too greedy, loading the boat to the brim, including piling up sacks of liquor on the decks and thereby reducing the advantage against pursuing Coast Guard vessels.

Many speedboats had low silhouettes. By riding low, so that the cases of liquor were carried below the waterline, the boats were hard to see on the horizon and difficult to hit with gunfire.

Rumrunners also invested in Maxim silencers, which muffled the sound of a boat's engines. Without them, the roar of three or four powerful engines would easily catch the attention of the Coast Guard. Some mufflers were reportedly so effective that the noise from multiple engines was no louder than a single automobile's engine.

Rumrunners on land also began hiring shortwave radio operators who used coded messages to communicate with their outside vessels. The parties would then agree on a time and place for the speedboat to meet the outside vessel. A mother ship might have been hovering fifteen to twenty miles off the East Coast, only to return within twelve miles on the night of the planned meeting. Unlicensed shortwave radio transmitters were illegal, but that did

The speedboat *Mary* of New York City, a rumrunner emphasizing speed more than cargo carrying capacity. *National Archives.*

not stop rumrunning syndicates from employing them. Some syndicates even purchased small, unregistered planes to spot Coast Guard vessels, but that only helped during the daytime.

Rumrunners adopted tactics to evade being spotted by Coast Guard patrol boats. For one, they preferred to choose moonless or foggy nights to make their runs out to the mother vessels. On the other hand, the weather could not be too rough—when a rumrunner came alongside the outside vessel to be loaded with cargo, no one wanted the waves to damage either vessel.

Rumrunners typically had to leave before midnight in order to reach their outside vessels, be loaded with a cargo of liquor, make the return journey to a drop off spot and have the liquor unloaded from the boat and onto waiting trucks, all before the sun rose. (In the summer months, with shorter days, the contact vessels often left before sunset, occasionally in full view of Coast Guard patrol boats.)

Speedboats carrying liquor on their return voyages at night operated without their running lights on. This was dangerous for both the rumrunner and other vessels operating in the area. The practice violated maritime laws and was one of the charges typically lodged against rumrunners if caught by the Coast Guard.

On return journeys, rumrunners sometimes followed the wakes of regular commercial vessels. This was in an effort to prevent Coast Guard spotters from seeing the tell-tale silver wakes of their speedboats.

In the event a rumrunner was spotted by a Coast Guard patrol vessel and chased, the rumrunner's captain typically adopted one or more of several tactics. First, naturally, the speedboat increased its speed. The captain could also take advantage of his intimate knowledge of shallow coastal areas with sandbars and rocks just below the water's surface, steering zigzagging courses, which could be dangerous for Coast Guard vessels in the dark.

If a speedboat was in danger of being captured, its captain might head for a shallow area along the coast and throw the sacks of liquor, weighted down to sink, into the bay. Many of the sacks were tied in such a way that when rumrunners returned on a subsequent night, hooks could be used to grab most of them that had been thrown overboard. Some outfits even hired scuba divers using breathing tubes to grab the rest.

If a rumrunner had no time to reach a shallow drop area, the captain might still want to throw the sacks of liquor overboard in an attempt to hide the evidence of a violation of the Volstead Act. In addition, casting the heavy cargo overboard made the rumrunner lighter and therefore faster. Finally, the floating cases of liquor were dangerous for pursuing Coast Guard craft, particularly at night when the cases were difficult to see.

A speedboat trailed by a Coast Guard craft could also throw out a smokescreen. This could be done by dropping used crankcase oil in front of a large fan or, more effectively, by injecting a mix of used crankcase oil, kerosene and pyrene directly into the hot exhaust manifold. A smokescreen would blot out the rumrunner, which would then change direction to evade the pursuing Coast Guard vessel. A smokescreen, combined with increased speed and running without lights at night, sometimes worked. If gas was used instead, the effect could temporarily incapacitate the Coast Guard crew. Gas was not often employed because its use made Coast Guardsmen angry, making them more likely to use deadly force.

If rumrunners were fired at, they had one key protective tactic. A knowledgeable source explained it in 1932: "Almost all rum runners plying inshore from the outside ships pile sacks of liquor four or five feet high and several sacks in thickness directly behind the pilot house. These sacks are as effective as sand bags in stopping machine gun bullets and are placed there as a precautionary measure against that very contingency."[40]

One defense mechanism Rhode Island rumrunners did not take was to use guns to threaten or fend off Coast Guardsmen. Admiral Billard testified in

Congress that rumrunning outfits employed "seagoing people, some of them desperate characters, many of whom served in the Allied armies and navies during the World War. These people are armed and will fight if there is chance of advantage by doing so." But there is no known incident in Rhode Island waters where a gun-wielding rumrunner fired at or even threatened a Coast Guardsman at sea. An assistant federal district attorney for Rhode Island who fought rumrunners in court wrote in the summer of 1932, "insofar as I am aware, no rum running vessel and no rum runner on the sea has ever fired a shot in his own defense against constituted authority."[41] Of course, rumrunners knew that if they did that and were caught, their punishment would be much more severe. In addition, with a Lewis machine gun and a one-pounder on board each Coast Guard patrol boat, the Coast Guard was always more heavily armed than the rumrunners.

Rummies sometimes carried rifles or pistols—and sometimes even illegal hand-held machine guns—on board their craft. But they did so in order to drive away hijackers who might try to steal their liquor at sea or at the drop zone. The rumrunners usually jettisoned any guns into the sea before they were captured by a Coast Guard vessel.

Equipment used to produce a smokescreen found on board the rumrunner *Dart* in 1931. *National Archives.*

If a captain and crew, and their boat, were captured by the Coast Guard, they also had mechanisms to get back into the rumrunning game. For one, the investors in rumrunning outfits typically hired experienced criminal attorneys in Providence and Newport to represent their crew members charged with violating federal laws. Investors would also provide bail money to release crew members from jail and would pay their fines.

Rumrunners had the benefit, particularly in the early years of Prohibition, of facing criminal penalties that were often mild. In the early years, a first- or second-time offender might receive a twenty-five- or fifty-dollar fine and no time in jail. A third-time offender likely faced some jail time, perhaps six months.

Rumrunning outfits also benefited from the unique laws that applied to their vessels when they were seized by the Coast Guard. Once seized, a rumrunning vessel could be forfeited to the federal government and auctioned off to the highest bidder. But the highest bidder was often a man representing the original owner. What's more, the price was often low, as rumrunners made it clear that they would challenge title to their boats purchased by others at auction—and perhaps potential buyers feared something worse.

It was common for a rumrunner to be caught by the Coast Guard with liquor on board, seized and returned to its former owners in short order. For the first two seizures, the rumrunning outfit could post a bond to free the vessel for its return to its owner. For example, the speedboat *Monolola* was nabbed by the Coast Guard in Narragansett Bay in February 1930 and again one year later, but both times the fast vessel returned to the rumrunning trade.

After a third seizure, the rumrunner could be forfeited and sold at auction to the highest bidder. Following another long chase, this one in January 1932, the Coast Guard found *Monolola* loaded with four hundred sacks of bottled liquor and ninety kegs of whiskey. On September 20 of that year, an attorney, likely representing its former New York City owners, bought the speedboat at auction for a mere $505.[42] The rumrunner was picked up a fourth time by a Coast Guard vessel in May 1933, about sixteen miles southwest of Gay Head on Martha's Vineyard, with $25,000 of liquor on board. Only the repeal of Prohibition finished *Monolola*'s career as a rumrunner.

Because the rumrunning business was so profitable for speedboats in the freighting business, the risk of getting caught was not always a deterrent. Assume that the average rumrunner carried 250 cases of liquor. At a pay scale of $5 per case for freighting, the rumrunner's crew could earn $1,250 for four to six hours work. If caught, experienced lawyers would come to their defense. If the boat was seized and put up for auction, the owners could often buy it back. Monetary penalties were relatively light. Thus, one successful trip could easily pay for one bad one. Still, nobody wanted to go to jail.

Who were the investors financing the rumrunners frequenting Rhode Island? No comprehensive study has been done. It is often difficult to tell because the "big money" men wanted to hide their participation from law enforcement authorities. Many of the wealthiest financiers likely were based in Boston and New York; some small-time investors hailed from Providence, Pawtucket and Newport, as well as nearby New Bedford, Massachusetts.

Who were the crew members operating the rumrunners? Again, no comprehensive study has been done. They were not, in Rhode Island at least, primarily or substantially from a criminal element. According to Charles H. Eden, an assistant federal district attorney who served in Rhode Island during Prohibition, "[t]he majority of the smugglers" were not "recruits from our chronically criminal elements. I know that some of them have entered the game for the adventure and high pay offered, I know others who were respectable fishermen before the advent of prohibition and who are still looked upon as respectable in communities where a man would be ostracized for stealing a chicken or pulling another's lobster pots."[43]

Rumrunner crews came from a variety of backgrounds. Daniel Okrent, in his superb study of Prohibition, wrote the following: "A study in the late 1920s established that roughly half of the professional bootleggers were eastern European Jews, another 25 percent Italian, and the remainder a mix of ethnicities, including Polish and Irish."[44] This percentage breakdown was not the case in Rhode Island, but many crew members on board rumrunners were immigrants or ethnic Americans. Several of the known small-time investors from Rhode Island were Jewish. The crews of the rumrunners likely largely reflected those on board the crews of Rhode Island fishing boats. The rumrunner Herbert Cavaca of Tiverton was described in a Coast Guard report as an "Italian fisherman." A substantial percentage of fishermen in Rhode Island and New Bedford were Portuguese immigrants. (One could not always tell the ethnic background of a man by his last name. One crew member who served as a deckhand on several rumrunners in Rhode Island waters, calling himself Henry Johnson, was a Norwegian immigrant.) Perhaps immigrants saw rumrunning as an easy, relatively low-risk and temporary way to gain some wealth in order to move up in the social order. Many social elites of the time, even if secretly, appreciated the efforts of the crews of rumrunners and their investors to bring them quality liquor to purchase.

Chapter 4

THE COAST GUARD IN 1929

ITS WEAPONS AND TACTICS

The efforts of the U.S. Coast Guard to enforce federal maritime laws at sea began with its bases. When it came to enforcing maritime laws in and near Rhode Island waters, the largest and most important station was Section Base 4 at New London, Connecticut. This base was the also a major Coast Guard base for New York and New Jersey waters, as well as for most of southeastern New England. Another major location that had vessels patrolling Rhode Island waters was Section Base 18 at Woods Hole, Massachusetts. Both locations sent out destroyers to Rum Row as well as patrol boats to patrol coastlines, bays and inlets.

During peacetime, the Coast Guard was not part of the U.S. Navy. Thus, its ships and other vessels did not carry the most up-to-date weapons of war. But they did carry plenty of lethal weapons sufficient to sink or destroy motorboats and fishing boats converted to rumrunners. The Coast Guard, compared to the U.S. Navy, possessed relatively small craft that could work in bays and small inlets on the coastline.

The most common patrol boats used by the Coast Guard in Narragansett Bay and other coastal waters were the 75-foot cutters (the 75s) and the 36-foot cabin picket boats. The 75s typically had a speed of about 15 knots (about 18 miles per hour). They had a draft of just 4 feet, allowing them to operate in shallow water. They displaced thirty-seven tons. The cabin picket boats were smaller, had a shorter draft and were much faster at 24.5 knots (about 28 miles per hour).

In early 1929, the Coast Guard stationed fifteen cutters and picket boats at Section Base 4 and twelve at Section Base 18. In addition, three picket boats were assigned for all of District 3, which included the nine Coast Guard lifesaving stations in Rhode Island and several more in southeastern Massachusetts.[45] The Brenton Point Coast Guard Station on Price's Neck, three miles southwest of downtown Newport, was primarily a lifesaving station, but it also had a picket boat, the only one in District 3 used to search for rumrunners.

In designing 75s and picket boats, as previously mentioned, while speed was important for chasing rumrunners, it was not the only important consideration. Seaworthiness and dependability were even more important. These vessels had to be out patrolling at sea almost constantly, even in poor weather conditions, and had to house comfortably the crew members for overnight stays. Thus, due to these design needs, the patrol vessels were never as fast as the fastest speedboats employed by rumrunners.

The Coast Guard could make up for lack of speed with large-caliber weapons. They were the equalizers for the Coast Guard. From 1929 to 1933, the 75s were typically armed with a mounted Hotchkiss one-pounder and a Lewis machine gun, while the cabin picket boats carried just the Lewis machine gun. Of the two weapons, the Lewis machine gun was the most deadly.

The Lewis machine gun was one of the outstanding weapons of World War I. It was also used in World War II and even in the Korean War. It was invented in 1911 by a U.S. Army colonel, Isaac Newton Lewis, but the U.S. military did not initially adopt it. Because he had invented his "Lewis gun" privately, he went to Europe and sold it successfully to Great Britain and Belgium. Ultimately, during World War I, more than 100,000 Lewis machine guns were used by the Allied armies, mostly manufactured and employed by the British. They were used primarily on land, but also in ships and on aircraft. The Lewis machine gun contributed substantially to making World War I the deadliest war in world history to that date.

The Lewis machine gun was a gas-operated system weighing about twenty-eight pounds. The American version used .30-06 Springfield cartridges that were fed by a top-mounted "pan" magazine. The pan would carry typically either forty-seven or ninety-seven rounds (usually forty-seven rounds on Coast Guard vessels). It had a voluminous fire capability and an impressive range. The rate of fire was from five hundred to six hundred rounds per minute, and the weapon could be fired at 2,440 feet per second. The effective range was 880 yards, but it had a maximum range of 3,500

Five Coast Guard 75-foot patrol boats are lined up at East Boston. A Hotchkiss one-pounder is at the bow of each boat, with four of five of them covered. The view of a Lewis machine gun on the port side of each boat is obstructed by the pilothouse. *Boston Public Library, Leslie Jones Collection.*

yards (almost two miles). The machine gun typically had a pistol grip as well as a solid wooden stock and had a sight to increase accuracy. On ships, the Lewis machine gun was mounted, typically on a tripod.[46] On the ubiquitous 75s, they were usually mounted on the port side.

The machine gun could counter the superior speed of the rumrunners. A veteran Coast Guard commander told a newspaper reporter in 1930 that the crews on the rumrunners "knew they could outdistance us [but] the Lewis machine gun on every Coast Guard boat put the fear of God in them." The former Coast Guard officer further said that the 75s were capable of only about fifteen knots an hour, or around eighteen miles an hour, and thus speedboats used by rumrunners could outpace them, even if they were heavily loaded with a cargo of liquor. He continued, "So when we spot a suspicious boat and want to look her over we fire a shot across the bow [as a] signal to heave to. If she wants to give flight, or run, we have the machine gun to show them we mean business."[47]

A navy gunner posing with a Lewis machine gun. *Naval History and Heritage Command.*

After firing some seven hundred rounds at the hull of a converted subchaser suspected of being a rumrunner, Coast Guardsmen bragged about the power of the Lewis machine gun. It could, they said, "penetrate an eighth of an inch of steel plate at a distance of a half of a mile."[48]

While the 75s and picket boats were not fast, they were usually fast enough to employ their machine guns effectively. This was a vast improvement from 1923, when the Coast Guard began using machine guns on some of its vessels against rumrunners, albeit not with great effect due to the slower boats it then used. A newspaper report stated that in early 1923, "Some of the incoming power boats brought news of a Coast Guard vessel, carrying machine guns, that had made several unsuccessful attempts to overhaul them. 'She is too slow,' they said. 'Makes only about 12 knots; poor speed against a boat that will do 22.'"[49] The speedboats in 1923 were so much faster than the Coast Guard pursuers that machine guns hardly fazed their crews. By 1929, those days were in the distant past.

A few Coast Guard boats, mainly captured rumrunners converted to Coast Guard use, carried mounted Browning machine guns. Browning machine guns, invented in 1917, were used by the U.S. armed forces in World War I, as well as in World War II and the Korean War.

The other large-caliber weapon 75s carried was a Hotchkiss one-pounder gun. It was a small 37mm cannon that shot a projectile shell weighing one pound. It was described as a "rapid-fire" gun. It was used by the U.S. Navy mainly as a saluting gun. On board Coast Guard vessels, the one-pounder was mounted in the bow and used primarily as a signal gun—for suspicious vessels to heave to and submit to inspection.[50]

The Hotchkiss one-pounder could be effective at blasting rumrunners speeding away in the distance. One report indicated that it had a range of from five to ten miles.[51]

Some Coast Guard officials claimed that the one-pounder was virtually harmless. That impression was not accurate. One-pounders fired at civilian vessels could cause significant damage. For example, in its February 1, 1926 edition, the *Daily News* of Brooklyn, New York, informed readers about a rumrunner named *Dorothy* that that fled a Coast Guard cutter the previous day. Then "the Coast Guard's seventy-five footer began firing her Hotchkiss one-pounder, tearing ugly gashes in the *Dorothy*'s hull."[52] Needless to say, the rumrunner was overhauled.

One unidentified Coast Guard officer observed how one-pounders on 75s could offset the slower speed of the cutters:

> *Their speed* [twenty-two knots] *is all right. But the chasers will have a one-pounder mounted on each bow and that will more than offset any handicap which the runners hold. I defy any engine in the world to outrun a one-pounder shell if we come within range. And, believe me, we are going to use those guns too.*[53]

In 1925, another unidentified Coast Guard officer told a newspaper reporter about an incident that demonstrated the effective range of one-pounders:

> *Recently an intermediary rumrunner that was once the pleasure yacht of a well-known man was hailed off Block Island. It refused to stop. It was brought to anchor by a shell fired at it from a distance of two miles and a half. The runner's captain lost a leg in the encounter and several others were injured. Twelve hundred cases of liquor, thirteen men, $2028 in cash and the boat itself were seized.*[54]

A navy officer fires a Hotchkiss one-pounder in 1918. *Naval History and Heritage Command.*

One-pound projectiles could be deadly, as was proven in the infamous case of *Josephine K.* The vessel was an outside Canadian schooner that had loaded on board a cargo of liquor from one of the French-owned islands off Newfoundland, St. Pierre. At about 8:00 p.m. on January 24, 1931, a Coast Guard cutter, *CG-145*, about ten miles to east of Rockaway, Long Island, spotted *Josephine K.*, reportedly within the twelve-mile limit from the U.S. coastline.

The captain of *Josephine K.*, William Pike Cluett of Lunenburg, Nova Scotia, Canada, tried to get away but failed. Drawing abreast of the schooner, *CG-145* sounded its Klaxon horn as a signal to heave to. According to his later testimony, *CG-145*'s commander, Boatswain Karl Schmidt, then ordered three blank shots fired from his vessel's one-pounder, to no effect.

Schmidt, manning the one-pounder himself and intending to use live ammunition, aimed it at *Josephine K.*'s pilothouse. He was at a distance of only 150 feet to the outside vessel but claimed to fear that his boat was being outdistanced. Schmidt fired two one-pound shells at *Josephine K.*, hitting the steering mechanism on one shot and the pilothouse with the other shot, the last to devastating effect. The schooner halted and its crew did not resist.

When Schmidt boarded it, a crewman yelled out, "You lousy [swear word], you shot a man." The victim was twenty-eight-year-old Captain Cluett, who died several hours later. A Coast Guard board of inquiry, reporting to Assistant Secretary of the Treasury Department Seymour Lowman, concluded that the death "though regrettable was unavoidable under the circumstances."[55]

Five months after the hearing, Wilbur P. Tally, second in command of *CG-145* when it ran down *Josephine K.* but who was not asked to testify at the hearing, made some spectacular accusations about the incident to a U.S. Attorney. First, Tally said that *Josephine K.* was actually outside the twelve-mile limit when it was attacked. Second, Tally claimed that firing the one-pounder was not necessary, as *Josephine K.* had given the signal that it would stop before Schmidt fired the one-pounder shell at the pilothouse that killed Cluett. Third, Tally asserted that the shooting was also unnecessary because it was apparent that *CG-145* was faster than *Josephine K.* and could easily overhaul the rumrunner. (This claim was proven true in a test race between the two boats in New York Harbor several days after the firing.) Tally added about Schmidt, "I knew his reputation for going gun-crazy, so I locked the machine gun. I was afraid he'd let loose with that too." Fourth, Tally said that Schmidt's claim that he had fired three blank shells as a warning before pouring in two shells with live ammunition at close range was untrue. "On the trip into Staten Island the next day," Tally added, "Schmidt then threw three solid shells overboard to bear out his story that he had fired the required number of shots" as warning shots.[56]

The *Josephine K.* episode revealed the problem that Coast Guard senior officials had of trusting boat commanders to follow Coast Guard policy on the use of large-caliber guns and to make wise decisions when it came to firing deadly projectiles at rumrunners. It also reflected a disturbing pattern of Coast Guard senior officials defending their officers and sailors in the field, no matter what the facts were.

The combination of machine guns and one-pounders was effective for the Coast Guard. An unnamed Coast Guard officer explained, referring to both types of guns on his 75, "[T]hese babies will stop 'em; we don't need speed when we've got these." "The machine gun," he added, "should be enough. We can fire 300 rounds so fast we'll be able to cut the rum boats in half at the water line. As for these steel-armored boats, the one-pounders will take care of them."[57]

While Coast Guard officials said that their boats had to fire live ammunition in order to stop faster speedboats that failed to stop and be searched when

Numerous bullet holes can be seen from machine gun fire that peppered the hull of the outside vessel *Josephine K. National Archives.*

signaled, that was not always accurate. Speedboats heavily laden with liquor, on their return voyages from the mother ships, could not attain anything close to their maximum speeds.

In addition, the Coast Guard could use multiple vessels to overhaul a rumrunner. The Coast Guard often had layers of support. In Narragansett Bay, for example, two Coast Guard vessels might patrol at the entrance to the bay, while two more patrolled several miles up the bay. So if a Coast Guard vessel spotted a suspected rumrunner racing up the bay, it could signal ahead to alert the other two vessels to cut it off. The Coast Guard had installed in some Coast Guard vessels wireless radio sets, a new development.

However, it does not appear that all patrol boats operating near the shore in Narragansett Bay had them from 1929 to 1933. Coast Guard officers lacking radio sets used flares to signal nearby Coast Guard vessels.

Coast Guard boats also had on board piercing searchlights. They were used to track rumrunners and to shine on the flag (known as the ensign) of the Coast Guard vessel, indicating to the crew of the suspect craft to heave to.

The use of informants was one of the Coast Guard's best weapons against rumrunners. Informers often worked for a rumrunning syndicate that competed against other syndicates in the local area. Syndicates sometimes sought to use the same drop sites. A syndicate sometimes paid law enforcement protection money to not raid a drop site and did not want other syndicates to get the benefit of those payments. By discovering when a competitor's rumrunner was expected to meet its outside vessel and return the same evening, the informer's bosses hoped that the competitor's rumrunner would be captured by the Coast Guard and driven out of business. Or informants could be out for a reward—in 1925, the federal government announced that tipsters could receive 25 percent of all fines on the boats captured as a result of the tips.[58]

When a credible tip was received, the Coast Guard could use layers of boats and lie in wait for the rumrunner to appear. This is what transpired, for example, with *Kelble* in March 1932.

It must also be kept in mind that Narragansett Bay—and Mount Hope Bay to the north—had finite lengths. For example, the distance from the entrance of Narragansett Bay to the mouth of the Providence River was about eighteen miles (the Providence River extended another eight miles). Accordingly, the rumrunners had to stop at a beach or dock at some point. The Coast Guard could even, and sometimes did, seize a rumrunner it had previously chased a prior night the next day or two tied up at a dock.

Nevertheless, many Coast Guard commanders of patrol boats preferred to use the Lewis machine gun or Hotchkiss one-pounder to fire at fleeing rumrunners. The results could be deadly.

By mid-1931, a somewhat larger and faster vessel than a 75-footer was operating in Rhode Island waters. It was a 78-footer with two engines providing a combined 1,160 horsepower and could travel at a speed of up to twenty-eight knots or thirty-two miles per hour. One 78-footer with twin Sterling Viking engines, *CG-403*, could make a speed of twenty-four miles per hour.[59]

In late 1925, the commander of Section Base 4 at New London was quoted as saying that the Coast Guard did not succeed in developing speedboats of its own.[60] But by then, the Coast Guard had another avenue to obtain speedboats to use against rumrunners: taking advantage of a new federal law enacted by Congress permitting the Coast Guard to take into its service rumrunners that had been seized and forfeited by court order.[61] When the Great Depression after 1929 also hit the Coast Guard's budget, the Coast Guard turned to converting forfeited speedboats to Coast Guard vessels. These speedboats could be refitted with machine guns (but not one-pounders). Several speedboats mentioned in this book were so forfeited, acquired and used by the Coast Guard against rumrunners in Rhode Island waters.

Chapter 5

LAWS AND POLICIES AUTHORIZING COAST GUARDSMEN TO FIRE THEIR LARGE-CALIBER GUNS

On December 31, 1929, U.S. Assistant Attorney General Gustav Youngquist, from his office in Washington, D.C., wrote a letter to Henry M. Boss, the U.S. Attorney based in Providence. It was only two days after the gunner on a Coast Guard cutter, *CG-290*, had fired at the rumrunner *Black Duck* in Narragansett Bay, killing three men and wounding another. Youngquist wrote, "Coast Guard authorities are apprehensive that [Rhode Island] state authorities may institute prosecution against the crew of the Coast Guard vessel." While Youngquist was not yet aware of the specific facts, he assumed, correctly, "that the facts in this case are such as usually pertain to and attend the chasing of a rum vessel which is trying, at all costs, to evade capture."[62]

Youngquist provided Boss with a brief summary of the law that authorized crews of the Coast Guard to fire their Lewis machine guns and Hotchkiss one-pounders at fleeing suspected rumrunners. He began with the following, citing a U.S. Supreme Court case as support:

> *The Government of the United States may, by means of physical force, exercised through its official agents, execute on every foot of American soil the powers and functions which belong to it. In re Neagle, 135 U.S. 1, 60. Control of importations into the United States is, of course, a constitutional function.*

Youngquist also cited a 1799 statute for granting Congress the power to "regulate the collection of duties on imports."[63] One of the laws rumrunners broke was not paying federal excise tax on imported alcohol.

Youngquist next turned to the authorizing statute most commonly cited for employing the use of force to halt, board and examine craft. This law, Section 2765 of the federal Revenue Statutes, provided:

> *Whenever any vessel liable to seizure or examination does not bring to when requested to do so, or on being chased by a cutter or boat which has displayed the pennant and ensign prescribed for vessels in the* [Coast Guard], *the master* [i.e., the commanding officer] *of the cutter or boat may fire at or into such vessel which does not bring-to, after such pennant or ensign has been hoisted and a gun has been fired by such cutter or boat as a signal.*[64]

Note that the last part of the quoted material required that before a machine gun or one-pounder could be fired at a fleeing rumrunner, the Coast Guard vessel had to show its flag and fire a gun as a warning signal in order to give the targeted vessel an opportunity to come to a stop (heave to) and submit to a search.

Section 2765 was then quoted regarding the federal government protecting Coast Guardsmen who participated in such authorized shootings where men were killed or wounded:

> [A]*ll persons acting by or under his direction shall be indemnified from any penalties or actions for damage for so doing if any person is killed or wounded by such fire, and if the commanding officer is prosecuted or is arrested therefore he shall be forthwith admitted to bail.*[65]

Youngquist added that by law, the Coast Guard was part of the military forces of the United States and that its officers were treated as officers of the U.S. Customs Service.[66]

These rules were set forth in a Coast Guard handbook that every Coast Guard officer had to be familiar with and was likely on board each Coast Guard vessel: *Instructions, Customs, Navigation, and Motor-Boat Laws and Duties of Boarding Officers.* This handbook, written in 1923, was not updated until 1932, so it applied during most of the period from 1929 to 1932. The handbook quotes from the statute almost word for word, requiring that before firing at a fleeing vessel, the commanding officer must hoist his vessel's flag and fire a gun "as a signal."[67]

Navy gunners in 1919 on board the troop transport USS *Kroonland* practice firing both a Lewis machine gun and a Hotchkiss one-pounder. *Naval History and Heritage Command.*

In addition, the handbook addressed the U.S. Constitution's ban on unreasonable searches and seizures by federal government officials. The handbook provided, "In all cases where the right to search is exercised, there must be responsible grounds for suspecting that there has been a violation of the law."[68] In the case of rumrunners, the Coast Guard generally had to see liquor on the boat.

Surprisingly, Youngquist cited a second federal statute for authorizing Coast Guardsmen to use guns to compel rumrunners to be searched. This statute was the subject of a recent re-discovery by federal attorneys looking into the *Black Duck* shootings. The Tariff Act of 1922 authorized the Coast Guard "at any time [to] go aboard…any vessel…within four leagues of the coast of the United States" in order to inspect and examine thoroughly the vessel. The same statute further authorized Coast Guardsmen to "use all necessary force to compel compliance."[69]

The Tariff Act thus also authorized Coast Guardsmen to fire their machine guns and one-pounders at rumrunners if that was necessary to prevent the boats from avoiding being searched. Importantly, unlike the first statute mentioned, Section 2765, the Tariff Act was interpreted by the U.S. Attorney General's Office as *not* requiring that a warning shot be fired prior to firing live ammunition. However, this statute was virtually unknown by Coast Guard officials before the *Black Duck* shooting. Further, it was not consistent with either Section 2765 or the Coast Guard handbook requiring commanding officers to show their flag and fire a warning shot before opening fire on a fleeing vessel.

To the extent the two statutes conflict, a court would likely apply the statute that was more specific on a point.[70] Here, because the Tariff Act did not address the matter, but Section 2765 did, that would mean the requirement to fire a warning shot as expressly set forth in Section 2765 should apply.

Youngquist turned his attention to the *Black Duck* incident. He concluded that if "the killings occurred while the officers [of *CG-290*] were acting under authority of either of these statutes, the homicides must be regarded as justifiable."[71]

While firing at fleeing rumrunners may have been lawful, it was not necessarily the policy of the Coast Guard to do so in all cases. The Coast Guard did not want the responsibility for killing crew members on rumrunners or accidentally shooting innocent bystanders or even nearby Coast Guardsmen. On the other hand, as Admiral Billard, the commandant of the Coast Guard, stated in a circular letter to all Coast Guard units, "Experience has shown that unless the use of force, which at sea is practically restricted to gunfire, is resorted to, it is impossible in the majority of cases to compel rum-running vessels to recognize governmental authority and heave to when challenged by a Coast Guard vessel." Still, Billard admitted that in order to save lives and injuries, care had to be taken when employing large-caliber guns, with the result that "there must be some sacrifice in efficiency."[72]

There remained two vital questions. First, where should the lines be drawn? Second, would these lines be respected by Coast Guard officers in the field?

On April 11, 1929, Billard sent a circular letter to each of the commanding officers of all Coast Guard units on the use of force against rumrunners. Before even firing blank warning shots, Billard advised, every effort should be made to overtake and signal the rumrunner, using either "the whistle, or klaxon, or megaphone, and visual signals such as the waving of arms or a signal flag should be freely and repeatedly used." If signaling did not work, Billard continued, three blank warning shots should be fired from the one-pounder. Only then could a projectile from a one-pounder be fired as a warning, but the shot had to be clear of the fleeing vessel. If these warning shots failed, then large-caliber weapons with live ammunition could be used.

Coast Guard commandant Rear Admiral Frederick C. Billard. *U.S. Coast Guard.*

The Coast Guard commandant emphasized the following: "Rifles or pistols shall never be used for the purpose of firing warning shots, with either blank or live ammunition." The reason given was that the reports of the small arms were not likely to be heard and the bullets were not likely to be seen by the crews of the rumrunners.

Billard then stated the following and, for emphasis, underlined the sentence: "Machine guns shall never be used for the purpose of firing warning shots." Unfortunately, for the next four years, the policies involving machine guns and one-pounders firing warning shots were often ignored in Rhode Island waters.[73]

The policy requiring three blank one-pounder shots was so universally ignored that the failures to do so in the shooting incidents described in this book will not always be noted—doing so would become too repetitive. The statutory requirement that at least one warning shot be fired before the Coast Guard could shoot at a fleeing vessel was also frequently not followed.

After more than three years of carnage, much of it in and around Narragansett Bay, and as it was becoming clear that Prohibition was coming to an end, in a letter dated September 7, 1932, Admiral Billard gave his strongest caution yet to Coast Guard units regarding the use of large-caliber guns. He concluded, "The best interests of the [Coast Guard] Service and public policy demand that the law enforcement duties of the Coast Guard be carried out in such a manner as to reduce to a minimum the probability of loss of life or injury to any person." Billard directed that "in every instance possible" when stopping suspected rum vessels, it should "be accomplished through warning shots and intimidation, and that actual firing at or into the vessel be resorted to only when it is certain that the authority of the Coast Guard cannot be otherwise imposed."[74] But again, many Coast Guard commanders operating vessels in late 1932 and in 1933 did not apparently read Billard's directive. Or they found it so vague or contradictory as to be almost useless guidance.

Chapter 6

SUMMER 1929

COAST GUARD FIRES MACHINE GUN, HITS HOUSE IN TIVERTON (*IDLE HOUR*)

T he Coast Guard in 1929, and for the next several years, opened up its machine guns on rumrunners it chased in Narragansett Bay and elsewhere near the Rhode Island shoreline. The policy change was likely caused by frustration in the ranks of Coast Guardsmen from the increasing use of speedboats as rumrunners.

In addition, Commandant Billard made Narragansett Bay a key focus of the Coast Guard's limited patrol boats. In a June 19, 1929 memorandum, Billard noted the "enormous amount of liquor known to have been coming into Narragansett Bay…for a number of years," contrasted with the few captures of rumrunners made by the Coast Guard. Accordingly, Billard ordered that Section Base 4 and Section Base 18 have a patrol boat guard the entrances to the East Passage, West Passage and Sakonnet River each night. The commandant recognized that the slower 75s were at a disadvantage when chasing faster rumrunners, but he thought that an increased "degree of vigilance" by personnel on the patrol boats would achieve better results than in the past.[75] Was Billard sending a coded message for the commanders of 75s to employ more freely their large-caliber guns?

The Coast Guard's new policy was implemented in the early morning of July 27, 1929. The Coast Guard vessel was the patrol boat *CG-290*, and its commander was Chief Boatswain's Mate Alexander C. Cornell. Cornell and his patrol boat, before the year was out, would earn nationwide notoriety. Indeed, he and his vessel would be involved in the next two major gunfights off Rhode Island's shores, starting with the early morning of Saturday, July 27.

Alexander Cameron Cornell was then thirty-nine years old. Standing five feet, six inches tall and weighing 125 pounds, he had by then long experience in the U.S. Navy and the Coast Guard. Raised in New London, Connecticut, he had enlisted in the navy in 1908 as an apprentice seaman and rose to the rank of lieutenant, junior grade, in the U.S. Navy Reserve by 1919. He ended his active service in 1923 and resigned as a chief quartermaster in 1925.

Perhaps seeking more action, Cornell enlisted in the Coast Guard in January 1926 as a chief boatswain's mate, with temporary status. He was transferred to Section Base 4 in New London on July 2, 1928, and assigned to command *CG-290*. Within two months, he was receiving praise from several of his superiors. The commander of Section Base 4 wrote, "Mr. Cornell is a very capable and efficient officer, neat in dress and appearance, and is a man of excellent character, and I consider him commissioned officer material. He has the faculty of getting along well with subordinates, maintains strict discipline, and holds the respect and confidence of his superior officers." Another officer agreed, adding that Cornell was "forceful in carrying out the work of law enforcement."[76]

Cornell would prove to be an aggressive commander who would not hesitate in employing his machine guns, which did not seem to bother his superiors. Indeed, Cornell may have decided that that to be promoted, firing machine guns at escaping rumrunners was what he had to do. (However, in the next several years, his promotion was held up by his poor teeth and untreated syphilis.)

CG-290 was a 75-footer. As with most 75s, it was armed with a one-pounder Hotchkiss cannon mounted forward and a Lewis machine gun mounted on the port side. Both would get warm in the morning of July 27.

At 12:15 a.m., Cornell, stationed in the Sakonnet River, saw the outline of a speedboat with no running lights on moving slowly up the channel north of Black Point on the Tiverton side. The mystery boat then turned and began heading, slowly, down the channel. Cornell approached within one hundred yards of the vessel, and then he ordered his searchlight turned on and pointed at the boat.

Cornell recognized the craft as the suspected rumrunner *Idle Hour*. Described as a gas screw yacht, *Idle Hour* was 50 feet long and 11 feet wide, had a draft of 5.4 feet and weighed 6 tons. It was built for the rumrunning trade in 1928 at Frederic S. Nock's shipyard at East Greenwich.

Idle Hour was registered to a "Mary Rittenhouse of Hempstead, Long Island, New York."[77] Mary Rittenhouse was the wife of the notorious gang leader Carl Rettich (Rittenhouse was Mary's maiden name).[78] The vessel was registered in Providence as a yacht, which meant it was not licensed for cargo. In the near future, Rettich would acquire an estate on Warwick Neck, called "Crime Castle," that would become his gang's hideout and would be famously raided by law enforcement in 1935. During Prohibition, Rettich started his criminal career from New York City as an active investor in rumrunners. He apparently was the main investor behind *Idle Hour*. A Coast Guard intelligence report in January 1930 identified Danny Walsh as the owner of *Idle Owner*.[79] While that information was not accurate, it does provide a tie between Walsh and Rettich. Rettich would be considered, infamously, as responsible for Walsh's disappearance and murder in 1933.

Both Cornell and the newspapers called the rumrunner the *Idle Hour* of New York City.

A Coast Guardsman blew his whistle for *Idle Hour* to heave to. Instead, the rumrunner's crew opened its engines, put on a burst of speed, threw out a smokescreen and began to zigzag while changing its course and proceeding north up the Sakonnet River. Cornell and *CG-290* followed.

Cornell ordered his gunner handling the one-pounder to fire a blank shell at the fleeing vessel as a warning (but not two more, as policy required). When that did not work, he ordered his machine gunner to fire a burst of rounds ahead of the bow as another warning (even though that order violated the Coast Guard's new policy not to use machine guns to give a warning). That move did not have the desired result either.

Cornell realized that *Idle Hour* was going about thirty knots per hour, while *CG-290* was proceeding at about thirteen knots per hour. He figured he would soon lose his prey. Cornell ordered his machine gunner to open fire again and aim for the vessel.

At the time, *Idle Hour* was proceeding up the west side of the Sakonnet River, while *CG-290* chased after it from astern to the west of the fleeing vessel. In his incident report, Cornell later wrote, "As she passed Fogland Point we made some direct hits with machine gun" on *Idle Hour*.[80] Bursts of machine gun fire appeared to strike the port side of *Idle Hour*'s aft cabin. Other shots struck the hull. The rumrunner put on more speed and south of Gould Island in the Sakonnet River disappeared up the river into the night.

A disappointed Cornell did not give up trying to seize *Idle Hour*. First, he placed a Coast Guardsman on Almy's Wharf in Tiverton, where *Idle Hour*

The *Idle Hour* of New York City, built for the rumrunning trade at East Greenwich in 1928. *National Archives.*

at one point seemed headed. Cornell thought it was the designated "drop" for the rumrunner. Next, after checking on some nearby coves and beaches, Cornell consulted with state policemen in Tiverton, who informed him that they had spotted a fast boat passing under the Stone Bridge. This was probably *Idle Hour* heading either northeast toward Fall River or northwest in the direction of the western side of Narragansett Bay.

The Stone Bridge over the Sakonnet River in northern Tiverton could be an obstacle for Coast Guard vessels. When the drawbridge was closed, it had a vertical clearance of just eight feet, enough for a rumrunner but not for Cornell's cutter. Just to the north, a railroad bridge spanning the river had an eleven-foot clearance when the drawbridge was closed.

Cornell was aware that *Idle Hour* typically moored at East Greenwich, on the west side of Narragansett Bay (conveniently close to Nock's Shipyard). He and his patrol boat arrived at East Greenwich at 4:15 a.m. that same morning. He found *Idle Hour*, but no one was on board and neither was any liquor. Cornell's crew discovered that the boat's engine was still hot and saw signs of a hurried departure. A close inspection also revealed two holes in the boat's aft cabin and numerous scars on its hull, all made by the machine gun fire. Cornell took *Idle Hour* in tow as a suspected rumrunner to bring it to his home port, New London.

Cornell next returned to the Sakonnet River to pick up his crew member left at Almy's Wharf. The man reported spotting two cars containing six men who had remained in the vicinity of the wharf until *CG-290* stood upriver. They then flew a kite with a red and white lantern attached and left. Presumably, Almy's Wharf had been *Idle Hour*'s planned drop, and the men who had been hired to load the cargo into their automobiles had signaled to *Idle Hour* that the drop had been compromised.

On Wednesday, July 31, the rumrunner was towed by a Coast Guard patrol boat back to Narragansett Bay and up to Providence, to await its fate—whether charges would be lodged against it by the federal U.S. Attorney. When it arrived at Providence and was inspected, the cabin of *Idle Hour* was found to have several bullet holes in it.[81]

In court in Providence, *Idle Hour*'s captain, Thomas Murray, of Fairhaven, Massachusetts, paid a $500 fine for failing to heave to in the Sakonnet River when ordered to do so by the Coast Guard. In addition, a $100 fine was imposed on the vessel for running without lights. The collector of customs of the port of Providence, Emory J. San Souci, dismissed two other charges.[82] *Idle Hour* would continue its career as a rumrunner.

A source not connected to the Coast Guard provided details of what transpired on the night of July 27–28. The information is fairly credible. The source was a Rhode Island rumrunner from Tiverton named Herbert Cavaca. In his written recollections, Cavaca stated that he had hired *Idle Hour* that night to pick up a load of liquor from an outside vessel.

The Tiverton rumrunner, using binoculars, watched the events from High Hill Point in Little Compton, just over two miles south of Tiverton Four Corners and on the east side of the Sakonnet River. He saw the Coast Guard cutter in the Sakonnet River head for *Idle Hour*. He later recalled:

> I knew she'd [*Idle Hour*] spotted the cutter and was trying to sneak away. But the patrol boat put chase to her and started shooting. From High Hill, you could see the tracer bullets skipping through the darkness and falling short….
>
> Over along the west shore, the 75 [*CG-290*] used her one-pounder several times and then, after getting in closer, opened up with the machine gun. My men lay down on the deck in the lee of the deck load of liquor. The captain, who was steering, folded up some heavy canvas and sort of draped it around his shoulders. Fifteen or 20 bullets hit this makeshift bullet-proof coat and fell on the deck.

Meanwhile, the Tiverton rumrunner drove to the beach at Seapowet Point on the Tiverton coastline. The crew of *CG-290* must have thought that the car on the beach was a boat, as the Coast Guard vessel shined its searchlight on the car and, according to the Tiverton rumrunner, "started to shoot. We laid down flat on the bank until they stopped firing." If true, Cornell had ordered his crew to fire machine guns on the mainland and failed to mention it in his after-action incident report. (Cornell's incident report did mention that after losing *Idle Hour*, he and his men searched Tiverton's coves and beaches, so this shooting incident could have occurred at this time.)

Cavaca later learned that *Idle Hour* had "gone up between Gould Island and Stone Bridge, dumped her load and then run for East Greenwich." This Gould Island, the second with that name in Narragansett Bay, was located on the east side of the Sakonnet River, about three-quarters of a mile south of Stone Bridge. The crew had thrown the sacks of liquor into shallow water, planning to fish them out later. (They were thwarted, as coastal residents from Tiverton and Portsmouth got there first.) The Tiverton rumrunner concluded, "The next morning, when the Coast Guard came to tow the *Idle Hour* to New London…they found that her hull was riddled with bullets."[83]

What really caught the attention of the public about the *Idle Hour* affair was the charge that one of the bullets from *CG-290* became embedded in a private citizen's home. A few days after the *Idle Hour* incident, returning to his summer house on Fogland Point, a peninsula jutting out from the eastern shore of the Sakonnet River, William B. Freeman found that a bullet had penetrated the outside wall of his house, smashed into a chair and table in his dining room and had lodged in a wooden floor in the house. Understandably, having heard about the machine guns fired on the Sakonnet River by a Coast Guard vessel a few night before, Freeman concluded that the high-powered bullet must have come from Boatswain Cornell's *CG-290*. Residents in the area thought the same.

Freeman contacted one of Rhode Island's U.S. senators, Jesse H. Metcalf, to lodge a complaint. Metcalf was likewise upset to learn that a Coast Guard bullet found its way inside the house of one of his constituents.

Senator Metcalf, in a strongly worded letter of protest to Admiral Billard, the Coast Guard commandant, declared that the "endangering of lives of innocent American citizens is intolerable" and requested a thorough investigation. Metcalf added, "According to residents in this section" of Fogland Point, the shot was fired from the rum chaser that was "shooting at" *Idle Hour*. Metcalf sternly wrote:

The Coast Guard patrol boat *CG-290*, with a home base of New London, was, under the command of Chief Boatswain's Mate Alexander C. Cornell, a terror to rumrunners in Rhode Island waters. A one-pounder is at the bow, and a Lewis machine gun is at the port side. It could well be Cornell standing on deck at the bow. *U.S. Coast Guard.*

I wish strongly to protest such careless action on the part of the Coast Guard and to get your assurance that shootings of this kind will not be repeated on the coast of Rhode Island. While all agree that all reasonable effort should be made to enforce the law, I think that endangering the lives of innocent American citizens is intolerable. A shot of this kind which penetrates a private home at 3 o'clock in the morning can be but the result of gross carelessness and ignorance on the part of the members of the Coast Guard.

I have received a protest from the residents of this section against this shooting and I most heartily agree with them that the action cannot and should not be tolerated.

Mr. Freeman, whose winter home is at 60 Forest Street, Providence, called personally at my office and asked that we get him assurance that the lives of his family and friends would not again be endangered by prohibition forces. I think every American citizen is entitled to this protection, and I most urgently request that you conduct a thorough investigation of this affair.[84]

Senator Metcalf's letter was quoted in Providence and Newport newspapers, as well as many newspapers around the country. Perhaps the best headline was from the *Hartford Courant*: "Senator Metcalf Protests Against Wild Shooting by Coast Guard."[85]

A rattled Billard opened up an investigation to determine if the Coast Guard had fired the shot into William Freeman's house. The Coast Guard's probe, not surprisingly, did not conclude that the shot that entered the Freeman house came from any Coast Guard vessel. The finding of the investigating officer was that it was "not certain beyond a reasonable doubt that the shot which entered the home of William M. Freeman at Fogland Point, Rhode Island, came from the *CG-290*."[86]

Malcolm F. Willoughby, who wrote a history of the U.S. Coast Guard's role chasing rumrunners during Prohibition that was published by the federal government, found that the Coast Guard had reached the following facts about *CG-290*'s chase of *Idle Hour*:

> *Both vessels were proceeding northward up the Sakonnet River, with CG-290 on the starboard bow of Idle Hour, and dropping astern due to slower speed. The direction of firing was obviously within the quadrant west to north.*
>
> *When firing commenced, the vessels were 1 mile down river from Fogland Point, a half-mile-long point jutting out from the river's eastern shore. It was at all times to starboard of the craft and, as they proceeded up the river, the angle to starboard constantly increased.*

Willoughby concluded:

> *Lt. Comdr. Clarence H. Dench conducted a thorough investigation at the scene; Boatswain Cornell attended and was cross-examined by the complainant. The investigating officer went on board CG-290 and had her re-run the course followed in pursuit of Idle Hour. The skipper showed that the line of fire was clear of shore and other vessels, and that when firing commenced, Fogland Point was northeast of CG-290.*
>
> *It was conceded that the shot could have come from CG-290, but as bursts of machine gun fire were being discharged at the rum runner, it seemed strange that one isolated shot of a burst should have found its way to the house. Boatswain Cornell was cleared of any culpable inefficiency or carelessness in directing his fire at Idle Hour. These conclusions seemed fair enough, but the Commandant issued instructions to the end that patrol boats operating in the vicinity of Sakonnet River exercise the utmost care so that there would be no possibility of any projectile striking persons or buildings on shore. It was an ever-present danger when pursuing rum runners in*

restricted waters, and a handicap to the Coast Guard which was fully recognized by the rummies.

It strikes this author that it was very likely (and is close to "beyond a reasonable doubt") that *CG-290* did indeed fire the bullet that had entered the Freeman house. Prior to Prohibition, it was, of course, extremely rare for a high-powered bullet to enter a summer home on the shoreline along Fogland Point. It is too much of a coincidence that the one time a bullet from the direction of the Sakonnet River did strike and enter a house, the firing of multiple rounds from a machine gun had occurred in the channel a few nights before. It seems most likely, then, that a stray machine gun bullet from *CG-290* had struck the Freeman house, perhaps directly or indirectly from ricocheting off the water. (In addition, recall the claim of the Tiverton rumrunner that *CG-290* had also fired at him and his men that night on a Tiverton beach, which, if true, was an example of "promiscuous" shooting).

Willoughby also did not mention that Cornell, in his after-action incident report, wrote that *Idle Hour*, as it sped northward up the Sakonnet River and arrived at Almy's Bell Buoy, "turned directly towards Almy's Wharf," which was to the east on Tiverton's shoreline. Cornell continued that, in response, *CG-290* "cut towards [the] wharf, firing burst of machine gun when line of fire was clear of shore and other vessels."[87] However, if *Idle Hour* was heading due east at this point, it is not clear how it could ever have been "clear" of the Tiverton shoreline at this time when *CG-290* fired its machine gun.

The Coast Guard investigation officer argued that the bullet could have been fired by a rumrunner using a rifle, but there were no reports of such firing from the Sakonnet River during that period. The author is not aware of any such shooting from the Sakonnet River in the entire period from 1929 to 1933.

In an internal Coast Guard letter, Commandant Billard seemed to question the quality of the investigation. He stated that the investigator had "somewhat inadequately, investigated the matter." In a transmittal letter to Senator Metcalf conveying the investigation's findings, Billard seemed to concede that the board of inquiry's conclusions may not be accurate, writing, "It is possible that the bullet in question did come from the patrol boat."

Ballard's main goal was to put an important U.S. senator at ease. He assured Senator Metcalf:

> *Our people are thoroughly indoctrinated with the determined policy of this office that innocent people or their property must not be endangered. I am today issuing instructions to the end that our patrol boats operating in the vicinity of the Sakonnet River shall exercise the utmost care so that there shall be no possibility of any projectiles striking persons or buildings on shore. I believe you will have no further occasion to complain of any stray, accidental shot from a Coast Guard craft.*[88]

Billard's fulsome promise was another indication that he was not fully confident of the board of inquiry's conclusion. The *Providence Journal* confirmed that all Coast Guard units operating along the Rhode Island coast were instructed to use "exceptional care" when firing machine guns.[89]

Billard passed on the instructions to the commander of Section Base 4 in New London and the man who led the board of inquiry, Clarence Dench, that patrol boats "operating in the vicinity of the Sakonnet River and Narragansett Bay shall exercise the utmost care, so that there shall be no possibility of any projectile striking on shore." Billard further excoriated Section Base 4's commander for Cornell firing only one blank shell from his one-pounder as a warning shot instead of the mandatory three and for using his machine gun for the purpose of firing warning shots. Both failures, Billard emphasized, ran counter to his directions in his April 11, 1929 circular letter on the use of large-caliber guns. Billard further complained that Cornell had not filed a report required when gunfire was employed, as mandated in a 1921 directive. (As a result, Cornell never details how many machine gun bullets he fired; to be fair here, Coast Guard patrol boat commanders would not consistently file these reports until 1931.)[90]

Despite Billard's firm tone, Dench strongly defended Cornell. Dench argued that it was not thought necessary to fire three warning shots from the one-pounder, as *Idle Hour*, after the searchlight was shown on it, must have realized a Coast Guard vessel wanted it to heave to, but instead the boat put on speed in an attempt to escape.

Dench also protested that imposing a standard on firing machine guns in the Sakonnet River so that there is "no possibility of any projectile striking on shore" was unrealistic if patrol boats were expected to stop the smuggling of illicit liquors in the river. Dench complained that this standard could not be achieved "without the prohibiting of all firing of projectiles in that river, because there will always be a likelihood of their landing on shore through aberrations of flight, faulty aim in darkness, or ricochet." The commander added, "The same condition would be present in regard to the narrow West

Passage of Narragansett Bay, and in a slightly less degree in the wider East Passage, depending upon position." He concluded, "Due to the superior speed of the illicit cargo carriers, the effect of such prohibition would be practically to nullify the preventative work of the patrols in those passages."

Readers of the *Providence Journal* would have been surprised to learn that Commander Dench informed his superior that, pending further clarifying instructions, he would not pass on the new firing directions to his vessel commanders. Dench thought it enough for his commanders to follow the directions of Billard's April 11, 1929 circular letter to balance "good judgment and discretion" with the necessity for Coast Guardsmen "actively and earnestly to carry out the law enforcement duties with which the service is charged."[91]

It does not appear that Billard responded to Dench's letter. If he had, and again insisted on patrol boats using three blanks shots as warning shots and taking care about firing machine guns in Narragansett Bay, it is possible that the tragedy perpetrated by Boatswain Cornell and *CG-290* described in the next chapter might have been avoided.

Chapter 7

WINTER 1929

MACHINE GUN KILLS THREE CREWMEN, WOUNDS ONE (*BLACK DUCK*)

The machine gunning and capture of the speedboat *Black Duck* on the night of December 29, 1929, by Boatswain Cornell and his crew on board *CG-290* was one of the most sensational incidents in the Coast Guard's campaign against liquor smuggling during Prohibition. The shooting resulted in the deaths of three crewmen and the wounding of a fourth. The dramatic incident was highlighted in newspapers across the country and helped to galvanize the "wet" forces in their campaign to overturn the Eighteenth Amendment. This chapter focuses on the shooting incident. The next chapter describes the reverberations from the killings in the political arena and on the issue of the Coast Guard firing large-caliber weapons at sea when enforcing suspected Prohibition violations.

Black Duck, with Charles ("Charlie") Travers as its master, was well known to the Coast Guard as a suspected rumrunner that operated in Narragansett Bay, but the speedboat had shown that it was too elusive and fast to be caught with a load of liquor on board. One Coast Guard officer testified that from May to August 1929, Coast Guard vessels stopped and searched *Black Duck* on four occasions, but in none of those cases was illegal alcohol found on board.[92]

The first time that Travers and Cornell encountered each other was during the night of October 12, 1928. While heading for the East Passage in Narragansett Bay some three miles away, and running without lights, Travers and *Black Duck* were intercepted by *CG-288*. Its commander, M.H.

Low, made signals for Travers to heave to, but Travers ignored the signals and instead tried to escape. *CG-288* fired several bursts of tracer machine gun bullets, and Cornell's patrol boat, *CG-290*, gained a position enabling it to cut off *Black Duck*. Travers stopped his craft and only grudgingly allowed his boat to be towed to Block Island. Travers was running "light," meaning without any illicit cargo on board. But because he did not stop when signaled and hindered Coast Guard attempts to attach the tow line to his boat, fines were imposed.[93]

The Coast Guard may have received a tip that on the night of December 28–29, 1929, *Black Duck* would make a run to its mother ship in Rum Row and return up the East Passage of Narragansett Bay, headed to unload its illicit cargo at Newport. Even if the Coast Guard had not received a tip about *Black Duck*, it was aware that two new outside vessels had just arrived at Rum Row off Block Island and Montauk Point. Moreover, it was a few days before New Year's Eve, when partygoers expected their parties to be lubricated with illegal liquor smuggled in by rumrunners.

Two Coast Guard vessels were ordered to guard the East Passage that night. One of them, Cornell's *CG-290*, at 9:00 p.m. arrived at Bell Buoy #1, which was about 240 yards from Bull Point at the southern tip of Jamestown. This location was near a remarkable rock formation on Jamestown known as The Dumplings and the U.S. Army's Fort Wetherrill. Cornell thought that the water was too deep to set his anchor, so he had his boat tied to the buoy. Cornell next had *CG-290*'s lights turned off to avoid being detected as it lay in wait, facing outward to the sea. A second 75-footer, *CG-241*, patrolled across the channel in the vicinity of Fort Adams.

Coast Guard boats sometimes tied themselves to buoys, with all lights out, while lying in wait for rumrunners. It was then permitted under Coast Guard policy, but it posed a potential danger to ships engaging in legitimate operations that often sought to locate buoys in foggy conditions.[94]

At about 2:00 a.m. on December 29, *Black Duck* approached Bull Point. The speedboat's captain was again Charlie Travers of Fairhaven, Massachusetts. His parents were first-generation immigrants from the Azores, a chain of islands in the Atlantic Ocean between Portugal and Africa, whose inhabitants (and Travers's parents) spoke Portuguese as their primary language. As a teenager, Travers had lied about his age and enlisted in the Life-Saving Service on Cuttyhunk Island, one of the Elizabeth Islands in Nantucket Sound. After his enlistment expired, he became a lobsterman working out of his home port of New Bedford. At the time, lobsters were selling for a pittance, ten to fourteen cents per pound.

In the 1920s, he discovered, along with many other local fishermen, that running rum was much more lucrative. In 1925, Travers was just nineteen years old when he was arrested aboard the rumrunner *Tramp* and charged with violating the National Prohibition Act. He was later convicted and sentenced to pay a fine of $500. But that did not drive him away from the rum business. Two years later, he was commanding the speedboat *Black Duck*, which had then been based in Gloucester, Massachusetts.[95] Travers used East Greenwich as *Black Duck*'s home base.[96]

The registered owner of *Black Duck* was Joe Williams of 78 Gay Street, Providence.[97] But according to a Coast Guard intelligence report, the boat was really owned by Joseph Dressler of West Warwick.[98]

Travers had three other crewmen on board: Jake Weisman of Providence, John Goulart of Fairhaven and Dudley Brandt of Boston. Weisman was the brother-in-law of Joseph Dressler, although Weisman was estranged from his wife at the time. Both Weisman and Dressler were Jewish American.[99] Given his relationship with Dressler and his prior bootlegging experience, Weisman was likely the representative of the rumrunning outfit that had invested in the voyage. Brandt served as the boat's engineer. Goulart was a friend and neighbor of Travers's in Fairhaven.

Travers and his crew earlier that evening had sped out from Newport (where they had parked their cars) to Rum Row to meet the outside British vessel *Symor* and had picked up 383 sacks of liquor.[100] Now they were headed back toward Newport to their designated drop zone to unload the sacks to a crew onshore.

Travers captained reputedly the fastest speedboat then operating in southeastern New England. The 50-foot *Black Duck*, powered with two new Detroit Aero Marine engines each producing three hundred horsepower, could achieve a speed of 32 knots (36.8 miles per hour). Thus, it was able to outdistance any Coast Guard vessel, even if loaded with cargo. The wooden-hulled speedboat, painted gray, had a low silhouette, making it hard to spot at sea. Its top deck was broken only by a small pilothouse where the crew sometimes gathered, as well as an even lower-profile engine room behind the pilothouse. A dory was secured on the afterdeck. There were other indications the speedboat was a rumrunner: its engines were heavily muffled with Maxim silencers, and it was fitted with a device to produce a smokescreen.

Cornell, in command of his 75-footer *CG-290*, waited patiently at the bell buoy off Bull Point. After firing its machine guns in late July 1929 at *Idle Hour* in the Sakonnet River, Cornell and his crew had experienced recent success.

On September 20, off Montauk Point, they seized a British "outside" vessel, the schooner *Vinces*. Cornell also furnished information leading to the seizure of the powerboat *William A. Landry*, which had been working with *Vinces*. On October 12, *CG-290* seized the American oil screw *Beatrice K*, with an astounding 1,600 sacks of liquor found on board. Just four days prior to December 29, on Christmas Day at Fort Pond Bay in New York, Cornell and his patrol boat had captured another "outside" vessel, this one the British oil schooner *Audrey B.*, with 2,800 sacks of liquor on board.

In addition to Cornell, *CG-290*'s crew consisted of seven other men: Chief Motor Machinist's Mate Louis Johnson, Boatswain's Mate First Class Louis W. Gavitt, Motor Machinist's Mate First Class Risden T. Bennett, Motor Machinist's Mate Second Class Andrew Rhude, Seaman First Class Lewis R. Pearson, Ship's Cook Second Class Arthur E. Dye and Seaman Second Class Frank W. Jakubec. Their Coast Guard experience ranged from one year and six months for Pearson to more than eleven years for Gavitt and more than sixteen years for Cornell (taking into account both his Coast Guard and navy service).[101]

As *Black Duck* neared, Cornell and Bennett were in the pilothouse and Pearson was standing on the aft part the deck on the port side. The rest of the men were sleeping below.

At about 2:15 a.m., as Travers approached the bell buoy off Bull Point, dense fog hung over the water. These were good conditions for a rumrunner to avoid being caught. However, in turn, the fog also made it difficult for the rumrunner to find its way safely up the East Passage. Travers decided to reduce his speed and engine noise and head toward the buoy so that he could listen to the clanging of its bell. Once he picked up the sound, he could mark where his vessel was in the channel.[102] The night was calm and the water smooth, so sound could be easily heard over the water.

Travers later said, "We were only going four miles an hour. I heard the gong ringing off the Dumplings. The first thing I knew I saw a dark object looming ahead. It was the 75. She had her lights out and was tied to the buoy."[103]

CG-290 had a rope at its stern tied to the buoy, and at the time its bow faced the sea to the southeast. *Black Duck* approached on *CG-290*'s port side.

Cornell spotted *Black Duck* at a distance of about five hundred yards, running without lights and on a course to cross *CG-290*'s bow. Cornell thought it was going fast. When the speedboat was about fifty yards from *CG-290*, Cornell, standing in his vessel's pilothouse and looking out the starboard window, said, "Here she comes. Don't let her get away." Cornell swung his searchlight on the oncoming vessel. Cornell and his crew immediately

TREASURY DEPARTMENT.
U. S. COAST GUARD
Form 2636.—Ed. Feb., 1923—6,000

U. S. COAST GUARD
R..0   DEC 31 1929   BY

REPORT OF VIOLATION OF CUSTOMS, NAVIGATION OR MOTOR-BOAT LAWS

U. S. Coast Guard _____ CG-290 _____

To the Commanding Officer:

The following report of violation is submitted:

The _____ Gas screw C-5677 _____ of _____ Providence, R.I. _____
    (Name)

length _____ 50 feet _____ documented, not documented;
    (To be measured, if a motor boat over 25 feet)   (Strike out term not applicable)

_____ Joseph Williams _____, owner

address of owner _____ 78 Gay Street, Providence, R.I. _____

in charge of _____ Charles Brown (alias Charles Travers) _____

address _____ 50 Clara Street, New Bedford, Mass. _____
coming to or leaving mooring
    underway,   in _____ at Dumplings Bell Buoy #1, Eastern Passage, _____
    at anchor,   _____ Narragansett Bay. (Place)

at _____ 2:15 a.m. _____, on _____ December 29 _____, 192 9.
    (Watch time)   (Date)

weather _____ obz (overcast & hazy); local time of sunset _____ 4:39 p.m. _____
    (State whether moonlight, cloudy, or dark)   (Hours and minutes)

Nature of violation:
    Running without lights,
    Failing to stop or signal, and
    loaded with sacks of liquor.

Sections or acts violated: Act, June 9, 1910,
                              R.S.2865, amended 27 Feb.1887,
                              as amended Jones' Act.
Remarks: R.S. 3069 Act March 4, 1909,Sec.65.
                              19 U.S.C.496.
                              27 U.S.C.40
                              R. S. 4377

Forwarded to—   Hdqtrs-3, Col.of Customs-3, Sec.of Commerce-1, Dist.Atty-1,
                Comdesfor-1, Files-1, CG-290-1.

R. C. JEWELL,   A. C. Cornell, Boatswain, U.S.C.G.
                                Officer in Charge.
Lieutenant, U.S.C.G.,
Acting Commander Base YOUR, Commanding.   Boarding Officer.

    (If violation of section 5, act June 9, 1910, is reported, state number of persons on board, whether carried for hire; and,
if so, whether operated by a person duly licensed.)

The incident report on the capture of the rumrunner *C-5677* (known as *Black Duck*) submitted by Chief Boatswain's Mate Alexander Cornell on December 29, 1929. *National Archives.*

recognized it as the gray speedboat *Black Duck* from its silhouette. As the boat got closer, despite the mist, they could also plainly see the boat's license number, *C-5677*, written in white paint on its bow, which identified the rumrunner as *Black Duck* (the boat did not have the name *Black Duck* written on it). Sacks of liquor were also spotted on its decks.

Cornell threw his searchlight alternately on the Coast Guard flag flying on his starboard yardarm and on *Black Duck*. At the same time, he sounded a Klaxon horn. The visual and sound actions were signals for *Black Duck* to heave to. Instead, the rumrunner responded by revving its engines and increasing its speed to about twenty-five miles per hour. Cornell ordered Seaman First Class Lewis Pearson to man the Lewis machine gun on the port side of the patrol boat.

Black Duck ran inside the buoy, between the patrol boat and the Jamestown shore. At a distance of about seventy-five feet, *Black Duck* passed the bow of *CG-290* and continued up the patrol boat's starboard side. No one was seen on the rumrunner's deck. Travers was at the wheel in the engine room, while the other three crewmen hid in the pilothouse. As *Black Duck* passed *CG-290*, Cornell yelled out from the pilothouse for the passing boat to heave to. It took under a minute for *Black Duck* to pass the Coast Guard vessel from the time it was spotted.

Cornell had to make a quick decision. His vessel was still tied to the buoy, its engines were not running and it would take many minutes to get the engines started and running at top speed. He must have figured that he had no chance to chase and catch the rumrunner, particularly with the foggy conditions and darkness. Moreover, based on his prior experience with *Black Duck* and other rumrunners, he figured *Black Duck* would not halt without a large-caliber weapon being fired at it. Given how close he was to the Jamestown shore, he ruled out firing live ammunition with his one-pounder. He estimated that at *Black Duck*'s current speed, the rumrunner would disappear in a fog bank in about fifteen seconds. Seaman Pearson, continuing to man the Lewis machine gun, stood by ready for orders.

Cornell also was aware that it was Coast Guard policy to fire three blank warning shots with his one-pounder before firing live ammunition at a fleeing rumrunner. He likely knew that at least one one-pounder had to be fired as a warning under Section 2765 of the federal Revenue Statutes. He was further aware that it was against Coast Guard policy to fire live machine gun bullets as a warning. But he must have been concerned that he lacked time to fire one or three blank one-pounder shells if he wanted to stop *Black Duck* with live machine gun bullets. Perhaps he also recalled how firing a warning shot at *Idle Hour* had provided valuable time for that rumrunner to escape. He probably further figured that he already given *Black Duck* plenty of warning with his searchlight and Klaxon.

Within five seconds of *Black Duck* passing *CG-290*, Cornell yelled from the pilothouse to Pearson, "Let her have it." Cornell did not give the order to fire a warning shot. Pearson said later that he had standing instructions from his New London gunnery instructor, and from Cornell himself, to fire his machine gun's first shots as warning shots either ahead of and over the rumrunner's bow or astern (that is, behind the rumrunner). Pearson intended, he later claimed, to fire astern of the fleeing rumrunner and over it; after that, if the vessel did not heave to, he would fire directly at the boat's stern to disable it. This could be accomplished by cutting the hawser line, ripping away the rudder or crippling the gas-powered engine system.

Alternatively, Pearson may have intended to shoot directly at the stern of *Black Duck*. After all, if he used his valuable time shooting a warning volley at a point astern of the fleeing boat, *Black Duck* could ignore the warning shots and escape into the fog. Even if Pearson had shot at *Black Duck*'s stern, that would not necessarily have been a deadly situation for the boat's crew; sometimes a crew was fairly well protected by sacks of liquor and small boats on the deck when machine gun bullets were directed at the boat's stern from a position directly behind the stern.

Pearson aimed the Lewis machine gun across his patrol boat by looking over its barrel and lined it up to a position astern of *Black Duck* or at its stern. He cocked the machine gun by pulling its charging handle back. He squeezed its trigger for about three seconds, firing a burst of twenty-one bullets. Then the weapon jammed. Pearson frantically tried to clear it. His pan of machine gun bullets contained forty-seven bullets, so Pearson had twenty-six more to let loose.

Just as Pearson fired his short burst, from only about seventy-five yards away, *Black Duck* swerved sharply to the left toward the Jamestown shoreline.[104] This exposed the port side of the rumrunner. The machine gun bullets fired by Pearson swept the vessel from stern to bow, above the line of the hull, including hitting the pilothouse and engine room. *Black Duck* then disappeared from view into the fog. Why Travers turned his boat to the left is not known. Perhaps it was an evasive maneuver to avoid machine gun fire.

Weisman, Goulart and Brandt had been inside the pilothouse crouching when the machine gun raked their boat. The bullets smashed into the windows and wood, killing each of the three men. Goulart and Brandt died instantly inside the pilothouse. The blood-soaked Weisman stumbled outside the pilothouse and collapsed on the deck near the wheel. Weisman succumbed within minutes.

One of the bullets struck Travers's right hand as he held the wheel in the engine room. Travers lost his grip. He must have used his uninjured left hand to switch on his boat's side running lights and turn his vessel back toward *CG-290*, which soon approached the stricken *Black Duck*. Meanwhile, Travers walked over to the boat's pilothouse and saw the carnage inside.

As *Black Duck* came along side *CG-290*, Travers was on deck. Cornell, holding a Thompson machine gun, hailed Travers and called for him to guide his boat alongside *CG-290*. Travers said, "I can't," but managed to do it anyway, according to Cornell. Travers yelled, "The rest of them are down and all shot up. Get us in somewhere, will you, as soon as you can."

Leaving his Thompson machine gun behind, Cornell and other Coast Guardsmen who had woken up and taken their stations on deck jumped on board the stricken *Black Duck*. Only Pearson remained behind in the pilothouse; he became sick, probably because of what he viewed on the rumrunner's deck. Seeing Weisman lying crumpled on the deck, Cornell ordered his men to "Pick him up." Weisman was laid out on the engine room hatch. He looked dead. Travers still pleaded, "For God's sake, do something for these men." Goulart and Brandt were seen lying in a heap in the pilothouse. Cornell ordered his crew to tow *Black Duck* to Newport to nearby Fort Adams, the largest U.S. Army fort protecting Narragansett Bay and the nearest location where medical assistance could be obtained.

The bullet that had hit Travers's right hand had injured his thumb, passed through his palm and shattered his wrist. Cornell had Travers brought aboard *CG-290* and noticed that the wound was congealing and not bleeding. Travers kept quiet and did not discuss the shooting or his boat's mission that night.[105]

Coast Guardsmen spent time putting out several small fires caused by the machine gunning. One sack of liquor inside a dory lashed to *Black Duck*'s deck had caught fire. Bottles of "Golden Wedding" whiskey were seen inside the sack.

About fifteen minutes after getting underway, at 2:45 a.m., *CG-290* arrived at Fort Adams. Cornell asked the fort's doctor if anything could be done for the three men laid out, but the doctor confirmed that they were dead. The doctor bandaged Travers's hand.

The three deceased men were taken to a makeshift morgue at the fort's medical quarters. The Newport coroner and his assistant soon arrived and conducted a quick autopsy. Another was conducted at Hambly Funeral

Front view of the rumrunner *Black Duck* after its seizure, tied up to a dock at Pawtuxet, January 8, 1930. *National Archives.*

Home in Newport. Weisman had been struck in his right shoulder, with the bullet fracturing ribs and vertebrae before lacerating both of his lungs, which was the cause of his death. Goulart had a bullet puncture wound in his chest, indicating that he had been facing *CG-290* when he was shot. The bullet lacerated his heart, severed his aorta and lacerated his kidney before exiting his body from the right loin. Brandt had two puncture wounds in his neck, just below his right ear. Bullets fractured his vertebrae and severed his jugular vein. Each man's death was believed to have been instantaneous (although Weisman had time to stumble out of the pilothouse and onto the deck).[106] Later in the morning, *Black Duck* was towed by a Coast Guard vessel to New London.

Lacking proper medical facilities, Charlie Travers was moved, under armed guard, to Newport Hospital. His room had iron bars, like a jail cell. Two Coast Guardsmen from *CG-290* guarded him. At first, they only allowed Travers's cousin and Reverend Roy W. Magoun, superintendent of Seamen's Church Institute in Newport, to speak to the patient. Charlie's lawyers, other family members and various Rhode Island state and local employees were barred from speaking with Travers pursuant to strict orders from the Treasury Department in Washington, D.C. One man, calling himself a police commissioner, insisted on speaking with Travers and would not leave, so one of the guards grabbed the man by the nape of the neck and seat of his pants and threw him out of the room.[107] Refusing Travers access to his attorney would have been a violation of his constitutional rights if done today, but the law was not as clear on that point back then. Until Travers was served a warrant for his arrest and charged in court, he could not be released on bail.

In the evening of December 30, Travers was allowed to speak to his attorney and a few newspapermen. To one reporter, Travers claimed that the Coast Guard fired on his boat without any warning. "They just loomed out of the fog and started to blaze away," Travers said. He added, "The Coast Guard cutter loomed up like a big mountain. We did not know what kind of craft it was, but I knew it was another ship and there was danger of collision and I swung our craft over." Travers continued, "Then they [the Coast Guard] commenced firing. My three comrades were hit at the same instant. They didn't even speak after they were shot."[108] Referring to his dead crewmates, Travers concluded, "Them three fellows were damn fine boys. I'm just sorry for them, that's all. They didn't give us a chance, not a chance, and they were right on us."[109]

The two interviews of Travers, both taken on December 30, helped inflame public opinion against the Coast Guard. He was understandably upset about the deaths of his three crewmen at the hands of the Coast Guard, but he was not a reliable witness. He was inconsistent on several points in the two interviews he gave, and some of his statements were untrue. For example, Travers's claim that he did not know that the boat tied to the bell buoy was a Coast Guard vessel is likely untrue, given that Cornell pointed his searchlight at *Black Duck* and sounded the Klaxon horn. But it is possible that with the night fog and short time elapsed that Travers did not realize he was being signaled by the Coast Guard to heave to. On the other hand, in his second interview, Travers did not claim that he did not know the vessel was from the Coast Guard. Travers also indicated in both of his December 30 interviews that *CG-290* had fired at his vessel head on, before it passed the Coast Guard vessel, but this was not accurate.[110] When *Black Duck* was examined by government inspectors at the State Pier in Providence, in the presence of newspapermen, it was apparent that the bullet holes came from the direction of the rear of the boat.[111]

Travers was not the only one who was not truthful about the events that evening. Crew members of *CG-290* unofficially informed newspaper reporters that they had fired a one-pounder across *Black Duck*'s bow as a warning.[112] That was not true either. The crewmen knew that a federal statute required a Coast Guard vessel to fire a warning shot with a one-pounder before firing live ammunition at a fleeing rumrunner, and to protect themselves, they lied about it.

During the day of December 30, the body of Jake Weisman was sent to the home of his father in Providence. He would later be buried at Lincoln Cemetery in Warwick. John Goulart's body was taken by undertakers to the home of his parents in Fairhaven. Later that night, Dudley Brandt's body was claimed by a family undertaker.[113]

Two federal government investigations commenced shortly after the shooting. The Customs Service formed an "independent committee" consisting of Customs Service officials to investigate the matter. They sent investigators to New London to take statements from Boatswain Cornell and his crew members on December 29. The next day, also in New London, the Coast Guard began its own investigation. Captain H.H. Wolf, commander of the Coast Guard destroyer force, created a board of inquiry to investigate the killings and appointed Lieutenant Commander Carl C. von Paulsen to lead it. The crew members of *CG-290*, including Cornell, were temporarily relieved of their duties and confined to their New London base. Each man testified at the board of inquiry hearing that concluded on January 6, 1930. After giving perhaps his first statement of the events, probably to the Customs Service, Cornell ended by saying, "We are very sorry that this happened. We'd have given anything not to have had these deaths occur."[114]

In Providence, Henry M. Boss, the U.S. Attorney for the District of Rhode Island, a federal government official, was deciding whether to bring charges against the Coast Guard crew. Rhode Island's assistant attorney general, Benjamin M. McLyman, was considering the same. In Newport, where the bodies of the three dead men were taken, a separate investigation was begun by the Coroner's Office.[115]

Rear view of the rumrunner *Black Duck* tied up to a dock at Pawtuxet, January 8, 1930, showing damage to its dory caused by machine gun fire. *National Archives.*

An ugly dispute between federal and state authorities ensued over both the handling of Charlie Travers and whether or not the slaying of the three crewmen should go before a state grand jury.

At first, the federal government seemed determined to maintain jurisdiction of the cases at the expense of the state and Travers. Coast Guardsmen, federal employees, continued to hold Travers at Newport Hospital and to restrict who could see him. Patrick Furey, an inspector of the Newport police assisting the state's case, was also denied admission to see Travers. In Providence, federal Customs Service officials refused to cooperate with the state investigation.[116]

"Our only interest is in seeing that the case gets to a grand jury," Rhode Island's Assistant Attorney General McLyman said. He did not care if it was a federal or a state grand jury.[117]

Meanwhile, on December 31, *Black Duck*'s wounded captain, Charlie Travers, while lying in bed at Newport Hospital, was finally served with a warrant for his arrest. Later that day, he was arraigned in Providence and charged with violating the National Prohibition Act. His right arm was in a sling, but he wore a nice suit. His bond of $10,000 was paid by a Providence man (presumably hired by Joseph Dressler), and he was released amid a throng of government officials and newspaper reporters. The burials of the three men killed on his boat occurred that day and the next.[118]

On January 3, 1930, *Black Duck* was examined in Providence by federal Customs Service officials. The inspectors found that all shots fired from *CG-290* had been fired toward the stern of the *Black Duck* and not head on, as Travers had asserted. The stricken vessel was then towed to Pawtuxet Cove, where it was held under a heavy guard.[119] (Two days later, one of the guards, a customs agent, waved two revolvers at a crowd that had gathered to view the famous boat; the guard was suspended from duty after he admitted that he had been intoxicated at the time from drinking "moonshine.")[120]

In short order, it became clear that federal authorities would not bring a case to a federal grand jury and instead would seek to protect *CG-290*'s crew from state authorities. On January 4, based on a review of some of the statements and testimony of *CG-290*'s crew, Boss issued a statement completely exonerating the crew. He declared that as the patrol boat's machine gun opened fire, the fleeing *Black Duck* veered and was raked from stern to pilothouse. Boss announced that the federal government would therefore not bring charges against *CG-290*'s crew. He added that the crew would not cooperate in any state investigation. Finally, Boss confirmed that *CG-290* had not fired any warning shots, either with the vessel's one-pounder or machine gun. But he added that in his view the Coast Guard was not required to do so under applicable law when dealing with rumrunners.[121] This position was in contrast with Boss's announcement several days earlier citing Section 2765 of the federal statutes, which required that the Coast Guard vessel fire a warning shot before using deadly force.[122]

Rhode Island authorities specially convened a Providence County grand jury to consider the evidence in the slaying of the three men aboard *Black Duck*. Federal authorities at first refused to identify the Coast Guardsmen from *CG-290* in an effort to protect them from the public. But they were forced to cooperate by producing the men at the grand jury hearing on January 14. The grand jurors heard testimony from Boatswain Cornell and the other seven crew members, from Charlie Travers and from thirteen other witnesses. Then the jurors retired from the courtroom to consider whether to indict Cornell, Pearson and other crew members for the charge of voluntary manslaughter.[123]

Chapter 8

WINTER 1930

THE AFTERMATH OF THE *BLACK DUCK* KILLINGS

The machine gunning and killing of the three crewmen on board *Black Duck* and the wounding of Charlie Travers created a sensation in the country, particularly in New England. It was front-page news in the *New York Times*'s December 30, 1929 edition, for example. The incident forced many to reconsider the advisability of Prohibition itself. It also resulted in some thoughtful leaders reevaluating the Coast Guard's policy of using deadly machine guns against rumrunners.

Still, Prohibition had many supporters nationwide, including in Congress. The Republican Party and Prohibition forces had combined to fail to reapportion federal election districts based on the 1920 census. Doing so would have resulted in a significant increase in new districts in urban areas. This outrageous and unprecedented situation meant that congressmen from rural districts in the South and West who heavily supported Prohibition still dominated Congress in 1930.

The *Black Duck* affair became the touchstone between those who sought more and tougher enforcement against Prohibition violators and those who wanted a lighter hand, as well as the end of national Prohibition. The dispute would be aired in competing statements, announcements, telegrams and rallies regarding the *Black Duck* incident.

News of the killings released pent-up anger at Prohibition and the means of enforcing it using large-caliber guns. The first to complain publicly was Reverend Roy W. Magoun, superintendent of the Seamen's Church Institute in Newport. On the morning of December 30, he declared in a

Sunday sermon at St. George's Church in Newport that the killings earlier in the day amounted to "downright murder." "Let us not forget," he said, "that the three men who were murdered this morning right off our shores by methods which would have made a German submarine commander proud, were our brothers. Their deaths must bring to us a little clearer the horrible price we are paying to attempt to enforce the laws which are fundamentally un-American."

Magoun vividly described Weisman, Goulart and Brandt huddled in a small cabin before they were "shot like rats in a trap to satisfy the frenzied fanaticism and smug hypocrisy" of the "dry" forces. "Surely we are not going to sit by and look on these things complacently," he said.[124] Magoun's words would help ensure that complacency would not be the order of the day.

The respected superintendent emeritus of Butler Hospital in Providence, Dr. G. Alder Blumer, also called the killings "murder."[125]

U.S. Senator David I. Walsh from Massachusetts sent a telegram on December 30 to Secretary of the Treasury Andrew W. Mellon requesting that a full investigation of the incident be conducted by officers not connected with the Coast Guard. Walsh referred to the considerable "public indignation in Massachusetts as a result of killing three citizens, alleged to be violating Prohibition law, by the Coast Guard off Newport Sunday." Walsh stated that an investigation should determine whether it was appropriate to "punish those who may be found to have exceeded their authority and used their official position to needlessly kill their fellow citizens, even though violating the law."[126]

Already feeling the heat, in Washington, D.C., on the day of the killings, Rear Admiral Frederick Billard, commandant of the Coast Guard, felt the need to issue a statement defending the Coast Guard's policy of using deadly force against rumrunners. He warned that the Coast Guard "means business" about enforcing "Prohibition in U.S. waters." He continued:

> The Coast Guard has the job of stopping liquor smuggling at sea. It is not a job that can be handled with soft words and amiable gestures….If a smuggler elects to defy the command of a Coast Guard craft to stop, he runs a serious risk of getting hurt through a course of action that the law has specifically authorized for 100 years.[127]

This statement satisfied those desiring a rigid enforcement of Prohibition laws but was seen by many others as inflammatory, being issued so soon after the killings.

Congressman John W. McCormack of Massachusetts supported Senator Walsh's call for an impartial and disinterested investigation. McCormack added, "A strong wave of public indignation properly exists as a result of what is considered unnecessary killings." Discussing the fatal shootings with newspaper reporters, McCormack said that the loss of human life brought to the minds of honest thinking persons that Prohibition was a farce and a failure and was fundamentally un-American and un-Christian.[128]

In Washington, D.C., Seymour Lowman, assistant secretary of the Treasury and in charge of Prohibition enforcement, issued a hardline statement supporting the Coast Guard. His statement, in part, read, "The loss of life at Newport the other day was unfortunate, but unavoidable. The laws of the United States must be maintained. The smugglers defied Government officers and took their punishment. They have no one to blame but themselves."[129]

Such an unyielding statement, combined with the killings of the three rumrunners, sparked much outrage. It was certainly a convenient opportunity for the many opponents of Prohibition to attack and place on the defensive both the supporters and enforcers of the Volstead Act.

At noon on January 2, a mass meeting was held at Boston's Faneuil Hall, sponsored by the Liberal Civic League, a national anti-Prohibition organization. Faneuil Hall had been the site of speeches in the days leading up to the American Revolution, where Patriots railed against British tyranny. An approving crowd of more than one thousand packed the hall and gallery on January 2, spilling into the hallways. Attendees cheered speakers who criticized the killings and Prohibition itself. Outside the historic building, red-lettered placards called the episode the "Newport Massacre." Inside, a speaker compared the Newport killings to the historic Boston Massacre of 1770, in which British soldiers armed with muskets shot at a crowd of protestors, killing five and wounding three. Both deeds, the speaker said, occurred under the guise of official authority.

Conrad W. Croker of the Liberal Civic League told the crowd, "The men who were killed were rumrunners, but they were also human beings and citizens." He added to applause, "If we're going to have law and order, we're going to insist on law and order on the part of our government." Croker ridiculed the claim of *CG-290*'s crew that it had fired its one-pounder as a warning shot. He demanded that Assistant Secretary of the Treasury Lowman "produce the empty shell." Croker further doubted that *Black Duck* had been properly warned before the machine gun opened on the fleeing rumrunner.[130]

One of several bullets found aboard *Black Duck* from machine guns fired by *CG-290*, presented as evidence in a Coast Guard investigation of *CG-290*'s shooting of *Black Duck* on December 29, 1929. This bullet was found in *Black Duck*'s forecastle. *National Archives.*

U.S. Congressman John J. Douglass from Massachusetts minced no words in denouncing the killings to the Faneuil Hall crowd. "The United States has no more right to kill a man unlawfully than has an individual," Douglass railed. "Men were slain feloniously Sunday morning by the Coast Guard of the United States. They were murdered."[131]

U.S. Senator David I. Walsh, in a letter, sent his regrets that he could not attend the meeting. His letter was read to the crowd, including Walsh referring to the killings at Newport as "cruel, if not murderous" and "shocking, apparently unwarranted."[132]

John F. ("Honey Fitz") Fitzgerald brought the meeting to a raucous conclusion. The smooth-talking former mayor of Boston and the grandfather of then twelve-year-old John Fitzgerald Kennedy called the Newport shootings a "horrible outrage." "If they can shoot at boats," Fitzgerald railed, "automobiles will be next." The former mayor wondered if the follow-up step would be "a general slaughter" in the restaurants and hotels of the country that serve liquor, so that "the most ardent Prohibitionist will be satisfied that the law is being carried out." Returning to the Newport killings, Fitzgerald passionately stated to the cheering crowd, "Human life is sacred, given by Almighty God, and should not be taken until after the most careful deliberation." He added, "Capital punishment is abolished in most places in the world now, and men who are found guilty…are given sometimes years before the sentence is carried out." By contrast, the three men off Newport were "shot down like rats in a trap."[133]

After the meeting at Faneuil Hall ended, the aroused crowd poured out into the streets. A small group proceeded to the Boston Common, where they tore up Coast Guard recruiting signs and posters. At South Street Station, another Coast Guard recruiting poster was damaged. The Coast Guard withdrew its recruiting posters from Boston.[134]

In Rhode Island on January 3, the local chapter of the Association Against Prohibition chose a propitious time to begin distributing ninety-four thousand questionnaires to state residents. The questions solicited their views on the constitutionality of federal enforcement of Prohibition, the feasibility of permitting sales of light wines and beer and the increase of "hypocrisy and general lawlessness under national prohibition."[135]

On the same day, Secretary of the Treasury Andrew Mellon issued a statement on the matter. A known opponent of Prohibition in his private life, he nonetheless supported the actions of the Coast Guard. He asserted that the eight-man Coast Guard crew of *CG-290* had done nothing that was not justified and authorized under the law in firing on *Black Duck*, even if it resulted in the three regrettable deaths. "They gave warning, the boat was endeavoring to escape, and they could not do less than they did," Mellon said. Referring to all Coast Guardsmen attempting to interdict suspected rumrunners, the statement continued, "If they could not shoot, they could not carry out their instructions" to stop boats suspected of smuggling.[136]

That same night, toughs on New London's waterfront seemed to respond to Secretary Mellon's statement. They beat up a Coast Guardsman, George A. Cadorett of Pawtucket, near the State Pier Headquarters at Section Base 4 in New London. Before being attacked, Cadorett had been asked, "Were you on the 290?" "No," Cadorett responded, but he admitted that he was a Coast Guardsman. "Well, that's good enough for us," one of the toughs replied, as the gang then administered the beating.[137]

Captain L.T. Chalker, a Coast Guard officer at the New London base, criticized inaccurate reports in newspapers for inflaming public opinion. "The readiness with which many papers have published the statements of liquor smugglers, cheap politicians and wet fanatics," he said, "has undoubtedly led many ruffians to believe that such actions as last night's cowardly attack on one of our men would meet with public approval."[138]

Violence and the threat of it in New London did not end. At about 2:30 a.m. on January 7, a gang of civilians threw stones at a houseboat owned by Boatswain Alexander Cornell that was moored in the rear of Howard Street. Cornell had been publicly identified as the commander of *CG-290* in the earliest newspaper accounts of the shootings. Cornell was not at home, as he was still confined to Section Base 4. His wife and five children were, however, in the houseboat during the stoning, and they understandably became terrified.[139] A few days earlier, Cornell had received a letter from Pawtuxet, Rhode Island, addressed to "Mr. Cornell, the Hun" that contained a death threat.[140]

On January 8, Customs officials in Providence asked Cranston police to reinforce customs agents guarding *Black Duck* at Pawtuxet Cove. The reinforcements were requested after customs officials had learned of a threat to blow up the rumrunner.[141]

The editorial pages in many of the nation's newspapers took sides. The *New York Herald Tribune* wrote, "It may be that bloodshed is inevitable in the enforcement of a law that large sections of the country treat with contempt. But does this excuse the raking of an unarmed rum-runner with machine guns at close range?" The *Washington Post* adopted a harsh law-and-order tone that even exceeded the Coast Guard's policy: "[T]he rumrunners got only what was coming to them....[W]hen smugglers are on open water...it is not only the duty of the authorities to pursue and search them, but to kill them if there is no other means of overhauling them."[142]

To the great embarrassment of Coast Guard officials, on the same night as the *Black Duck* shooting, an outside vessel had been captured and brought into New London, but Coast Guardsmen broke open many of the confiscated liquor bottles, got drunk and engaged in a major brawl. Calling this affair "disgraceful," the *New York Herald Tribune* continued, "The public is asking itself why men of this caliber should be sent forth to hunt suspected vessels with machine guns."[143]

The *Black Duck* controversy found its way to the floor of the House of Representatives in Washington, D.C., on January 7. The day before, Representative Fiorello La Guardia of New York City had recognized the political value of the *Black Duck* incident in the effort to repeal Prohibition, declaring in a statement that "for the first time the drys are on the defensive."[144] On the House floor, La Guardia spent thirty-nine minutes speaking against the *Black Duck* killings, the uselessness of trying to enforce Prohibition and the deleterious effect Prohibition had on the previously pristine reputation of the Coast Guard. In response, Representative Carroll L. Beedy of Maine defended the actions of the Coast Guard in firing on fleeing rumrunners, to the applause of most House members.[145]

Attorney General Oscar Heltzen of Rhode Island collected information on the shootings that he planned to introduce to a grand jury. On January 2, he declared that he had plenty of evidence to show that the one-pounder on *CG-290* was never fired as a warning to the crew of *Black Duck*.[146]

Finally, on January 14, 1930, a Providence County grand jury was presented evidence in connection with the slayings of the three *Black Duck* crewmen. The primary question was whether there was sufficient evidence to return an indictment charging voluntary manslaughter by the Coast Guard crew of *CG-290*. The proceedings began at 10:00 a.m., with jurors hearing from twenty-two witnesses, including Charlie Travers and the members of the patrol boat's crew. The jurors did not visit the *Black Duck* but were shown photographs of it and the bullet holes. They began to confer at 5:00 p.m. and returned forty-eight minutes later. The jurors reported no indictment. The foreman of the grand jury read the following statement to the presiding judge, A.A. Capotosto:

> *In view of the great public interest in the matter under investigation by the Grand Jury, involving the so-called Black Duck shooting, its members feel that a statement should be made at this time. We believe that the Attorney General's Department has fully and thoroughly presented to us all the evidence available which would assist us in arriving at a decision in the matter. The investigation and consideration has been completely carried out. We accordingly report that we find no true bill.*[147]

The Customs Service and Coast Guard board of inquiry investigations also exonerated the crew of *CG-290*.[148]

Paulsen's investigation discovered that at least nineteen bullets struck *Black Duck*. Remarkably, almost all of these bullets hit the boat above the hull, striking the pilothouse, engine room, dory and other parts on the deck of the rumrunner. Gunner Pearson would have avoided the tragedy had he aimed lower or higher.

The grand jury made the correct decision. The members of *CG-290*'s crew did not commit the crime of voluntary manslaughter. Voluntary manslaughter, also called intentional manslaughter, typically involves a killing in the heat of passion without prior intent to kill. The crime still requires an

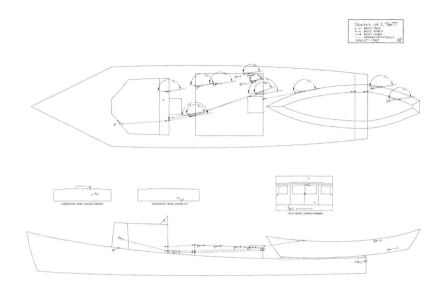

"Sketch of C-5677," showing the probable paths of machine gun bullets fired from *CG-290* at *Black Duck* on December 29, 1929, prepared for a Coast Guard investigation in late December 1929 or early January 1930. *National Archives.*

intent to kill at the time of the killing.[149] None of the crew members intended to kill Weisman, Goulart or Brandt.

The jurors were not asked whether or not the Coast Guard crew was entitled to fire and use deadly force against a suspected rumrunner that refused to halt when signaled by a searchlight and a Klaxon horn. That was not the standard for involuntary manslaughter. While Cornell should have made a better effort to fire a warning shot with his vessel's one-pounder, as Coast Guard policy required, it seems unlikely that would have resulted in Travers cutting his engines and heaving to.

Sometimes a terrible thing happens and the perpetrators of it did not commit a crime. This was one of those instances.

Still, it is very possible that Cornell and Pearson had an understanding that Pearson was to fire his machine gun burst directly into *Black Duck*, thus endangering the lives of the rumrunner's crew. A serious problem for Cornell was that *CG-290* was tied up to a bell buoy, with its engines not running. As a result, it had no chance of chasing and running down *Black Duck*, and there was no other Coast Guard vessel up the bay to assist. Thus, Cornell and Pearson may well have decided that they had no choice but to fire directly at *Black Duck* if they wanted to force it to heave to. (On February 6, 1930, the

Coast Guard prohibited its boats from tying up to buoys, ostensibly for the safety of legitimate civilian boats.)[150] Cornell also admitted ordering Pearson, "Let her have it." That did not sound like an order to fire a warning shot or a shot over the rumrunner or behind the rumrunner. And Pearson wound up firing on a line just above *Black Duck*'s deck, an extremely dangerous level for the rumrunner's crew, whether or not Travers had turned his vessel to the port side.

Everett S. Allen, in his book *Black Ships: Rumrunners of Prohibition*, published some of the formal statements and testimony of the crew of *CG-290* regarding the *Black Duck* affair. In one of the statements, Cornell essentially admitted that he had Pearson fire directly at *Black Duck*'s stern and hull at deck level and made no mention of a warning shot. He said:

> *Realizing that the rum boat had twice the speed of our craft and was sure to escape in the fog unless she could be made to lie to, we started firing the machine gun across her stern and hull. We knew that the cargo in the stern protected the crew. We saw no one except the man at the wheel and he was protected by the piled cases.*[151]

Allen did not provide a citation for this statement, and the author did not find it in Coast Guard records. The author suspects that the statement is credible and was taken on December 29, prior to the later statements by Cornell and his crew. By the time of these later statements and testimony, Cornell and Pearson may have agreed to say that their understanding was that Pearson was first to fire warning shots astern or over *Black Duck*.

The *Providence Journal* reported in its December 30 edition, based on reports taken on December 29 and 30, "20 shots were fired, with the intention, Coast Guard officials said, of disabling the fleeing boat." New London Coast Guard officials further explained that the burst of machine gun fire was "to try to cut the hawser line, rip away the rudder or cripple the machinery of the rum runner."[152] This was another admission that the Lewis machine gun was fired directly at *Black Duck*.

However, an assistant federal district attorney on the case argued that *Black Duck*'s crew failed to take the precautionary measure of stacking sacks of liquor in rows behind their boat's pilothouse. Failing to do so, and presenting the boat's stern to *CG-290* at close range, were "fatal errors," according to the attorney, Charles H. Eden.[153]

The standard line among *CG-290*'s crew members and their superiors at New London was that *Black Duck*, as it fled, unexpectedly turned left, resulting in Pearson's machine gun bullets pouring into the port side of the rumrunner. But this author, based on a review of the Sketch of Probable Action, showing the movements of *Black Duck* in relation to *CG-290*'s station, and the Sketch of C-5677, showing the paths of the machine gun bullets that struck *Black Duck* on it starboard side, both prepared by the Coast Guard for Paulsen's investigation, believes that the deadly machine gun bullets hit the rumrunner seconds before it turned to the left.[154] However, this author does not consider this point is crucial. The key to the incident was that Pearson fired directly at *Black Duck*.

In any event, the blame for the three deaths should be laid primarily at the feet of the Coast Guard's policy of allowing large-caliber guns to be fired at fleeing rumrunners. As a result of this policy, it was just a matter of time before unintentional deaths occurred. With deadly machine gun fire peppering small, wooden rumrunners, it was a wonder that more accidental deaths did not happen.

Captain Wolf, an officer at Section Base 4 at New London, recognized that accidental deaths would occur as a result of the Coast Guard's policy, but he blamed the rumrunners for not stopping their boats:

> *Small vessels engaged in smuggling are willing to take the chance of running from vessels on patrol and very often do not heed the warning to stop. The well-known smuggler, C-5677, took this chance and as a result three men were killed. Accidents of this kind are deeply regretted, but will happen from time to time if vessels engaged in smuggling do not heed the warnings of Coast Guard vessels to heave to when so directed.*[155]

Boatswain Cornell made the same point when he was interviewed during the Coast Guard's detailed investigation. Cornell mentioned that after the capture, he had said to Travers, "I guess this will learn us all a lesson." When asked by the investigator to explain what he meant by that, Cornell said, "I meant that the conditions that existed that night were bound to happen at some time, the way that these [rumrunning] boats have been operating in the past and failing to stop when signaled by vessels of the Coast Guard."[156]

Lieutenant Commander Paulsen, after his investigation of the shooting, made a similar point more bluntly. He concluded that based on the Coast Guard's experience pursuing rumrunners and his own experience, "a speed boat… cannot be stopped except by such machine gun fire as will endanger life."[157]

At the January 2 meeting at Faneuil Hall, Conrad Croker of the Liberal Civic League shouted at the packed crowd, "The boy who fired the shots is not responsible, those in command of 290 are not responsible. It's the system of hypocrisy which is responsible."[158]

The Coast Guard had authority to employ deadly weapons in order to force a vessel suspected of violating federal laws to stop and be searched. The problem was that the laws being enforced involved Prohibition, which was a deeply unpopular law and widely violated nationally. In this circumstance, it was simply bad policy to fire large-caliber weapons at fleeing rumrunners.

Some sharp observers at the time made this subtle connection. Senator David Walsh of Massachusetts was one of them. In his first statement on the incident, on December 30, 1929, he questioned whether it was appropriate for Coast Guardsmen acting in "their official position to needlessly kill their fellow citizens, even though violating the law."[159] The next day, he said, "It is a murderous act to kill the unarmed whose attempted crime is aided and abetted and encouraged by overwhelming numbers of our citizens, especially in the large centers."[160] By large centers, Walsh meant New York City, Boston, Baltimore, Miami, Chicago, Detroit, Los Angeles, Seattle and other cities. On January 6, 1930, Walsh suggested that the U.S. Senate's Commerce Committee, which had jurisdiction over the Coast Guard, consider "investigating the whole question of killing alleged law breakers by Coast Guardsmen in connection with the enforcement of the Prohibition laws."[161]

"Honey Fitz" Fitzgerald, at the same Faneuil Hall meeting, focused on the hypocrisy of the situation. He said that Weisman, Goulart and Brandt "were killed in such an outrageous manner that we must consider the… atmosphere concerning Prohibition, particularly in this section of the country." He continued, "Everyone knows that liquor was drunk openly in practically every hotel in this part of the country on New Year's Eve, and that a large part of the supply came in the same manner as these boys were slaughtered for doing."[162]

It was a subtle point that the hard-line law enforcement types in the Coast Guard did not appreciate. To the Coast Guard officers, they had the task under federal law of interdicting smuggling of illegal liquor, and they would do it using all force necessary, even if it meant endangering the lives of men who could hardly be called criminals deserving to be shot.

Many, perhaps most, crew members working on rumrunners were former fishermen or young men seeking adventure and a quick buck. They were not hardened or dangerous criminals. Sometimes Coast Guard officials liked to portray some rumrunners as "desperate characters," but

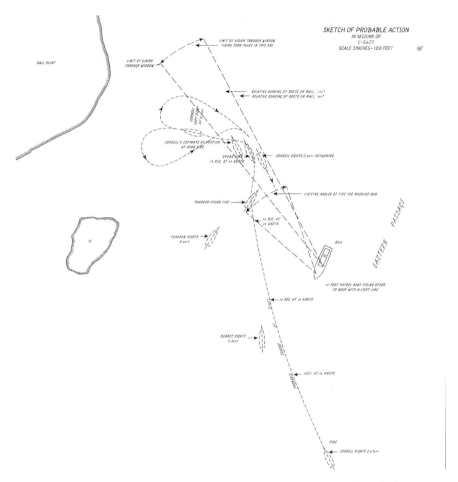

"Sketch of Probable Action in Seizure of C-5677," otherwise known as *Black Duck*, prepared for a Coast Guard investigation in late December 1929 to early January 1930. *National Archives.*

that rarely fit the description of rumrunners operating in Rhode Island waters. No guns were found aboard the *Black Duck*, and there were no known successful or attempted shootings of Coast Guardsmen in Rhode Island waters during Prohibition.

Still, the Coast Guard had underwater divers search near the dock of Fort Adams for a gun Charlie Travers might have thrown overboard. The *Providence Journal* reported, "Newport fishermen yesterday said that it was unusual for small rumrunners to carry weapons, as they were frequently searched by Coast Guard vessels on their outward trips to Rum Row."[163] It is interesting that the *Journal* turned to fishermen for the true story about rumrunners.

A review of the backgrounds of the three men killed by *CG-290*'s crew does not reveal that they were dangerous criminals who deserved being shot at with machine guns. Of the four crewmen on board *Black Duck*, Jacob "Jake" Weisman of Providence had the most experience in the illegal liquor business. His parents were Jewish immigrants from Austria whose primary language was Yiddish and who operated a restaurant at 78 Gay Street in Providence (which was the address given for the registered owner of *Black Duck*). Weisman was described in the *Boston Globe* as a leader in the Rhode Island beer rackets. This prominent and likely exaggerated title was apparently based on his indictment in connection with a raid on a bootlegging operation in a farm at Portsmouth on the evening of March 14–15, 1929, at which six hundred cases of liquor were seized, as well as a prior arrest and fine for transporting Canadian beer.[164] At the time of his last rumrunning cruise, the twenty-eight-year-old Weisman was married and had children, but he was separated from his wife and consorting with a young mistress in New Bedford. The mistress, tellingly, said of him to a newspaper reporter that the rumrunning business "was the breath of life to him. His heart and soul were in it. He loved excitement going out and clipping in again. He made good money at it, he had an expensive car. He used to say that if anything ever happened to that business and he couldn't get on, he'd just [as well] be dead. He'd been in it so long, you see."[165] But there was no indication that Weisman was a dangerous criminal who presented a risk of engaging in gunplay.

John Goulart may have had the least experience in the illegal liquor business. As was the case with Charlie Travers, his parents were immigrants from the Azores. His parents worked on their farm on Sconticut Neck Road in Fairhaven. Goulart and his family were longtime neighbors and friends of Charlie Travers and his family. Goulart had two brothers enlisted in the navy. After graduating from Fairhaven High School, where he played on the football team, he worked on his father's dairy farm and later was engaged as a lobster fisherman.[166] His mother informed a newspaper reporter that her deceased son had been working for Travers for some time.[167] Again, there was no indication that Goulart had a dangerous disposition.

Dudley Brandt of the Dorchester neighborhood in Boston had served in the navy in World War I, but he was also not particularly experienced in the rum business. Brandt was married but had not lived at his Dorchester home for several months. However, his wife did say that he regularly sent her money. The *Boston Globe* wrote that Brandt was well known in the Savin Hill District in Dorchester and was a skilled marine engineer and a specialist in testing engines. He was hired as *Black Duck*'s engineer.[168]

The crew members were representative of rumrunners in southeastern New England. Two, Travers and Goulart, were former fishermen. Two were ethnic Portuguese (Travers and Goulart), and Weisman was Jewish. Each of the three men had parents who were first-generation immigrants. Along with Brandt, none of the men was known to have a history of violent behavior.

Elsworth Latham, a veteran Coast Guard officer based in Newport who in 1931 would order his picket boat's machine gun to be fired at five rumrunners in Rhode Island waters, had come across the *Black Duck*'s crew earlier in 1929. In in an interview late in his life, Lathan had only kind thoughts about them. He recalled, "You've got to remember, we're talking Prohibition; there weren't many jobs to be had, people had families to feed. A lot of those fellows that were running rum weren't true criminals or bad men, they were trying to survive. It was a means to an end. As for Charlie [Travers] I always found him to be pleasant and congenial. All of them were good boys on that boat [*Black Duck*]."[169]

Charlie Travers was an experienced commander of rumrunners, even though he was only twenty-three years old at the time of the *Black Duck* shooting. A Providence County grand jury must not have been convinced that the former Coast Guardsman and fisherman was a dangerous criminal. On March 6, 1930, the grand jury failed to indict him for his role in attempting to smuggle 383 cases of illegal liquor found on board *Black Duck* after its capture. The grand jurors must have felt that being shot by the Coast Guard and seeing three of his crew killed was punishment enough for Travers.[170]

Chapter 9

WINTER 1930

THE SHOOTINGS RESUME
(MONOLOLA AND MADAME X)

T
he Coast Guard never halted or even deferred its policy of machine
gunning rumrunners in or approaching Narragansett Bay. Within a few
months following the *Black Duck* tragedy, the *rat-tat-tat* of machine guns
could again be heard along miles of Rhode Island waters. In these next two
incidents, however, the machine gun fire did not stop the fleeing rumrunners.
Was this an indication that Coast Guard gunners were demonstrating more
care in their shooting?

Besides the ill-fated *Black Duck*, perhaps the most famous rumrunner
operating in Narragansett Bay during Prohibition was *Monolola*, a 50-foot
powerboat built at the Crowninshield Shipyard at Somerset, Massachusetts.
It was involved in three wild chases from 1930 to 1932.

The first incident in Rhode Island waters occurred on February 24, 1930.
The Coast Guard, adopting a new policy since the *Black Duck* killings of
keeping mum about the details, did not offer any information to newspaper
reporters, who had to rely on rumor and those who heard shots fired.

Coast Guard patrol boat *CG-234*, a 75-footer, spotted *Monolola* running
without lights on the east side of Rose Island in the East Passage of
Narragansett Bay at about 2:15 a.m. on February 25. The patrol boat threw
its searchlight on the mysterious boat and saw that it was *Monolola*, with its
deck piled high with sacks of liquor. *CG-234* fired two one-pounder blank
shells, followed by a burst of machine gun fire, as signals to stop, but they
were ignored. Instead, *Monolola* revved its engines and increased its speed,
proceeding to the north toward Gould Island.

CG-234 fired live machine gun bullets at the fleeing craft. Crew members saw that the fire shattered glass in the wheelhouse door, and other shots were seen striking sacks of liquor on the vessel's deck. *CG-234* fired a total of 260 bullets at *Monolola*, but the fast speedboat escaped into the darkness.

According to U.S. Navy personnel present on Rose Island and Gould Island at the time, as reported by the *Boston Globe*, "the chase started about 2 a.m. When the vessels went past the islands the fugitive boat was about 600 feet in the lead. It was then that the shots were heard."[171]

The *Newport Mercury*, with the benefit of writing several days after the event, reported, "The Marine Guard on Rose Island heard [the first shots], and the government forces at the Training Station and Gould Island heard the shots, as the Coast Guard cutter repeatedly fired in an attempt to make the rumrunner stop. At the time it was said *Monolola* was about 200 yards in advance of the pursuing Coast Guard vessel, both proceeding at a rapid rate." The Newport newspaper continued: "Further shots were heard from the Middletown shore, and the men on duty at the Mount Hope Bridge heard shots as the chase continued relentlessly under that structure."[172]

The *Providence Journal* reported in its February 26 newspaper, "The shots of the patrol boat were heard by numerous residents along the eastern shore of the bay, as well as by officials at the Government reservations on Rose and Gould Islands, off Newport, and by a bridge policeman on the Mount Hope bridge." The Providence newspaper added that observers thought they had heard the firing of a one-pound gun as well as a machine gun. The report concluded that the rumrunner had "led the Coast Guard boat on the longest race that has ever been staged in Rhode Island waters."[173] The twenty-five-mile chase up Narragansett Bay and into Mount Hope Bay was also said to be the longest chase ever made by a Coast Guard vessel from the New London base.

CG-234 lost *Monolola* in Mount Hope Bay. *CG-234* spent the rest of the night looking at various coves and ports in the eastern part of Mount Hope Bay, until the rumrunner was found at Crowninshield Shipyard, across from downtown Fall River, at 7:40 a.m. Its cargo, crew and registration papers were gone. It was not known if the crew had dumped the liquor in shallow water around Fall River or managed to unload it onshore.

The official incident report filed by the commander of *CG-234* described the damage done by the machine gun fire:

A port glass was found missing from the wheelhouse with shattered glass on deck. One machine gun hole was found alongside engine room trunk and

The notorious and speedy rumrunner *Monolola*, with a low silhouette, making it hard to see from a distance. *National Archives.*

another in her starboard quarter. Blood was splattered on the afterside of the wheelhouse by outside wheel. Her decks had been freshly washed down but particles of glass were scattered around.

It appears the rum boat had been washed down by the crew, but one bloodstain was missed.[174] Whether the blood was from a wound caused by a bullet or flying glass is not known.

This was the first time the Coast Guard had come across *Monolola*. The boat was initially thought to be owned by New York interests, but the *Providence Journal* reported that it "was said by Coast Guardsmen to have been owned by the Capone syndicate."[175] Alphonso ("Al" or "Scarface") Capone, the famous Chicago beer bootlegger, once visited Providence during Prohibition. The boat was registered to a Harry Bennett of 80 Plenty Street, Providence, but there was no one at that address by that name.

The *Newport Mercury* reported, "It is known, also, that a number of interests in this vicinity [Newport] are concerned with the boat, which is said to have cost in the neighborhood of $50,000." The newspaper added that *Monolola* "was a new craft and had made but one or two trips. It was equipped with two Liberty motors and a 400-horse-power Flat motor, generating a total of more than 1,100 horse-power. It was said to be the fastest craft in these waters, and capable of a speed in excess of 45 knots."[176] If the forty-five knots claim was true, *Monolola* may have been the fastest rumrunner in Rhode Island's history.

The Coast Guard towed *Monolola* to New London. While it was tied up at the State Pier in New London, reporters could see that the rumrunner's sides had been dented by machine gun bullets, and the window glass on the port of its pilothouse was shattered. A *Providence Journal* reporter wrote that the rumrunner "bore evidence of the machine gun fire that had swept its decks during the chase."[177]

Commander L.T. Chalker, chief of staff of the Coast Guard's New London base, informed reporters that charges could be brought of not stopping when ordered, running without lights and resisting arrest. Eventually, with little proof of rumrunning, *Monolola* was released back to its owners. The speedboat would cross paths with Coast Guard machine gunners a year later.[178]

Interestingly, Coast Guard officials at New London said that the Coast Guard fired on suspected fleeing rumrunners only when there was visible evidence of contraband on board.[179] *CG-234*'s crew did report seeing sacks of liquor piled high on *Monolola*'s deck before firing at it. The Coast Guard believed that *Monolola* was captained by Harry Kembarn, who was given a dishonorable discharge from the Coast Guard in December 1929.[180]

Shockingly, the next report of the Coast Guard firing its machine guns at a boat traveling to Rhode Island waters had a *Black Duck* connection. The targeted vessel was reportedly owned by none other than Charles Travers, the sole survivor of the *Black Duck* shootings.

On the night of February 27, 1930, the Coast Guard destroyer *Downes*, cruising about five miles east of Block Island, spotted a motorboat traveling with speed and without lights. The destroyer turned on its searchlights and pointed them at the distant boat; Coast Guardsmen reported seeing sacks of burlap bags on the deck of the speedboat. The vessel failed to heed a signal to stop and be searched and ignored more than three one-pounder blank shells fired by the destroyer.

The Coast Guard vessel gave chase and the motorboat fled. The *Downes*'s official report indicated that the destroyer fired live one-pounder ammunition at the fleeing vessel. But according to a newspaper account, the Coast Guard vessel opened fire with its machine guns, and the targeted vessel began "zig-zagging away from a shower of hot lead." But the suspected rumrunner was fast—it sped away from the Coast Guard vessel into the night at an impressive nineteen knots an hour and avoided capture.[181]

The next day, Coast Guardsmen searched for their prey in coves and behind islands. The patrol boat *CG-283* found a fishing boat abandoned at a dock at Newport. No crew members were around, and no liquor was found on board. It was *Madame X*, a speedy boat owned by Charles Travers of New Bedford. The Coast Guardsmen seized the vessel, insisting that it was the same one that had eluded them the night before and that had been spotted with liquor piled on its deck. Coast Guardsmen brought *Madame X* to New London, where it was charged with running without lights, failing to stop when ordered and resisting arrest.

The American gas screw *Madame X* was 58 feet long and 13 feet wide and had a depth of 5.5 feet. The 26.5-ton vessel, built of wood at Casey Boat Building Company at Fairhaven, Massachusetts, in 1930, had a single mast but was powered by two 150-horsepower Lathrop engines.[182] The boat's name was inspired by a 1929 movie of the same name directed by Lionel Barrymore. It had been licensed for fishing (Travers had been a fisherman). Its master was Arthur "Frank" Butler from New Bedford—he would play an important role in the sinking of the steel-plated *Nola* at the end of 1931.

The March 1, 1930 edition of the *Hartford Courant* waxed eloquently about the irony:

> *Just two months after he groped over the bodies of three of the crew of the rum-runner "Black Duck," whose pilothouse was suddenly turned into a death chamber by a torrent of machine-gun bullets from the Coast Guard patrol boat "290," the name of Charles Travers, of Fairhaven, Mass., lone survivor of the smuggler, went into Coast Guard records again today, when a New London patrol boat paraded into the harbor with Travers's brand new speed modeled fishing sloop, "Madame X," a captive….*
>
> *Less than a week ago, the man whose arm was badly torn by machine-gun fire December 29, purchased the new "Madame X." Beautifully designed, nearly 60 feet from bow to stern, and powered by two 200-horsepower Sterling engines, the suspected rum boat is considered the fastest boat of its kind in the water.*

This was not the last of *Madame X*'s run-ins with the Coast Guard. On September 30, 1932, near Mishaum Point, Dartmouth, Massachusetts, the vessel and its crew were captured by *CG-2296* after the cabin picket boat fired twenty-one rounds of machine gun fire at sacks of liquor piled on the rumrunner's deck. *Madame X* was found to have been registered as a fishing boat in the name of Jesse Silvia of Newport, and three crew members gave Newport as their residence (the fourth named Fall River as his residence). A total of 914 sacks of liquor was seized from *Madame X*.[183]

The Coast Guard's firing of machine guns and one-pounder cannons at *Monolola* and *Madame X* established that the controversy over the *Black Duck* shootings had little or no effect on its use of large-caliber weapons in Rhode Island waters.

Chapter 10

SUMMER 1930

THE CARNAGE CONTINUES (*MARDELLE*)

A shooting incident in Narragansett Bay that occurred in August 1930 again revealed that the *Black Duck* tragedy did not deter the Coast Guard from riddling the fleeing rumrunner *Mardelle* with machine gun fire, even if it caused a severe injury to one of the crew. After this latest wounding, a revelation made this episode even more startling.

Mardelle's tenure as a rumrunner was brief. The boat had been constructed by Crowninshield Shipbuilding Company at its shipyard in Somerset and delivered to rumrunners in late July 1930.[184] The 65-foot boat, powered with three Liberty engines, was fast.

While most rumrunners were disguised as fishing boats or as small cargo haulers, *Mardelle* was the first one in Rhode Island waters to employ a disguise as a luxury yacht. *Mardelle*'s interior included fine mahogany wood, and it was elaborately fitted out. Its hull was painted a mahogany color. To carry out the impression that the yacht was a simple pleasure boat, all members of the crew were arrayed in uniforms. On the stern of the vessel was written in large gold letters "Mardelle, New York." In actuality, it was reportedly owned by Boston bootleggers and operated out of Fall River.

Mardelle's disguise as a luxury yacht did not help it at night. At about 2:00 a.m. on August 26, 1930, off Dyer Island in the East Passage, in between Prudence Island and Middletown on Aquidneck Island, the Coast Guard's *CG-808* spotted *Mardelle* moving at about twelve knots and signaled the boat to heave to for inspection. *CG-808* flashed its searchlight, fired a rocket into the dark sky, sounded its Klaxon horn and then fired a burst of machine gun fire in front of the rumrunner's bow. *Mardelle* responded by throwing out a smokescreen, increasing its speed and turning south toward Jamestown.

To the surprise of the crew of the *Mardelle*, the speedy Coast Guard vessel *CG-808* stayed with their speedy rumrunner and splattered it with machine gun bullets. Bullets exploded liquor bottles stored in burlap bags on its deck and splintered the boat's wood.

According to the *Providence Journal*, "hundreds of cottagers on Prudence Island witnessed the chase," which included "soaring rockets and red stabs of machine gun fire."[185] The rockets fired were flares intended to illuminate the scene for the pursuing Coast Guard boats.

CG-808's incident report fills in details missing from the newspaper articles.[186] When the machine gun bullets caused some of the contraband on the deck of *Mardelle* to catch fire, the machine gun fire stopped, but the chase continued. *Mardelle* proceeded south toward, remarkably, a fleet of U.S. Navy vessels anchored off the east side of Jamestown. According to the incident report, *Mardelle* started to circle various navy ships anchored in the bay, ten in total, all the while throwing sacks and kegs of liquor overboard. Some of the kegs were intended to impede *CG-808*'s progress, but the Coast Guard vessel maintained its pursuit of the rumrunner, at all times shining its searchlight on it.

Suddenly, at about 2:30 a.m., *CG-134*, a 100-foot all-steel Coast Guard vessel that carried a three-pound rifle as well as machine guns, likely under the command of Lieutenant Robert C. Jewell, appeared on the scene. The patrol boat boxed in *Mardelle* and fired a warning shot with its machine gun. The crew of the rumrunner finally surrendered. When Coast Guardsmen from *CG-134* boarded the vessel, they found sacks of liquor on fire on top of the deck and another fire in the engine room. Both blazes were put out by the Coast Guardsmen.

The Coast Guardsmen then found below decks a wounded William "Chips" Munson of Fall River. A bullet had penetrated his back, punctured a lung and exited under an armpit. Munson, known in Newport, was the boat's chief engineer. Another crew member, Henry Chapman of Fairhaven, was injured in his finger, but not seriously.

CG-808 took the severely injured Munson to Fort Adams in Newport. Munson was immediately sent to the meager emergency army medical facilities at the army fort. Perhaps Coast Guard officials wanted to avoid sending Munson to the better-equipped Newport Hospital, where newspaper reporters would have access to him. They did not like it when Charlie Travers had been interviewed shortly after he was shot on *Black Duck* and blasted the Coast Guard for shooting his crew.

Coast Guard officials refused to provide any information regarding the identities of the commander or crew of *CG-134*. According to the *Boston Globe*, Coast Guardsmen "who man ships involved in machine gun skirmishes with rumrunners are heckled when they go ashore and their families also suffer, according to the authorities, and their names are not being made public for this reason." The Coast Guard spokesman also did not identify the second Coast Guard vessel that participated in the capture, *CG-808*, and denied a rumor that it was the converted rumrunner *Black Duck*.

Dr. E.V. Murphy, port physician of Newport, announced that a Coast Guard bullet went through Munson's chest an inch and a half from his spinal column and came out three inches from his heart. Munson had barely avoided instant death or permanent paralysis. Dr. Murphy added that the patient was suffering from shock, but his condition was not regarded as unduly serious unless complications developed. In the afternoon of August 27, under a heavy guard, Munson was finally transferred to Newport Hospital for better care. Coincidentally, the wounded rumrunner stayed in the same room in the hospital in which Travers spent a week in early January. As with Travers, Munson's room was guarded, this time by a crew member of *CG-808*.

Machine gun fire all concentrated into Area bounded by red rectangle on both quarters in order to disable machinery or to explode gas tanks.

This drawing and handwritten note by Louis Gavitt, in command of the speedboat *CG-808*, informed his Coast Guard superiors of his strategy of firing machine guns at fleeing rumrunners in order to disable them or "to explode" their "gas tanks." *National Archives*.

While *Mardelle* was originally towed to Section Base 4 by *CG-134* to New London, it was later towed to Providence, with its cargo of whiskey, as well as three handcuffed crewmen, still on board. The whiskey that remained intact was taken in charge by employees of the collector of customs after it had been carefully checked, while heavily armed guards supervised the proceedings. No visitors were allowed aboard the boat. Still, reporters could see that the boat's ports were splintered, and the deck showed signs of a fire, caused by the bullets that hit sacks of liquor.[187] A *Providence Journal* reporter stated that "[f]rom the view of the *Mardelle* at the pier" in the Providence River, "it appeared that the coast guard shots were fired from at least three angles, forward aft, and from starboard, or the right side." The reporter further described the damage he saw:

> *Of the three port-holes in the forward side of the pilot-house, two were shot away and the third was splintered by bullets. At least nine bullets were in evidence in the woodwork on the forward side of the pilot-house.*
>
> *Other bullets from a machine gun had clipped the starboard gunwale in several places. The quarterdeck was in chaos. Broken bottles, partly burned sacks and scorched deck told their own story; that of hot fire of machine guns setting fire to the sacks and smashing the bottles of choice whiskey.*
>
> *The small slight mast of the yacht was splintered in one place by a bullet and another shot had damaged the lone, small lifeboat, near the keel.*[188]

Aboard *Mardelle*, federal authorities counted 575 cases of William Penn and Golden Wedding rye whiskey, done up in burlap bags, and its decks were strewn with broken bottles. Federal officials in Providence claimed that much of *Mardelle*'s liquor cargo had been thrown overboard. Brooklyn, New York's *Daily News* supported the claim, colorfully reporting in its August 28 edition:

> *Champagne—For Nothing!—All you had to do yesterday to get whiskey or champagne was to leave your estate down in Newport, R.I., and stroll over to Belmont Beach. The stuff was floating ashore in cases. It was believed to have come from rum ship Mardelle, seized in Narragansett Bay.*[189]

CG-134 towed *Mardelle* to Section Base 4 in New London. Chapman refused further treatment for his injured finger. He and two other crewmen from Fall River were arraigned in Providence.

On August 28, three sensational disclosures were made. First, there were reports of a possible fifth man aboard *Mardelle* who had served as the boat's master but was not captured. It was thought that the man may have fallen overboard after being shot, he may have drowned in an attempt to swim ashore or he may have reached the shore and escaped. Federal investigators received no assistance from any of the captured rumrunners, including from Munson; they maintained their silence, as was their right under the Fifth Amendment of the U.S. Constitution (the right not to incriminate oneself).[190]

Another sensation was created when crew members of *Mardelle* asserted that they had heard no warning shot fired from the Coast Guard boat and that their first indication of pursuit came with the rattle of machine gun fire. A Coast Guard spokesman at New London headquarters claimed that the customary warning shots had been fired over *Mardelle*'s bow. However, *CG-808*'s incident report indicated that only a burst of machine gun fire was shot across the rumrunner's bow. This was against two Coast Guard policies: first, the one that required that three blank warning shots from a one-pounder be fired before live ammunition from machine guns was employed, and the second that prohibited machine guns from being used to fire warning shots. The Coast Guard spokesman was not relaying a complete, accurate story.

An even greater clamor arose when federal officials in Providence admitted that the Coast Guard vessel that had showered *Mardelle* with machine gun bullets and had made the capture was indeed the former *Black Duck*. It had been forfeited to the federal government, taken into the Coast Guard's service on March 27, 1930, and renamed as speedboat *CG-808*. It was assigned to Section Base 4 in New London.[191] When *Black Duck* had been ordered by Judge Ira Lloyd Letts turned over to the Coast Guard at a hearing in Providence in March 1930, an Associated Press report succinctly summarized the rationale as follows: "The *Black Duck* is one of the fastest boats ever used in the rum smuggling service and was by far speedier than the usual Coast Guard patrol boat. It is reported here that the Coast Guard will arm the craft and use it to pursue smugglers."[192]

Once *Black Duck* was acquired by the Coast Guard and taken to Section Base 4, it was, according to the *Newport Mercury*, camouflaged, and its decks were equipped with two Browning machine guns. Presumably, the Coast Guard believed that with *CG-808*'s speed and firepower, it could be effectively utilized in the war against rumrunners. Prior to the action on July 26, *CG-808* had sped over the waters of Narragansett Bay and the Sakonnet River, and even out to Long Island, in search of rumrunners.[193]

Newspaper reporters asked for more information about the identity of the crew of *CG-808*, but the Coast Guard refused, out of concern that crew members would be abused by rumrunners and their friends. Federal officials noted that the members of the crew of *CG-290*, as well as members of their families, "have lived more or less in fear their lives since the shooting in the bay seven months ago." An official of the Coast Guard in Providence added that the Coast Guard had been protecting the identity of *CG-808* as the former *Black Duck*, for fear rumrunners or bootleggers might attempt to destroy the vessel.[194]

Coast Guard records show that the commander of *CG-808* was Louis W. Gavitt. Coincidentally, he had been a member of the crew of *CG-290* when it had machine gunned *Black Duck* that fateful morning in December 1929, although he was not the gunner. Gavitt would prove to be an aggressive pursuer of rumrunners.

Mardelle itself would be captured again with an illicit load of liquor on board and forfeited to the federal government. On March 22, 1932, it would be taken into the service of the Coast Guard as *CG-832* and assigned to Section Base 4.[195]

The most important development about the *Mardelle* incident was that it clarified that Coast Guardsmen operating in Rhode Island waters would not be deterred from using deadly force when chasing a fast rumrunner. Unlike the *Black Duck* incident, there were no civilian protests after the public learned of the shooting of Chips Munson in his back and lung. State Attorney General Benjamin McLyman said that he would investigate the shooting if information at the federal court hearing merited it, but he took no action. Rhode Islanders must have been upset by the continuing policy of the Coast Guard to use its machine guns against rumrunners in Narragansett Bay. But perhaps they were distracted by greater fears. By the fall of 1930, the country was in the grips of a severe economic downturn, with high unemployment and continuing job losses, called the Great Depression.

Chapter 11

FALL 1930

MACHINE GUN TRACERS FILL THE NIGHT SKY AT WATCH HILL (*HELEN* AND *HIGH STRUNG*)

R hode Islanders began expressing their distaste for Prohibition in official ways. In November 1930, the General Assembly permitted a statewide referendum on Prohibition to go forward, even though it had no legal effect. The wets crushed the drys, winning 172,545 votes for repeal of Prohibition to 48,540 for retaining it. The cities of Providence, Pawtucket, Woonsocket and Newport were strongholds of anti-Prohibition sentiment. On Providence's Federal Hill, a bastion of Italian immigrants, the tally against Prohibition in one voting district was 2,005 to 3. Hopkinton was the only community in the state to support the dry side.[196] Even U.S. Senator Jesse Metcalf, a Republican, announced that he would vote for the repeal of the Eighteenth Amendment and the Volstead Act.[197]

This vote did not have any influence on the Coast Guard's enforcement activities against rumrunners. Prohibition remained the law of the land. Alexander C. Cornell, still in command of the feared *CG-290* cutter, would do his best to see to it, even if it meant firing his machine guns and putting the lives of rumrunner crews at risk. In March 1930, a senior officer at Section Base 4 praised Cornell for making his "fifth seizure of liquor laden vessels…since September 1929. His success is due to zeal, initiative, excellent judgment, tireless industry, and hard work."[198]

Rumrunners did not utilize only coves and drops along Narragansett Bay and the Sakonnet River. There was also a long shoreline on the southern Rhode Island mainland coast from Point Judith to the east to Napatree Point near the summer resort town of Watch Hill to the west. Rumrunners who utilized the drops on the southern shore tended to hail from outfits based in New York City.

The beach at Napatree Point is perhaps the most beautiful sandy beach in Rhode Island, if not in all of New England's mainland. To the west of Napatree Point is so-called Little Narragansett Bay. It is a small inlet located on the northeast side of Stonington, Connecticut. The Pawcatuck River leads into the bay; just up the river on the eastern side is Westerly, Rhode Island, and on the western side is Pawcatuck, Connecticut.

On the night of October 24, despite a raging storm, Coast Guard vessels maintained a picket line in the approaches to Little Narragansett Bay. More Coast Guard vessels operated to the south.

A new outside vessel from Europe had arrived at Rum Row off Block Island and Montauk Point, and Coast Guard officials expected several contact boats to meet up with the new arrival, be loaded with illicit liquor and run for the Rhode Island or Connecticut shores. Moreover, Coast Guard officials, after several years of experience, were aware that increased efforts to smuggle liquor into New York City would be made in preparation for the upcoming holidays—Thanksgiving, Christmas and New Year's Eve.

On the stormy night of October 24, a lookout spotted the steam trawler *Penguin* headed eastward. Knowing that sometimes rumrunners followed in the wakes of civilian cargo ships in the hopes of avoiding suspicion, Cornell and his crew on *CG-290*, patrolling in the area, kept a sharp lookout. Sure enough, crew members spotted a speedboat following in *Penguin*'s wake, running without lights. It was the 67-foot *Helen* of Newport.

Boatswain Cornell set his vessel's course to head off *Helen*, and when seven miles east of Race Rock off Fishers Island (in New York waters just southeast of Stonington, Connecticut), he signaled *Helen* to heave to. The rumrunner merely put on speed, hoping to escape. Cornell ordered his gunner to fire a warning shot from his one-pounder, but it did not have the desired effect.

As *Helen* sped away in the storm, *CG-290* gave chase. Cornell sent a spray of shots at the rumrunner using live ammunition with his boat's one-pounder and his patrol boat's infamous Lewis machine gun. Hearing the firing, *CG-289*, another 75 that was then patrolling east of Fishers Island and commanded by Chief Boatswain's Mate John Lenci, closed in on *Helen* and also opened fire.

Soon, both Coast Guard vessels were blasting away with their one-pounders and machine guns as they continued the chase, approaching Napatree Point to the west of Watch Hill. Several shots found their mark,

The beach at Napatree Point, next to Watch Hill, where a crew grounded the rumrunner *Helen* to escape furious machine gun fire from Coast Guard patrol boats. *Photo by author.*

and *Helen* began taking on water. Two more Coast Guard 75s appeared on the scene, *CG-134* and *CG-241*, as well as picket boat *2235*.

Helen's crew, realizing that they could not avoid all of the Coast Guard vessels, and despite the high seas from the storm, ran their speedboat onto the sandy beach at Napatree Point. They ran aground near the former fortification from the Spanish-American War called Fort Mansfield (cement remains from the fort exist today, but the area is fenced off).

Somehow, the crew escaped being injured from the bombardment. Machine gun bullets had pierced the pilothouse, and one-pound shells had torn holes in the deck planking and the wooden hull on the sides. The boat's "mast was struck several times, one of the running lights was shot away, and one bullet left a hole through the glass [window] in the pilot house at approximately the height of a man's head," the *Providence Journal* reported.

The crew members scrambled out of *Helen* and tried to escape on foot. Eventually, four of them were captured. Three hailed from New York City, and one came from New Jersey.

Coast Guardsmen from the Watch Hill Station reported seeing seven or eight men leave *Helen*. If the report was accurate, several crew members escaped capture. But four crew members typically manned a rumrunner the size of *Helen*.

On shore, when the sun rose, Coast Guardsmen found that the bottom of *Helen*'s hull was ripped open. Whether that was due to exploding one-pound shells or the vessel scraping rocks on its way to the beach is not certain. The *Providence Journal* said it was both. The Associated Press reported, "Inspection of the *Helen* after the craft had been beached, showed that the pilothouse was well peppered with bullets and a one-pounder ball had struck the hull."[199]

Cornell credited his one-pounder cannon fire for sinking *Helen*. It was his seventh rumrunning boat seized. Lenci also filed an official report stating that *Helen* "was cornered and sunk by gunfire close in on Napatree Point, Rhode Island."

The Coast Guard estimated the loss to the rumrunners at $100,000. *Helen*, which was powered by two three-hundred-horsepower motors, was valued at $40,000 by Coast Guard officials, and it was reported to have been carrying one thousand cases of liquor, valued at $60,000. The next day, Coast Guardsmen from their nearby station at Watch Hill, assisted by others from Coast Guard Stations at Quonochontaug and Fishers Island, unloaded the listing *Helen* and transported the sacks of liquor to Providence as evidence of violating the Volstead Act.

Federal authorities provided information about *Helen* of Newport. According to customs officials in Newport, *Helen* had been registered on June 19, 1930, as being owned by William Henry of Newport. The master of the ship when the vessel was registered was Charles David of Newport.

It was also disclosed that *Helen* had been built in the spring of 1930 in New York City and that it weighed fifty-two gross tons. It was sixty-seven feet long and fifteen feet wide, with a depth of eight feet. Curiously, even though it had been constructed in 1930, presumably for the "rum" trade, the boat had a mast. Perhaps that was to disguise it as a fishing vessel, or the decision may have been made that having the ability to sail the boat would be useful in case all of its engines stopped working. Now *Helen* was stranded on a beach with a large hole in its hull.[200]

The *Hartford Courant* wrote about the *Helen* incident, "The boom of one pound guns and the rattle of machine gun fire awakened residents in Stonington....Coast Guardsmen estimated that 500 rounds of machine gun bullets and about 40 rounds of one-pound shells were fired during the engagement."[201]

The *Providence Journal* described the damage done to *Helen* from the large-caliber guns:

> *Capt. George W. Streeter, in charge of the Watch Hill station, estimated the rum boat was hit at least 50 times by machine gun bullets and one-pounders. Bullets tore into the hull on both sides and there were eight in a dory lashed to the deck. The forward part of the boat and the pilothouse were the most badly damaged.*[202]

An extraordinary aspect of the chase and capture of *Helen*, in addition to the fact that the incident was covered in more than one hundred newspapers nationwide, was the vivid descriptions of the gunfire published in the October 25 edition of the *Providence Journal*. The most thorough description of the gunfire was provided by Chrystin McConnell, a former captain of artillery in the U.S. Army in World War I. McConnell viewed the gunfire from his Watch Hill home. He described seeing tracer bullets shooting through the dark night in all directions during the firing off Napatree Point. He also explained how, fearing that the bullets were getting close to his house, he had sent his wife and daughter away from a window, where they had been watching the bombardment, to a safe place until he was satisfied that the danger was over.

McConnell informed the *Providence Journal* reporter, "I heard the sound of firing shortly before 2 o'clock" in the morning. He continued:

> *I went to my window, which looked out across Little Narragansett Bay, toward Napatree Point. I could see the lights of a number of boats, I think four or five. I heard the firing plainly and saw green and red streaks of flame as tracers started shooting from all directions toward the bulkhead on Napatree*
>
> *I could see the flash of the one-pounder and I think they must have fired it 50 times. Searchlights were flashing along the beach and the reports of the one-pounder and the rat-tat-tat of machine-guns sounded like a battle.*
>
> *I called my wife and daughter to the window and we watched for some time. The tracers looked just like roman candles shooting into the darkness.*
>
> *Then one of the boats changed its course and the bullets started coming directly towards our house but were falling short. I had not decided yet whether the boats were battling a rum boat, each other or just holding night practice.*

I called the Coast Guard in Watch Hill on the telephone and told them that if they were just having a little fun with each other to send them a message with their blinkers to change the range a bit. I was afraid we might be in his range. The man at the Coast Guard station told me that the Coast Guard had caught a rum boat, but there was no danger. However, I told my wife and daughter to get away from the window.

I don't want anyone to get the idea that I am criticizing the action of the Coast Guard for firing on the boat, for I understand it is their duty. I will criticize their shooting, however. I never saw worse shooting anywhere in my experience. They don't shoot straight or that boat would have been sunk by all the shots they fired.[203]

The Associated Press wrote, "A man on shore at Watch Hill claimed that bullets spattered houses there and pointed to marks on his own cottage to support this claim."[204] But the *Providence Journal* could not confirm that "homes of summer visitors had been struck by machine gun bullets during the 'naval battle.'"

The fates of *Helen* and its crew following the shooting incident were disastrous. *Helen* sank in Block Island Sound while being towed by the Coast Guard, and three members of its captured crew pleaded guilty to rum charges on February 9, 1931.

The same syndicate may have lost another rumrunner in the same area in Block Island Sound. At about 8:30 p.m. on November 15, in a dense fog, while cruising near Cerberus Shoal, Boatswain Cornell on *CG-290* spotted a boat running to the north without lights. Cornell moved to cut off the vessel. The beam of the Coast Guard vessel's searchlight revealed sacks of liquor piled up on the decks of the now fleeing boat.

Cornell ordered a blank warning shot from his ship's one-pounder be fired across the rumrunner's bow, and a siren blew and the Coast Guard vessel's searchlight was shown on the boat, all as signals to heave to. The rumrunner's crew failed to heed the warnings and sped on, north toward Fishers Island. Cornell wrote in his official report that "eleven service shells all told were fired from the one-pounder and several hits were made." One of the live one-pounder shots fired by *CG-290* tore through the tiller rope of the fleeing vessel, disabling it. Cornell and his crew were then easily able to overhaul the speedboat and capture it. After the crew members were handcuffed, the captured vessel was towed into New London. It was Cornell's ninth capture.

The rumrunner was *High Strung*, whose twin engines made it capable of attaining a speed of thirty knots when unloaded and twenty knots with a full

The captured rumrunner *High Strung*, tied up at a wharf in the Providence River near the federal customs office in Providence. *National Archives.*

cargo of liquor on board. Built at Brooklyn, New York, earlier in 1930, it was 47.8 feet long and 11.8 feet wide, had a draft of 5.6 feet and weighed 13 tons.[205] The registered owner of the vessel was Jacob Teitelbaum of North Main Street in Providence.

The members of *High Strung*'s crew, three New Yorkers, were arraigned in New London. Their cargo of about six hundred cases of liquor was seized by the Coast Guard.[206] From interrogating the prisoners, it was reported that the main investor in *High Strung* and other rumrunners that were recently seized could be Waxey Gordon, a notorious gangster heading a large rum ring operating out of New York City.

Boatswain Cornell, in his official report, wrote that *High Strung* had "turned and headed for" *CG-290* at twenty knots and that he kept his own vessel going about fifteen knots right at the rumrunner. When the boats were within twenty-five feet of each other, according to Cornell, *High Strung* veered to the right in an attempt to ram the rumrunner. Cornell then claimed that at this moment, his vessel suffered a broken wheel rope, but that the rumrunner must have had an accident too since it spun out of control and began to circle the patrol boat. According to Cornell's account, as *High Strung* circled, the Coast Guard vessel pummeled it with one-pounder shells. Once an auxiliary tiller was rigged, Cornell's *CG-290* went along side *High Strung* and made the capture.[207]

Apparently, Boatswain Cornell, in his official report, either concocted a story about the attempted ramming or was confused about what happened. Multiple newspaper reports, based on information provided by the Coast Guard, made it clear that one of the one-pounder shots (some said the second one) fired at *High Strung* had torn off its tiller rope. This resulted in the rumrunner losing control of its steering mechanism. The *Hartford Courant* even reported that *High Strung* had been "floundering in a circle" after its "tiller rope was parted by a one-pound shell."[208] Cornell thought that its captain was trying to ram his Coast Guard vessel. Perhaps Cornell was trying to justify his firing eleven projectiles from *CG-290*'s one-pound cannon by making the rumrunner seem like the aggressor.

Not surprisingly, on occasion, a Coast Guard vessel fired large-caliber guns at a fleeing rumrunner without the Coast Guard either capturing or identifying the rumrunner. This happened to *CG-289* just after midnight on September 28, 1930. While patrolling in the vicinity of Sandy Point off Block Island, *CG-289* spotted a speedboat running without lights. A searchlight was shown on the speedboat, the Klaxon horn was sounded and a single one-pounder blank was fired as a signal to heave to. Instead of stopping, the unidentified boat increased its speed. Chief Boatswain's Mate Theodore C. Losch had his patrol vessel fire about eight pans of machine gun bullets and seven one-pounder projectiles directly at the rumrunner. But after a one-hour chase, even though the barrage had started a fire on the fleeing vessel, the rumrunner escaped into the night "due to superior speed."[209] Its identity was never determined.

In the coming months, the action would return in a spectacular way to Narragansett Bay.

Chapter 12

WINTER 1931

MACHINE GUN FIRE INTERRUPTS THE NIGHT ON AQUIDNECK ISLAND (*MONOLOLA* AND *ALIBI II*)

The winter of 1931 did not indicate any slackening of the Coast Guard's willingness to fire its machine guns at rumrunners in Rhode Island waters. Indeed, during the early morning of February 23, 1931, in two spectacular chases in Narragansett Bay, Coast Guard vessels fired hundreds of rounds of machine gun bullets, as well as one-pounders, at fleeing rumrunners, to the surprise of civilians once slumbering in residences on the bay's coasts. The results for the rumrunners involved were mixed.

The Coast Guard must have received several tips that rumrunners would be operating in Narragansett Bay in the evening of February 22 and 23. Coast Guard 75-footers and 36-foot picket boats from Section Base 4 at New London and Section Base 18 at Woods Hole stood guard in the Sakonnet River and in the East Passage of Narragansett Bay north of Newport Harbor.

CG-234, a 75, while moored at Gould Island in the East Passage, at about 12:15 a.m. on February 23, spotted a boat running without lights moving north toward its location. The patrol boat threw its searchlight on the mysterious boat and saw that it was *Monolola* of Newport with its deck piled high with sacks of liquor. *CG-234* and *Monolola* had been involved in a sensational chase in Narragansett Bay a year earlier almost to the day and in the same area.

The rumrunner, now commanded by James A. Baker of Newport, sped about twenty-three or thirty knots (sources vary), compared to less than twenty by the Coast Guard vessel. The patrol boat made up for its lack of speed by firing its large-caliber weapons.

According to the incident report submitted by F.D. Overhauser, *CG-234*'s commander, the cutter fired three one-pounder blank shells, followed by a burst of machine gun fire, as signals to stop, but they were ignored. Instead, *Monolola* threw out a dense smokescreen, increased its speed and changed its course to the east toward Coddington Cove.

At first, *CG-234* did not employ its machine gun, as the rumrunner was hugging the coast near a beach that had houses on it. Once *Monolola* was clear of the beach, the 75's gunner fired live machine gun bullets at the fleeing craft. Crew members saw that the fire shattered glass in the wheelhouse door, and other shots were seen striking sacks of liquor on the vessel's deck. *CG-234* fired more than two hundred bullets at *Monolola*, but the faster speedboat sped beyond the range of *CG-234*'s searchlight.

Monolola then crossed paths with *CG-289*, which had been stationed at the south end of Prudence Island. While the two Coast Guard vessels thought they had *Monolola* "dead to rights," the desperate crew members on board the speedboat had other ideas. Its captain, Baker, began zigzagging at top speed.

About one mile south of Carr Point off Portsmouth, *CG-289* fired a burst from its machine gun and fired shells from its one-pounder at the fleeing rumrunner, which then changed its course and headed across the bay south toward Potter Cove off Conanicut Island. *CG-234* continued its pursuit, and *Monolola* actually crossed its bow when the two vessels were just fifty feet from each other and one hundred yards from the shore. The speedboat came so close to the Coast Guard cutter that Coast Guardsmen could read the words "Golden Wedding"—a famous brand of whiskey— on the boxes used as a barricade.

Because *CG-234*'s machine gun had jammed due to faulty ammunition, the patrol boat fired thirteen shells from its one-pounder at *Monolola*. The Coast Guard vessel ceased firing when a tanker drew near, and the rumrunner escaped into the darkness. According to the Associated Press, "Twisting and turning to escape the shots, the speedboat continued down the bay and was lost to the patrol boats" near Potter Cove at 1:10 a.m.[210]

After the wild chase, in which "hundreds of shots were fired," *Monolola* made good its escape. The *Newport Mercury* reported, "Local residents watched the battle between the Coast Guard and the rumrunners from the Cliff Walk and discerned the escape of a craft, which was picked up in the rays of a Coast Guard searchlight, according to reports, but finally swept out to sea under a hail of bullets and disappeared."[211]

Commander M.J. Ryan at Destroyer Force Headquarters at New London said that while he had received reports that *Monolola* had been hit "several

Part of a drawing of a Coast Guard patrol boat firing its machine gun from the bow of the vessel at a fleeing rumrunner. *From* St. Louis Globe-Democrat, *April 5, 1925.*

times," he suspected no one on board was hurt, as the crew was protected by a "barricade" of wood cases and burlap sacks of liquor.[212] But wood, burlap and glass did not provide secure protection against large-caliber machine gun bullets.

CG-234 and *CG-289* spent the rest of the early morning hours searching Crowninshield Shipyard and beaches around Fall River until 3:40 a.m. when another patrol boat, *CG-134*, captured *Monolola* running without lights north of Mount Hope Bridge. Its holds were inspected, but no liquor was found by the Coast Guard. The rumrunner must have reentered Narragansett Bay and dropped off its load before it surrendered.

The speedboat was taken to Providence. A few days later, the collector of customs at Providence, Emory J. San Souci, imposed fines totaling $600, $100 of which was against the motorboat itself for running without lights and $500 of which was against James Baker for failing to heave to when ordered by the Coast Guard. Customs records still showed that the rumrunner was registered to Harry Bennet, 80 Plenty Street, Providence. But this time the deputy collector announced that the registration papers were false, as he found no person by such name or address in Providence.

As it did in 1930, the Coast Guard claimed that *Monolola* was owned by Al Capone's syndicate.[213]

Monolola was machine gunned and captured one more time, but in Vineyard Sound, not Narragansett Bay. On January 12, 1932, *CG-405*, a new 78-footer, spotted *Monolola* near Nomans Land island and gave chase. After *Monolola* ignored signals to stop, *CG-405* fired five rounds of projectiles from its one-pounder, and machine guns on each side of the patrol boat were fired as well at the fleeing vessel. In about five minutes, the rumrunner stopped and surrendered. According to the *Providence Journal*, "more than 100 machine gun bullets" had been shot at *Monolola*, where "500 sacks of choice liquors" were found on board. Three of the crew hailed from New York City and one from Boston.[214]

The chase of *Monolola* was not the only action that stirred excitement in Narragansett Bay in the early morning of February 23, 1931—there was also the pursuit of *Alibi II*. It was 42.2 feet long and 12.4 feet wide, had a depth of 4.8 feet and weighed 6 tons. Built in 1930 at the Crowninshield Shipyard, it was owned by Thomas W. Powell of Edgewood, Rhode Island.[215] It was registered in Providence to its captain, Rico de Nadal of Fall River. The *Providence Journal* called *Alibi II* the "pride of the New England rum fleet."[216]

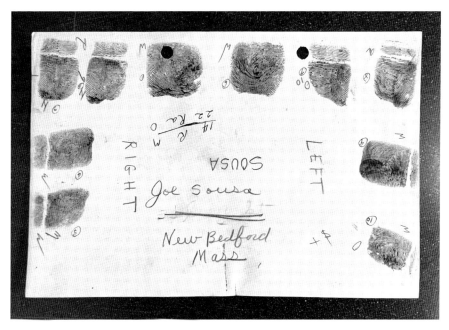

Fingerprints of Joe Sousa of New Bedford, Massachusetts, after his arrest for rumrunning on board the captured *Monolola*. *National Archives.*

Coast Guard cutter *CG-235*, a 75 commanded by Boatswain W.W. Prentice, first spotted *Alibi II* in the Sakonnet River. *Alibi II* was known as a rumrunner to the Coast Guard. *CG-235*, according to Coast Guard reports, sounded a whistle and Klaxon horn, played its searchlight on its flag and fired three blank warning shot across the bow of the rumrunner with its one-pounder. Prentice reportedly decided to open fire after de Nadal turned his boat around and started to head back toward the open ocean at full speed.

During the five-mile chase, according to the *Newport Mercury*, residents near the shoreline of the Sakonnet River in Newport and Middletown "distinctly heard" a "bombardment of one-pounder and machine-gun fire."[217] According to a Coast Guard incident report, *CG-235* fired two solid shots from the one-pounder, one striking the rumrunner's bow and the other the stern. After *CG-235* began to gain on the heavily-laden powerboat, according to the *Newport Mercury*, "a flame shot from the gasoline tank, and the crew of four men immediately" jumped into a dory. *Alibi II* burst into flames and sank before *CG-235* arrived at the scene. Its cargo of liquor, estimated as being worth at least $25,000, was lost. The four crew members, three hailing from Fall River and the other from Brighton, Massachusetts, were rescued by the Coast Guard and transported to New Bedford, where charges were prepared against them for violating the customs laws.[218]

Whether cannon or machine gun fire caused *Alibi II* to explode is not known for certain. The rumrunner twice before had been seized by authorities and released pending bail. The *Newport Mercury* speculated that "*Alibi II* is believed to have been scuttled, owing to the fact that the craft was under government bond for two alleged previous violations of the liquor laws."[219] The crew may have determined that since the boat and its cargo would both be lost to condemnation proceedings, it would be best for them to sink the ship so that the evidence of illegal liquor on board would disappear under the waves.

Still, the Coast Guard reported that its one-pound cannon struck the craft twice, so one of those shots, or machine gun bullets, could well have broken a gas line and started a small fire, with the fire ultimately igniting the gas tank and causing an explosion. Such an event was not uncommon aboard rumrunners. It seems unlikely that *Alibi II*'s crew members would intentionally set fire to their gas tank with them still in the vessel.

Stories about the chases of *Monolola* and *Alibi II* made front-page news in dozens of newspapers across the country. The *Newport Mercury* ran one of the

Part of a drawing of a rumrunner, having just departed its "outside" supply vessel hovering in the background, fleeing from a Coast Guard patrol boat firing its machine gun at it. During the shooting, a crew member throws cases of liquor overboard to get rid of the evidence of transporting illegal liquor. *From* St. Louis Globe-Democrat, *April 5, 1925.*

best headlines: "Alibi II, Rumrunner, Is No More." More colorful reporting was published about the remarkable chase of *Monolola*. The *Providence Journal* wrote:

> *Residents of Newport, who went to the cliffs overlooking the sea, witnessed the battle between the Coast Guard vessels and one of the rum ships. They say a rum-runner dodged in and out of the beams of the patrol boat's searchlights and disappeared in the dark, only to be picked up again as the patrol boat maneuvered into position.*
>
> *As soon as the rumrunner came under the ray of the light, the firing from both Government vessels started again. The rumrunner, however, made a dash to the open sea and swept out of the bay as the firing from the patrol boats was renewed.*[220]

The Associated Press report provided colorful details for hungry readers:

> *The dark waters of Narragansett Bay echoed early today to the dull boom of one-pounders and the rattle of machine gunfire as Coast Guard patrol boats and rumrunners fought it out to a finish....*
>
> *The gunfire was heard by scores of Newporters, who hurried to the high bluffs at the outskirts of the city to watch the guardsmen and the runners maneuver about the inner harbor. For an hour two patrol boats and a small power boat sped about the harbor firing random shots. The crowds that gathered to watch saw the power boat dodge in and out of the circle of the guardsmen's searchlights time and again and finally sweep out into the bay.*[221]

Reading the Associated Press report, one might be forgiven for assuming that the gun battle was a two-sided affair. But the rumrunner, of course, did not fire any shots at the Coast Guard vessels.

Chapter 13

SPRING 1931

JUDGE LAMBASTS THE COAST GUARD FOR ANOTHER DEATH (868-G, *FOLLOW ME* AND *WHISPERING WINDS*)

B y the spring of 1931, Rhode Island's General Assembly had begun to consider legislation to get out from under the Eighteenth Amendment and the Volstead Act. By a vote of 88 to 1, the state's House of Representatives instructed the state's members of Congress to initiate legislation for a constitutional convention for the purpose of repealing or modifying the Eighteenth Amendment. Only a Hopkinton delegate voted against it. The resolution then passed the state senate on a voice vote without a single member dissenting. Another provision of the bill legalized wine and beer prescribed by physicians "for medicinal purposes."[222]

Meanwhile, Coast Guard patrol boats continued to enforce federal Prohibition laws with vigor. The next incident, an extraordinary one, earned the Coast Guard a tongue-lashing by a federal district court judge.

In the early morning of Saturday, April 11, 1931, picket boat *CG-2343* patrolled the northern part of the Sakonnet River. *CG-2343* was under the command of Chief Boatswain's Mate Elsworth Lathan of the Brenton Point Coast Guard Station south of Newport. Just before 3:00 a.m., off Common Fence Point in Portsmouth near the entrance to Mount Hope Bay, a lookout on Lathan's boat spotted a motorboat pulling two motorless boats, each piled high with sacks of liquor. *CG-2343* sounded its siren for the motorboat to heave to, but it refused. Three one-pounder blank shells (or one, accounts differ) were fired across the motorboat's bow as a signal for it to stop.

The motorboat was called *868-G*, and Raymond Coleman of Tiverton, an experienced commander of rumrunners, was its captain. Despite pulling the two small, heavily-laden small boats, Coleman refused to heave to when signaled. Instead, he sped away, this time south down the Sakonnet River. *CG-2343* pursued and opened fire with its machine gun. A burst of about twenty bullets poured into directly into the craft. One of Coleman's crew suddenly writhed in pain, shot in the leg just above the knee.

Coleman stopped fleeing and heaved to. Before doing so, Coleman ordered another crewman, Warren Mosher of Fall River, to cut the lines to the two motorless boats being towed, which was done. Coleman hoped to get rid of the evidence that he and his crew were participating in rumrunning.

As Lathan drew his boat near *868-G*, one of the crewmen aboard the rumrunner, probably Mosher, shouted, "There's a man shot aboard here." Lathan immediately boarded the vessel and removed the wounded man, Leonard (or Leopold) Mousseau of Tiverton, to *CG-2343*. Coast Guardsman Charles F. Beaumont then jumped from his picket boat onto *868-G*.

What happened next was not part of the usual pattern. At 3:12 a.m., off Common Fence Point, a few minutes after Beaumont came aboard, *868-G* exploded. The blast blew Beaumont, Mosher, Coleman and another man accompanying Coleman, Cornelius O'Brien of Tiverton, off the boat and into the water. Lathan supervised his men picking Beaumont and Mosher out of the water. Coleman claimed that he yelled for a life preserver to be thrown to O'Brien, who was struggling in the water. But in the darkness, despite likely using his searchlight, Lathan could not locate Coleman or O'Brien. He figured they had disappeared into the darkness and escaped from him by swimming ashore.

Lathan then had the two smaller boats, which had been cast adrift, seized and towed. However, rough water led the two boats to take on water and start to sink. Three sacks of liquor were removed to *CG-2343* as evidence before the two boats sank in about forty feet of water off Sakonnet Point. Accordingly, the remaining 597 or so sacks of liquor, representing a small fortune, went down with the small boats.

Lathan continued his journey back to Newport and arrived at Newport Harbor at about 7:30 a.m. Mousseau, who had been handcuffed, was rushed to Newport Hospital. The physician who looked after Mosher said that his condition was not considered serious. Mosher then limped on board a Coast Guard vessel, which took him and the other crewmen to Providence for arraignment. Meanwhile, Beaumont had suffered burns to his head from the explosion on board the boat, but the injuries were not deemed severe enough for him to require treatment at Newport Hospital.[223]

What Boatswain Lathan did not know was that while Coleman and O'Brien had been thrown from the boat by the blast, Coleman had survived and swam ashore, but O'Brien had been killed. Later that morning, two Tiverton quahog fishermen found O'Brien's lifeless body floating in eighteen feet of water some one hundred yards from the Tiverton shoreline, midway between two wharves, one operated by Liberty Oil and the other operated by Sinclair Oil.

O'Brien's case was particularly tragic, as he was not a rumrunner. Friends of O'Brien said that he operated a profitable gasoline station in Tiverton and had only accompanied Coleman on the voyage for the excitement.

When the press learned about O'Brien's death, speculation abounded about whether or not O'Brien had been killed by machine gun bullets. The autopsy of O'Brien that was conducted at Hambly Funeral Home in Newport the day after the explosion was closely watched by the press and others. Among those who attended the autopsy were two local physicians and the state pathologist and his assistant.

The autopsy did not reveal any trace of bullet wounds. Both of O'Brien's lungs were filled with water, indicating that he had drowned. There were some wounds on his face and hands, likely caused by the explosion.

O'Brien was found heavily dressed, in a sweater, woolen trousers, heavy socks and high rubber boots. His heavy coat was missing, probably discarded in an attempt to swim ashore. But the other water-soaked garments, with the boots, would have been heavy enough to drag down even an experienced swimmer.

Raymond Coleman later charged that *CG-2343*, because of its superior speed, could have forced *886-G* to heave to without resorting to machine gun fire. Lathan's picket boat could run at an impressive twenty-five miles per hour, and Coleman was towing two boats filled with sacks of liquor. Coleman also claimed that the Coast Guardsmen intentionally had left O'Brien and him, after the explosion had hurled them into the water, to fend for themselves and drown.

While Lathan, who spent most of his career trying to save persons in jeopardy at sea, did not intend O'Brien to drown, it does seem to have been a dereliction of his duty to have left the scene so quickly in light of the violent explosion, knowing that there were two men unaccounted for. He and his fellow Coast Guardsmen may have felt that the rumrunners would likely have tried to escape by swimming to the shore, but that was just an

The speedy rumrunner *Whispering Winds* of Bridgeport, Connecticut, in the control of the Coast Guard and customs office at New London, July 18, 1931. Note the broken glass of the windows to the pilothouse, caused by machine gun bullets. *National Archives.*

assumption. They could not have been sure whether one or both of the men had been so injured by the blast that they could not swim.

Emory J. San Souci, collector of customs of the port of Providence and a future Rhode Island governor, took it upon himself to defend the Coast Guardsmen's conduct. San Souci was a federal appointee, and of course, Coast Guardsmen were federal employees.

San Souci asserted that ample warning was given to the rumrunners before the machine gun was brought into play. He expressed doubt about Coleman's claim that the patrol boat deliberately left Coleman and O'Brien to drown. "The public must not forget the fact that the Coast Guard has a serious duty to perform in the enforcement of laws relating to smuggling and unlawful transportation of liquor in the territorial waters of the United States," said San Souci. "There is no question but that on Saturday morning the rumrunners off Common Fence Point not only were warned, but were ordered to stop."

San Souci continued:

> *When rum runners openly and flagrantly disregard commands to halt, they do so at their own peril. Regardless of what rum runners, bootleggers, lawyers of bootleggers and those who are against the Prohibition law think, Coast Guard officers and men as rule do not stand by and deliberately let men drown.*[224]

San Souci declined to comment on Coleman's other charge—that the pursuing Coast Guard vessel, because of its superior speed, could have the forced the rumrunner to heave to without resorting to machine gun fire. The collector of customs explained that he had not received any official report of the incident. But the lack of a report had not prevented San Souci from defending the Coast Guard on Coleman's first charge.

The *Newport Mercury* article that discussed the aftermath of the sorry *868-G* episode speculated that the explosion could have been caused by the rumrunner's crew intentionally setting off a bomb or dropping a match into

Sacks of liquor piled high on the deck of *Whispering Winds*, July 18, 1931, at New London. *National Archives.*

the boat's gasoline tank.[225] This speculation was irresponsible. Why crew members would want to do that, when every crew member except one was still aboard and the liquor was never on board (so that there was no need to destroy evidence), was never explained. Apparently, neither the Coast Guard nor any other government office investigated the incident, and therefore the cause of the explosion can never be known for certain.

The evidence strongly points to the Coast Guard's machine gun fire causing the deadly explosion. Each speedboat employed as a rumrunner was gas powered. Therefore, each one had a tank full of gas and gas in pipes leading to the gas tank. When high-powered bullets strike metal gas tanks and gas lines, explosions can occur. After being hit by machine gun fire and one-pounder shells, *Alibi II* had exploded a few months earlier in February 1931 (although it is possible that the crew sabotaged its own boat). Later in 1931, a machine gun bullet would puncture the rumrunner *Eaglet*'s gas tank, causing a violent explosion.[226] In the *868-G* incident, because *CG-2343* only fired twenty machine gun bullets and yet quickly wounded a crew member, the gunner must have aimed at the side of the boat and not its stern, making the gas lines more vulnerable. Thus, it is more than conceivable, and indeed more than probable, that the Coast Guard's machine gunning of *868-G* caused a small fire on board the targeted vessel that was not immediately noticed and that the fire ultimately ignited the gas in the vessel's punctured gas tank or lines.

It appears that some commanders of Coast Guard vessels intentionally fired at the gas tanks of rumrunners that refused to heave to. Indeed, the commander of speedboat *CG-808*, Louis Gavitt, in an August 1930 memorandum, explained to his Coast Guard superiors how he had "concentrated" all of his boat's "machine gun fire" on the fleeing rumrunner *Estelle*'s port side toward the stern "in order to disable machinery or to explode the gas tanks."[227] The machine gun fire, in fact, caused *Estelle* to catch fire and burst into flames off Long Island, but its crew managed to beach the vessel before it exploded. (As a reminder, *CG-808* was the former *Black Duck*, and Gavitt had been a member of the crew of *CG-290* when the deadly shooting occurred.)

The explosion of *868-G* and death of Cornelius O'Brien can be viewed as another tragedy that was bound to happen at some point as a result of the policy of Coast Guard vessels of indiscriminately firing machine guns at fleeing gas-powered rumrunners.

Jude Ira Lloyd Letts of the federal district court in Providence agreed with Coleman's view of the incident. At a hearing addressing the charges against Coleman, Mousseau and Mosher, Letts condemned the conduct of the Coast Guard. The *Providence Journal* reported:

> *Judge Letts excoriated the Coast Guard for "indifference to human life" and warned* [that] *the court would not support them in "acts of lawlessness."*
>
> *Judge Letts contended that the Coast Guard, equipped with a faster vessel, could have overtaken the smaller motorboat without resorting to gunfire and the resultant loss of life.*

The defendants pleaded guilty to a charge of attempting to import contraband liquor, but Judge Letts imposed a fine of just one dollar on each man.[228]

Many machine gun shootings never made the newspapers, particularly if the rumrunners were not captured. For example, sometime in May 1931, Chief Boatswain's Mate Elsworth Lathan, again commanding his picket boat from the Brenton Point Coast Guard Station, *CG-2343*, spotted a speedboat whose crew was unloading sacks of liquor on the Little Compton shoreline at Warren Point. It was the rumrunner *Follow Me*. Lathan, according to a Tiverton rumrunner's recollection, "opened up with a machine gun, hitting *Follow Me* several times but injuring no one." *Follow Me* then slipped its cable and headed away from Lathan, paralleling the beach and throwing out a smokescreen. The smokescreen worked, and Lathan lost the rumrunner.[229]

The next incident was of interest because the speedboat in question was perhaps the fastest ever to ply Rhode Island waters. Reportedly, it was even speedier than the former *Black Duck*.

On the early morning of June 18, 1931, off Watch Hill at about 1:30 a.m., Coast Guardsmen on board *CG-401*, commanded by Chief Quartermaster Arthur Gibbs, heard the whirring of a high-speed motor. The patrol boat gave chase, but the unidentified speedboat turned and headed east for Gardiners Bay, disappearing into the night. *CG-401* continued its pursuit and a few hours later again heard the sounds of a speedboat heading its way. The patrol boat's searchlight was turned on, and a motorboat without lights was sighted. The patrol boat pursued, illuminated its ensign with its searchlight and fired a blank one-pounder shell, both signals for the vessel to heave to. When these efforts proved fruitless and the speedboat increased its speed, Gibbs ordered his gunners to fire its one-pounder and machine gun with live ammunition into the fleeing vessel. After scoring a number of hits during a thirty-minute chase, *CG-401* overtook the rumrunner in Long Island Sound north of Plum Island. Sacks of liquor were piled outside the

A federal customs official checks on a hole in a dory made by a machine gun bullet fired from a Coast Guard vessel at *Whispering Winds*. The sacks of liquor piled high on the deck may have helped stop or deflect a few bullets. *National Archives.*

deckhouse for the crew's protection, and its hold was full of contraband liquor. The weight had slowed down the speedboat, and *CG-401* was one of the new, fast 78-footers.

Once the Coast Guardsmen saw the vessel in the daytime, they were impressed. It was the speedboat *Whispering Winds*, whose homeport was Bridgeport, Connecticut. It had been built in Mystic and was on its maiden voyage. Its four-man crew included two Massachusetts men, engineer Robert Wilson from Providence and deckhand Roy White of Wakefield (or Wyoming, accounts differ), Rhode Island.[230] On August 19, 1932, the Coast Guard added the 50-foot speedboat to its fleet, calling it *CG-986*.[231]

The Coast Guard's New London base now had at its disposal perhaps the two fastest speedboats ever to ply the waters of southern New England. One was the former *Black Duck*, now *CG-808*, and the other was the former *Whispering Winds*, now *CG-986*. Coast Guardsmen claimed that only *Whispering Winds* could outrun *Black Duck*.[232]

Chapter 14

SUMMER 1931

TWO RUMRUNNERS ARE MACHINED GUNNED, CATCH FIRE AND SINK (*YVETTE JUNE* AND *EAGLET*)

Stunningly, in the summer of 1931, two notorious rumrunners operating out of Rhode Island, *Yvette June* and *Eaglet*, were riddled with machine gun bullets by Coast Guard vessels, caught fire and sank. The unfortunate *Eaglet* was machine gunned at close range even after it had burst into flames. Remarkably, none of the crew members on board either boat was killed or seriously wounded.

The speedboat *Yvette June* was launched at Fall River in early July 1931. The 60-foot rumrunner was reported to have cost its Fall River owners $60,000. While the future looked bright for the motorboat, disaster struck on its first voyage as a rumrunner.

At about 1:00 a.m. on the morning of July 14, two Coast Guard patrol boats, *CG-400* and *CG-284*, spotted what they believed to be a rumrunner motoring without lights near the entrance of the Sakonnet River. They gave chase. *CG-400* was temporarily commanded by Alexander Cornell, who had commanded *CG-290* when it had fired on the rumrunner *Black Duck* in Narragansett Bay in December 1929, killing three of its crew and wounding a fourth. *CG-400* was a new 78-foot cutter, which was faster than the 75s.

A one-pounder was fired in the general direction of *Yvette June* as a signal to pull up, but without effect. The rumrunner began to speed away, north up the Sakonnet River. Not only that, but it threw out a smokescreen. Only then, according to Coast Guard authorities, did the two Coast Guard vessels fire their machine guns at the fleeing *Yvette June*.

According to the version of the incident the Coast Guard told to newspaper reporters, after a chase of five miles, *Yvette June* slowed down considerably around Church's Point, was overtaken and then rammed *CG-400* when making a sharp left turn in a final, desperate attempt to escape. After another flurry of machine gun fire, the rumrunner caught fire and began to sink. "Flames were already shooting high from her engine room and her after deck and cargo were ablaze," reported the *Providence Journal*. How the fire started was not reported. The Coast Guard did not claim, as it sometimes did, that the fire was started by crew members in order to destroy the evidence of their rumrunning.

One of the Coast Guard vessels came alongside the stricken vessel, sent Coast Guardsmen aboard and removed from the vessel five men and three sacks of liquor. Then *Yvette June* sank, taking the rest of its cargo to the bottom of the river. The location of the sinking was 1,700 yards from the Ole Bull Buoy north of Church's Point.

Rico de Nadal of Fall River, the captain of *Yvette June*, was one of the men taken into custody. He was an experienced boat master, having commanded *Alibi II* in February 1931 when it had also been machine gunned, caught fire and sunk. Also in custody were his brother William de Nadal, of Tiverton, the boat's registered owner; Charles B. Bachman of Newport; Helo Lachapelle, also of Newport; and Emile Larchevesque of Fall River. (The surname of Nadal was likely Spanish or Portuguese, while the surnames of Lachapelle and Larchevesque were French Canadian in origin.) Bail was set for $5,000 for each of them, except the amount was $3,000 for Larchevesque. A sixth man was reported to have jumped off the rumrunner, swum safely to shore and escaped capture.

Captain de Nadal told a story to reporters that conflicted sharply with the official Coast Guard version of the sinking of *Yvette June*. He said that his boat was pursued by three Coast Guard vessels, two of which subjected *Yvette June* to a withering crossfire from their machine guns, while the third vessel raked his boat from its stern. So thick was the shower of machine gun bullets, according to de Nadal, that the trunk of *Yvette June*'s cabin had been cut off clean and the vessel had caught fire and started to sink. De Nadal added that he had to jump away from the boat's wheel to dodge the bullets and that it was a miracle none of the crew was killed by the gunfire. Finally, he claimed that it was Cornell's vessel, *CG-400*, that had done the ramming, finishing off *Yvette June* and sending it to the bottom of the Sakonnet River.

There was strong evidence that de Nadal's version was more accurate. When *CG-400* arrived at the municipal dock at Providence later in the morning of July 14, with the five prisoners in tow, its officers, according to the Associated Press, bragged that their vessel had just "sunk" *Yvette June* in the Sakonnet River. The Associated Press report added, "A dent in the cutter's bow gave weight to unconfirmed reports the rum boat was sunk by ramming."[233] The first Associated Press report of the incident stated that *CG-400* had rammed the rumrunner and that "the Coast Guard said the ramming was entirely accidental and followed when the *Yvette June*, which had refused to stop, frantically maneuvered to get away."[234] In follow-up reports, the *Providence Journal* began to describe the incident as follows: "Last July the *Yvette June* was shot, rammed and sunk by a Coast Guard boat."[235] Moreover, in Coast Guard records there is a comment that a Coast Guard report stated that *CG-400* had rammed and sunk *Yvette June*.[236]

Attempts to salvage *Yvette June* added to the controversy surrounding the vessel. Its stern was at the bottom of the Sakonnet River in about fifty feet of water, and its bow showed above the surface, near Church's Point. On July 15, Coast Guard divers began diving to bring away the sacks of liquor left on board. If the Coast Guard did not do that, many others in the area would. Three divers spent most of the day bringing up 538 sacks of liquor with an estimated value of $29,500.[237]

The Coast Guard also made repeated attempts the next several days to refloat the boat and tow it to Providence. Lightening its load helped, but it was not enough. A line was hitched to the boat's forward mooring post on five occasions, but the line failed to hold each time. The last time, *Yvette June* was towed as far as Common Fence Point in Portsmouth, but it sank again, this time in seventy feet of water, making it even more inaccessible than it had been originally. Eventually, the Coast Guard gave up trying to surface the rumrunner and announced that it had abandoned the effort.

Two weeks later, enter Crowninshield Shipbuilding Company, which had a history of building and repairing speedy rumrunners, as well as constructing patrol boats for the Coast Guard. Its main shipyard was directly across the Taunton River from downtown Fall River, less than a mile north of what is now the Braga Bridge. After being hired by *Yvette June*'s registered owner, William de Nadal of Tiverton, and without informing the Coast Guard, Crowninshield employees successfully raised *Yvette June*.

After being repaired, *Yvette June* was taken on a trial run off Newport. The vessel was spotted and identified by an alert Coast Guardsman, seized and taken to New London. A court case ensued at the federal courthouse in Providence. Crowninshield had the stronger case, arguing that under admiralty laws the federal government could not charge a former rumrunner with a violation of the Prohibition Act resulting in its forfeiture because the boat's current owner, the shipbuilding company, had salvaged the sunken vessel only after the Coast Guard had publicly announced its abandonment of *Yvette June*.[238] Federal district court judge Ira Lloyd Letts, in Providence, ruled against the government.[239]

After the boat was raised and inspected by a newspaper reporter, the *Newport Mercury* wrote that *Yvette June*'s pilothouse had been "sheared right off by machine gun bullets."[240] The physical evidence thus supported Captain de Nadal's version of the July 14 chase. This report suggests that perhaps the machine gun fire had so devastated the rumrunner that it went out of control and accidentally rammed *CG-400*. If so, it was not the first time that that had happened to a rumrunner.

The Coast Guard convened a board of inquiry to investigate the ramming incident, but the transcript is missing from the Coast Guard's board of inquiry file.

While newspapers reported that *Yvette June* had been captured and sunk on its first voyage as a rumrunner, it may have been the boat's second. A newspaper report stated that on the night of July 7, 1931, a rumrunning speedboat had laid down a smokescreen after a twenty-mile chase by a Coast Guard patrol boat in Narragansett Bay. The newspaper wire service further stated, "Three hundred rounds of machine gun bullets were fired at the rumrunner. Some of the shots are believed by Coast Guardsmen to have found their mark."[241] Given the time frame and use of the smokescreen, this boat may have been *Yvette June*.

Yvette June continued to be used as a rumrunner until April 4, 1932, when picket boat *CG-2343*, commanded by Boatswain Lathan of the Brenton Point Coast Guard Station, machine gunned the boat and forced it onto a beach near Westport, Massachusetts, next door to Little Compton. Westport policemen later found on board the rumrunner more than one thousand cases of liquor. In order to assist in towing the beached boat back into the water, Section Base 18 at Woods Hole sent *CG-974*, the former notorious Rhode Island rumrunner *Good Luck* of Newport, which had been captured off Warren Point carrying a load of illicit liquor and taken into the Coast Guard's service two weeks earlier on March 22 (it was seized without resort to firing large-caliber guns at it).[242]

Yvette June's days as a rumrunner were over. It was taken into the service of the Coast Guard as *CG-994* on October 14, 1932.[243]

Before it was the target of machine guns in the summer of 1931, the Rhode Island rumrunner *Eaglet* had had a long and successful career

The crew of the rum boat *Linwood* was accused of setting fire to the vessel to destroy evidence of illegal rumrunning before its seizure by the Coast Guard in 1923. In Narragansett Bay, fires were typically started by machine gun bullets puncturing the rumrunner's gas lines or hitting flammable sacks of liquor. *Library of Congress.*

carrying illegal liquor up Narragansett Bay. The 80-foot-long vessel, built in 1911, was a former navy cutter. It was powered with gas engines generating an impressive 1,130 horsepower. It weighed 26 tons and had a 15-foot beam and a depth of 6.8 feet. The vessel was larger than the typical rumrunner but had the engine power to make it fast.

Eaglet was first seized by the Coast Guard off Block Island in 1925 with a load of alcohol on board. In late September 1929, off Long Island, *CG-284* reported firing fourteen one-pounder shells and five pans of machine gun bullets at a fleeing vessel that escaped, which the commander of the patrol boat thought was "the *Eaglet* of Providence, Rhode Island." In early June 1930, *CG-283* cornered *Eaglet* in Fall River when the vessel was seen to have sacks of liquor piled on its deck. But *Eaglet* rammed the patrol boat, escaped and beached itself in the Kickemuit River to the east of Warren. The rumrunner was found with no crew in sight but with 242 sacks of contraband still on board.

The boat was registered to an individual residing in Providence, but it typically operated out of Tiverton. At some point, *Eaglet* became owned by Tiverton's Raymond ("Ray") Coleman, who had commanded the rumrunner *868-G* in April 1931 when it was machine gunned by the Coast Guard in the Sakonnet River and exploded.[244]

In August 1928, Lieutenant Commander Charles S. Root, a Coast Guard intelligence officer, wrote two memoranda on the 80-foot *Eaglet*, which provide a good summary of its offshore-inshore operations. Root wrote of *Eaglet*:

> *This vessel has successfully operated for a year and uses a wharf in the Sakonnet River, just north of the Stone Bridge. This is the "drop" most frequently used. The owner buys his merchandise from a Providence man and "bulls"* [hard liquor] *from the* [outside vessels] *Good Luck, Lucky Strike, and Firelight. He has no storehouse, but sells his goods at the drop.*
>
> *The Eaglet is capable of carrying 1,400 cases, but the owner usually runs about 800, in order not to hamper the speed of the boat.*
>
> *The Lucky Strike and Good Luck, believed to be owned by a Rhode Island man, have a carrying capacity of about 2,500 cases and have been very successful. They are double-enders and can turn so rapidly that they are easily able to elude destroyers when visibility is low. They usually take station off the coast and are believed to be in constant communication with Providence, where their owner maintains a* [radio] *station which was especially built for this purpose.*
>
> [These outside vessels] *also are unloaded by the speedboat C-4809 and another speedboat called the Tramp, with the Eaglet....It is said these boats can unload the seagoing vessels in three nights, if they can make contact before 10 p.m. This early contact is necessary because the offshore vessels owned by this person almost invariably hover east of the longitude of Nantucket.*[245]

In another Coast Guard intelligence report, Root indicated that *Eaglet*'s reputed owner, Sam Ruskin, working from a hotel in Attleboro, Massachusetts, purchased some of his stock from Danny Walsh of Providence, the "Providence man" noted in the above description. Yet a third Coast Guard intelligence report stated that "Dan Walsh controls Fire Light, Good Luck and Lucky Strike. Walsh does business along the entire coast, especially from Point Judith to Watch Hill."[246]

The rumrunner *Tramp* would subsequently be captured and pressed into the service of the Coast Guard, becoming the nemesis of *Eaglet*.

At about 1:20 a.m. on June 13, 1931, three miles south of the Sakonnet Lighthouse, Chief Boatswain's Mate Charles H. Bartlett, commander of the 75-foot cutter *CG-287*, saw a steamship. Knowing the rum boats often followed in the wake of steamers, Bartlett strained his ears to listen to what would come next. He heard a distinct noise of engines and spotted a vessel running without lights. Coast Guardsmen recognized the unique shape of *Eaglet*, with its torpedo-shaped stern, low pilothouse and turtle-back deck forward of the pilothouse. With its one-pounder out of order, *CG-287* fired a warning shot using its machine gun, but to no avail. *Eaglet* increased its speed and headed north for the Sakonnet River.

Bartlett ordered the machine gun fired at *Eaglet*'s stern. A burst from the machine gun was fired at the fleeing vessel as it disappeared from sight. The rumrunner then released a smokescreen, becoming invisible to the Coast Guardsmen. *Eaglet* escaped up the Sakonnet River.

At 5:45 a.m. the same morning, *CG-287* found *Eaglet* in the Sakonnet River heading northward. This time, the vessel stopped to be inspected. The rumrunner had had time to drop off its load of liquor, so no contraband was found on board. But the Coast Guard boarding party saw that the captured vessel "had been damaged on the port bow and that she had been hit by machine gun fire." Bartlett reported later that day that "machine gun bullets holes were found by members of the boarding party in the port side of the *Eaglet* in and near the damaged portion of the turtle back deck."[247]

The *Eaglet* was seized and charged with failing to stop and running without lights. Its owner was then George Davidson of Tiverton, and its master was Percy King of Newport. But with no liquor on board, the vessel was subsequently released.

Two months later, in the late afternoon of August 8, 1931, *Eaglet* was moored at Seaconnet Fish Pier in the Sakonnet River in Tiverton. On board were George Davidson, forty-seven years old, its owner; Leory W. Fitzler, twenty-five, its engineer; Patrick Connors, twenty-three, its captain; and crew members Percy King (thirty-seven), Edmund Sunderland (twenty-three), George Sunderland (twenty-five) and George McGraw (thirty-two). All hailed from Tiverton, except King of Newport and McGraw of Fall River.

Connors steered *Eaglet* down the Sakonnet River, where it was spotted by a Coast Guard 75-footer, *CG-235*, then stationed at the mouth of that river and half a mile off shore. *CG-235* stopped and first looked over the rumrunner *Monolola*, which was on its way out to sea. While *Monolola* was tied up to the patrol boat, *Eaglet* came down the river and brazenly tied itself up to *Monolola* at 5:18 p.m. *Eaglet* was also inspected by the Coast Guardsmen. No liquor was found on board either boat, but everyone knew that the rumrunners were set to meet up with an outside vessel on Rum Row that evening. With the short summer nights, rumrunners had to depart for Rum Row with some light remaining in the day in order to return and make the drop off that night in darkness before the sun rose the next morning. Both boats were released and headed out to sea.

All this rumrunning activity in broad daylight alerted Coast Guard commanders to be on the lookout that evening. Chief Boatswain's Mate Cecil MacLeod at the time commanded *CG-813*, the former 40-foot rumrunner *Tramp* (also known as *C-5691*) that had been converted to a Coast Guard vessel after its capture. *Tramp*, built at the Lawley Shipyard at Neponset, Massachusetts, was reputedly *Black Duck*'s sister ship. MacLeod operated out of Section Base 18 at Woods Hole.[248]

MacLeod had also heard of rumrunners adopting the new tactic of following closely in the wake of legitimate commercial vessels, hoping to hide the tell-tale white streak of wake trailing the rumrunner. Shortly before midnight on August 8, MacLeod spotted the freighter SS *Muncove* plowing through Nantucket Sound coming toward *CG-813*. The location was fourteen miles southwest of Cuttyhunk Island, in the entrance to Buzzards Bay. MacLeod maneuvered his vessel so as to cut in behind the freighter unexpectedly. Sure enough, his searchlights picked up the silhouette of *Eaglet*, running without lights. According to MacLeod's later report, *Eaglet* was so loaded down with sacks on its decks and riding so low that it "looked like a hay-wagon coming down the road." It was on a course for the Sakonnet River and was then about eight miles from Sakonnet Point.

Eaglet was the much heavier craft at 80 feet compared to the 40-foot *CG-813*, and *Eaglet* was slowed by a heavy load of contraband liquor. *CG-813* also had the advantage of being armed with two automatic Browning machine guns.

MacLeod signaled for *Eaglet* to heave to. The rumrunner's captain, Connors, ignored the order. MacLeod next ordered his machine gunner to fire a burst of bullets across *Eaglet*'s bow. That did not work either. *Eaglet* continued to follow in the wake of the freighter. This tactic inhibited MacLeod from indiscriminately firing his boat's machine gun at the fleeing vessel, for fear of hitting the commercial vessel. It appears *Eaglet* then swerved into the wake of another freighter, the steamship *Boston*.

MacLeod ordered his machine gunner, Archie Dickinson, to fire at *Eaglet* when he had a clear shot into the rumrunner's engine room. (In his incident report, MacLeod did not mention his order to fire at the engine room.) The machine gunner saw an opening. Suddenly, a hail of bullets ripped into the port side of *Eaglet*'s hull. Continuing the chase, Dickinson waited two or three minutes, allowing time for the rumrunner to surrender, before firing another pan of machine gun bullets. According to Coast Guard crew member Charles Rucker, Dickinson fired "several pans" of machine gun bullets into *Eaglet*, with the result that "she then caught fire and her engine stopped."[249] MacLeod later reported that ten pans were fired into *Eaglet*'s hull (each pan held about forty-seven bullets).[250]

The disabled *Eaglet* stopped and began to drift. The *Boston Globe*, no doubt based on information from MacLeod or others from his crew, reported:

> *A tongue of flame licked out from aft on her deck. The dry straw casing of the bottles was like tinder, and in no time the boat a mass of flames. MacLeod brought the CG-813 neatly alongside the burning vessel, where seven trapped men lined the rail, eager for rescue. Resistance was forgotten as they piled over the rail onto the patrol boat's deck, amid broken glass that sprayed Coast Guardsmen and prisoners....Before MacLeod cast loose from the burning Eaglet, despite the danger of an explosion in her gasoline tanks that might blow up both vessels at any second, his men secured a number of sacks of contraband liquor to be used as evidence in court.*[251]

The *Providence Journal* reported:

> *The Eaglet, many times the target for Coast Guard bullets during a spectacular career of rum running off the southern New England coast and in Narragansett Bay in the past six years, was set afire by a machine gun bullet which punctured her huge gasoline tanks after she had refused to heave to when ordered and her deck was raked by gunfire according to the report of the crew of CG-813, which made the capture.*[252]

The crew on board the SS *Muncove* transmitted by a wireless to a Coast Guard destroyer a description of the following disturbing scene:

> *That boat [Eaglet] that shot flares up at ten pm and again at eleven pm was burning and was all in flames. Some small boat was shooting at the burning boat with rockets or machine guns ten miles west south-west of Vineyard Light Vessel.*[253]

This description indicates that, shockingly, *CG-813* machine gunned *Eaglet* even as it burned. (Testimony at a subsequent trial of the crew members confirmed that a Coast Guard boat "emptied many steel jacketed bullets into the vessel after it had burst into flames."[254])

Eaglet, in flames, sank. It was judged to have on board a large cargo of liquor with an estimated value of $80,000. The rumrunner itself was valued at more than $25,000, making a total loss of more than $100,000.

CG-813 brought the new captives to Section Base 18 at Woods Hole. One of the crew members, Leroy Fitzler, had an injured hand. According to the *Boston Globe*, "the surgeon R. Henry V. Stroupe, dressed the wound and found it only superficial."[255]

Not for the first time, the Coast Guard had, in its initial statement, understated the injuries suffered by rumrunners who had been subjected to fusillades of machine gun fire. In fact, three of the seven crew members exhibited wounds. Fitzler was the most severely wounded—his right hand had been shattered by a bullet. Both the *Providence Journal* and *Newport Mercury* reported that Fitzler might have to have his hand amputated. Edmund Sunderland had a sear across his shoulder, where, he said, a bullet from the Coast Guard machine gun grazed him. George McGraw had a scratch on his right side, which he believed had been inflicted by a bullet, although it may have been from when he fell in the engine room trying to avoid being hit by the gunfire.

Eaglet crew members claimed that one of the bullets fired from *CG-813* had punctured and ignited the gasoline tank and that the explosion had sprayed the boat with burning gasoline. Their craft was ablaze from stem to stem when the Coast Guard boat came alongside and removed them from their stricken vessel. Customs agent William J. Fitzgerald claimed that the men had set fire to their own craft when they saw their capture was inevitable, but no one gave this view any credence.[256]

The *Newport Mercury* reported, in its article published five days after the incident, that during *CG-813*'s chase of *Eaglet*, "the Coast Guard is reported to have fired 1,000 machine gun bullets." Earlier, the day after the incident, a United Press International report indicated that "more than 500 machine gun shots were fired by the pursuing Coast Guard boat."[257] The latter report was more accurate.

At trial, the nine sacks of liquor removed from *Eaglet* before it sank were introduced as evidence. It proved to be Canadian whiskey. On March 24, 1932, the jury returned a verdict of guilty as to each defendant. Connors and King were each sentenced to pay a fine and costs of $400; Edmund and

George Sunderland and McGraw were each sentenced to pay a fine and costs of $300. Davidson and Fitzler received harsh sentences. Davidson was sentenced to prison for six months and Fitzler for three months; both were remitted to the Providence County Jail.[258] In addition, the federal court in Providence later ordered that the $9,500 bond given for the release of *Eaglet* in 1930 be paid to the federal government.[259]

Still, the trial judge in Providence, U.S. District Court judge Ira Lloyd Letts, felt compelled to state in court that the evidence submitted that *CG-813* had fired 470 machine gun bullets at the *Eaglet* presented "a rather sad commentary on the administration of law in this country." He added bitingly, "Here it is evident the Coast Guard continued to fire upon the vessel after it had burst into flames." Judge Letts further criticized the Coast Guard for firing a machine gun as warning shots, rather than firing a one-pounder over the bow of *Eaglet*.[260] Meanwhile, *Eaglet* lay undisturbed under two hundred feet of water some eight miles southwest of Sakonnet Point.

Chapter 15

SUMMER AND FALL 1931

MORE COMPLAINTS OF MACHINE GUNS ENDANGERING CIVILIANS IN NARRAGANSETT BAY (*MITZI*)

Relatively early during the night of September 1, 1931, the notorious rumrunner *Mitzi* was machine gunned in the narrow West Passage of Narragansett Bay by picket boat *CG-2343*, leading to complaints that the Coast Guard had endangered civilians onshore between Saunderstown and Plum Beach south of Wickford.

Mitzi was well-known to "rummy" hunters for operating out of East Greenwich. Described as a "gas yacht," it was built at Morris Heights, New York, in 1931. It was 53.5 feet long and 11.5 feet wide, had a depth of 6.2 feet and weighed a hefty 16 tons. It had two engines capable of developing a total of 1,080 horsepower. Once owned by a New Yorker, it was acquired by Nicholas Gaul of Providence in May 1931.[261]

Mitzi previously had a run-in with *CG-2343* on July 5, 1931. That night, the picket boat, under the command of Boatswain Elsworth Lathan and operating from the Brenton Point Coast Guard Station in Newport, was patrolling near Dutch Island in the West Passage of Narragansett Bay. At about 11:30 p.m., a speedboat running without lights was spotted coming up the bay. Lathan ordered the usual signals to be made, but they were ignored. Using his searchlight at a distance of only twenty yards, Lathan could plainly see that it was the rumrunner *Mitzi* of Providence and that it had tell-tale sacks of liquor piled on its decks.

Mitzie released a dense smokescreen and sped away to the north. Lathan ordered his machine gunner to open fire with live bullets. According to

Lathan, his boat fired "approximately three hundred rounds of machine gun ammunition…at the fleeing boat in order to damage her or put her out of commission." But *CG-2343* was not fast enough to keep up with *Mitzi*, which disappeared into the darkness.

The next day, crew member Michael Mackin saw *Mitzi* at a shipyard in East Greenwich, where it had been hauled out of the water for repairs. Mackin saw that the rumrunner's deck had been "shattered by machine gun bullets" and that "pieces of bullets were picked out of her holds where they had penetrated her deck." Mackin also dug some bullets out of the hull and kept them as evidence.[262]

The author interviewed Irving Sheldon when he was ninety-five years old about his memories of seeing a rumrunner being fired on in Narragansett Bay. It could well have been the attack on *Mitzi*. Sheldon, who resided with his family in a summer house called Spindrift on the coast at Saunderstown, still vividly remembered a summer night in the early 1930s when he saw from his family's house on Narragansett Bay an attack on a rumrunner by a Coast Guard vessel. Sheldon recalled that as a child, his older brother Rhody came into his bedroom one night and woke him up so they could watch from his third-floor bedroom windows the gunfire on the bay. He can remember seeing tracer bullets pierce the dark night and the red glow of bullets hot from barrel friction from a machine gun. The rumrunner was getting battered, he recalled.[263]

Virtually the same scene with the same players was replayed the night of September 1, 1931, at approximately 9:30 p.m., in the West Passage. This time, Lathan fired 350 rounds of machine gun bullets at *Mitzi*, in a chase covering five miles, from Dutch Island to Wickford. *Mitzi* again released a smokescreen and disappeared up the West Passage. Lathan did not see *Mitzi* at East Greenwich Bay that night, but he then motored across to Mount Hope Bay to the Crowninshield Shipyard and in the early morning saw the rumrunner being hauled out of the water. The boat was inspected for bullet holes, but this time none could be found.[264]

Because the machine gun fire occurred relatively early in the night near populated areas, this incident caught the attention of the public. A former state representative, Manuel Talcott, wrote a letter to U.S. Senator Felix Hebert, complaining that at the time, many civilians were meeting at Plum Beach, including children, whose lives were endangered by the gunfire.

Coast Guard commandant Admiral Billard responded to Senator Hebert himself, denying the charge. The picket boat, Billard declared, fired at the stern of the *Mitzi* only as it was speeding northward, and since Plum Beach

A drawing of a Coast Guard patrol boat pursuing and firing at a rumrunner, titled "Naval Manoeuvers [*sic*] in the Atlantic Too," by Rollin Kirby and dated March 11, 1923. Two crew members on the rumrunner fire pistols back at the Coast Guard boat (which is not known to have ever occurred in Rhode Island waters). *Library of Congress.*

ran north–south, there was no danger to the civilians. The commandant emphasized, "During the entire [chase], the rumrunner motor boat was headed due north with the Coast Guard picket boat directly astern, so that the there was no possibility of any shots reaching either shore, either directly or through ricochet."[265]

Calling the admiral's statement "mostly hooey," Talcott added that it was "exactly what I anticipated when I entered my complaint." Talcott explained that *Mitzi* probably zigzagged to evade the machine gun fire, which would have accounted for some of the bullets going toward the shore. Talcott added, "If any man can tell how a bullet is going to ricochet on the water and the amount of deflection, he knows more about guns than any other man who has ever handled a gun."[266]

Lathan's immediate superior, the commander of the Third District, located in Wakefield, performed an investigation. He concluded that Lathan had complied with the Coast Guard policies and had not endangered any lives. Nonetheless, he cautioned Lathan and the rest of the Brenton Point Station Coast Guardsmen regarding the direction of firing machine guns in the narrow confines of the West Passage, as well as in the Sakonnet River. He wrote that "it is the opinion of headquarters" that not shooting at a rumrunner in restricted areas in Narragansett Bay and thus allowing it to escape "is preferable to the death or injury of any innocent person by gunfire from the Coast Guard vessel."[267] Admiral Billard, after reviewing the report, responded to the report's conclusions by sending a mixed message:

> *Headquarters has noted with approval the activities of the Brenton Point Station in patrolling the waters in the vicinity of Narragansett Bay to prevent violations of the Customs laws, and does not desire to take any action which might tend to discourage the personnel of Brenton Point Station in waging this vigorous offensive against rum-running vessels in Narragansett Bay. Nevertheless, Headquarters agrees with you that too much caution cannot be used in connection with the use of gunfire in restricted waters.*[268]

Mitzi found more trouble on the night of October 2, 1931. The ubiquitous Alexander Cornell and his *CG-290* were at anchor in the West Passage of Narragansett Bay, just off Bonnett Point in Narragansett, when at 9:19 p.m. the crew saw a vessel running without lights. *CG-290* slipped its anchor and steamed toward the unidentified vessel. But at a distance of five hundred yards, the target vessel spotted the patrol boat, turned around and headed out to sea. While turning, Cornell put his searchlight on the boat and had a gunner fire three blank one-pounder shells across its bow as a signal to heave to, but the boat just put on more speed. *CG-290* then fired two one-pounder live shells and about forty-five machine gun bullets at the fleeing vessel. But due to the distance and vessel's greater speed, the patrol boat lost its mark. Coast Guard officials thought that the unidentified vessel was *Mitzi*, which had been spotted at 3:00 p.m. that afternoon exiting the East Passage, giving it time to meet its outside vessel beyond the twelve-mile range and motor back that evening into Narragansett Bay for its drop off.[269] This would not be the last time Coast Guard machine guns would be employed against *Mitzi*.

Chapter 16

FALL 1931

FOUR RUMRUNNERS ARE MACHINE GUNNED ON THE RHODE ISLAND–MASSACHUSETTS BORDER (*RHODE ISLAND, OVERLAND, JE T'AIME* AND *NOLA*)

Rumrunners did not necessarily stick to Rhode Island's borders, even if they were operating out of Newport, Providence, East Greenwich, Tiverton, Little Compton or another port in the state. In four incidents in the fall of 1931, Rhode Island rumrunners operating out of Rhode Island were machine gunned in waters near the Rhode Island and Massachusetts border. In two of the incidents, the rumrunners (*Rhode Island* and *Nola*) were sunk. During or after another incident (*Overland*), a crew member drowned.

What made two of these incidents remarkable were the steps crew members on the rumrunners took to avoid being killed by machine gun fire. On *Je T'Aime*, the third rumrunner, crew members wore bulletproof vests. In *Nola*'s case, the owner went further, affixing on his boat's structure steel plates. But the armor did not work—the Coast Guard machine gunner must have fired hundreds of rounds at *Nola*, giving one crew member on board a life-threatening wound and inflicting wounds on two others.

As a result of a newspaper reporter interviewing a Coast Guard officer, a detailed, marvelous narrative of the chase and attack on the rumrunner *Rhode Island* was published. It included a startling admission by the Coast Guard officer about the use of his vessel's deadly machine guns.

The *Rhode Island* had a long career as a rumrunner operating out of Newport. It was first captured in February 1925, unloading cargo at a wharf at Rocky Point in Warwick. Charles Allen Jr. of Providence was then listed as its registered owner, and Ira McVey of Providence was listed as its master.[270] A Coast Guard intelligence report indicated that its real owner was Dutch Reitzmuth, a gangster from Pawtucket.[271]

On the night of October 6, 1931, *CG-2297*, a new Coast Guard speedboat, was on its first patrol operating out of Section Base 18 at Woods Hole. A lookout spotted *Rhode Island* outside New Bedford Harbor, running a zigzag course without lights two miles off Hen and Chickens Lightship.

When the rumrunner refused signals to heave to, the commander in charge of *CG-2297* ordered his machine gunner to open fire. *Rhode Island* responded by throwing up a smokescreen, but to no avail. *CG-2297* was fast, able to achieve thirty-five miles per hour, while the otherwise speedy *Rhode Island* was slowed by its heavy cargo. One newspaper report indicated that the machine gunner aboard *CG-2297* fired a well-directed shot that penetrated the side of the speedboat. The Coast Guard boat finally overhauled its prey.

When *Rhode Island* was seized near the Hen and Chickens Lightship and its crew removed from their speedboat and taken aboard the Coast Guard vessel, the rumrunner was sinking. It eventually sank. Coast Guard officials, as usual, claimed that the crew of the rumrunner intentionally sank it, while the crew members countered that machine gun fire sank their vessel. No one was injured, and six cases of alcohol were removed from the boat by Coast Guardsmen as evidence. The prisoners were carried to Providence for arraignment. It was reported that the *Rhode Island* speedboat was worth $25,000 and that the liquor it carried had a value of $40,000.[272]

After the capture, an enterprising newspaper reporter was able to obtain a detailed description of the chase, machine gun fire and capture from Lieutenant Donald Hesler, second in command at Section Base 18 in Woods Hole. Hesler was asked to ride on board *CG-2297* that night because the Coast Guard vessel was on its first patrol. It may have been a new Coast Guard speedboat. The boat's skipper was twenty-five-year-old Chief Boatswain's Mate Irwin T. Yost.

The crew of the Coast Guard vessel was on alert because supplies were expected to be brought into shore for the upcoming Columbus Day holiday. As *CG-2297* patrolled leisurely, southwest of Hen and Chickens and near Gooseberry Neck at the Massachusetts–Rhode Island border, the lookout spotted a decent-sized ship roaring along and noticed something shining on the water in its wake. Peering closer, the Coast Guardsman saw phosphorescence churning up in the wake of the large boat. It was a speedboat following in the wake of the larger ship, and the speedboat had no running lights turned on.

The rumrunner *Rhode Island*, shown in the photo in a harbor tied to a dock, was captured on October 6, 1931. *National Archives.*

The Coast Guard vessel's searchlight was switched on and pointed at the speedboat. It revealed, Lieutenant Hesler said, that the boat (*Rhode Island*) was "loaded like a haystack with burlap bags" full of liquor. *CG-2297*'s Klaxon horn blared out, and the searchlight was turned to show its Treasury Department flag. These were signals for *Rhode Island* to heave to, but the suspected rumrunner instead responded by speeding up. Tracer bullets were fired over the escaping craft as another warning.

The article continues Lieutenant Hesler's story:

> *Up to 35 miles-an-hour went the two boats, with the high-speed Coast Guard boat easily keeping pace. A smokescreen swept out aft from the first*

boat, choking the pursuers. But they still could follow the trail by the sparkle of the choppy waters.

Yost manned the Lewis machine gun. It was blowing such a gale that he had to brace himself, legs wide apart, and hang on with main strength.

Gradually [CG-2297] ate up the distance apart. Lieut. Healer shouted at Yost: "Can you put a shot through that port hole?" He indicated the porthole in the little wheelhouse.

Without a word, Yost aimed his gun. It was a bulls-eye, a clean shot through the glass window. Dismayed at the barrage of bullets that had formed a necklace around the freeboard, the skipper of the "rummy" bellowed an order for "stop." The engines kept turning. He rang his engine-room signals frantically, with no slowing up.

So close was the distance between the two boats that the Coast Guards could hear the skipper again yell: "Stop those engines!" He ordered his lieutenant [his second-in-command] *to "get down there and stop them yourself."*

The lieutenant then did a nervy thing. He walked the length of the deck in direct line with the trained guns on the Coast Guard boat. Yost yanked his finger from the trigger and watched him go.

"And in the engine room of the boat he found the engineer crawling on the deck, literally clawing his fingers into the boarding," declared Lieut. Hesler. "Yost's gun had encircled the room completely."

Already the speed boat was half submerged by the gunfire. The crew ran aft and leaped into a dory. The Coast Guards took them aboard. In a minute, Yost, not wanting to lose his prize, quickly boarded the abandoned boat and attempted to stem the flow of water.

He found, however, that his efforts were in vain. The scuttling valves in the engine room had been opened and the wheels tossed away. There was nothing he could do but return to his boat and watch the craft sink to the bottom, 2½ miles southwest of Hen and Chickens.

Coffee and sandwiches were given the five men as they were carried to the Section Base here [at Woods Hole]. *Questioned by Commander* [R.J.] *Hatch and Customs Inspector William J. Fitzgerald, they said the boat was named the Rhode Island and that they sailed from Newport.*[273]

A startling facet of this report was that Lieutenant Hesler admitted asking the machine gunner to aim for the porthole inside the wheelhouse, knowing that crew members could be wounded or killed by that course of action. Furthermore, Hesler and the newspaper reporter both found it amusing that as a result of this order, the engineer lay prostrate on the boat's deck, trying to avoid the machine gun fire and save his life. In addition, even with an officer on board, Yost had violated Coast Guard policy by firing live rounds as warning shots. These types of issues may explain why the Coast Guard infrequently allowed its officers to discuss missions with the press corps.

Hesler also conceded that when the rumrunner was overtaken, it was already half-submerged as a result of machine gun fire puncturing holes in *Rhode Island*'s hull. The rumrunner ultimately sank.

From the perspective of the rumrunners, it must have been disconcerting that *CG-2297* could run as fast as thirty-five miles per hour.

In the next incident, the rumrunner escaped from a furious fusillade of one-pounder and machine gun fire. A crew member died of drowning that morning, but it is not known if the death was related to the gunfire.

The rumrunner was *Overland*, whose registered owner was Wilfred Corriveau of Woonsocket and which generally operated out of Newport. It had three four-hundred-horsepower Packard engines and was regarded as one of the fastest rumrunners in the state. *Overland* was 52.4 feet long and 12.4 feet wide, had a depth of 5.6 feet and weighed about 14 tons. While originally built at Beals, Maine, in 1925, it had been refurbished at the Crowninshield Shipyard at Somerset in 1930. Early in the morning of January 27, 1931, *Overland* surrendered with liquor on board after *CG-2343* fired a burst of machine gun fire in its direction as it was entering the Sakonnet River.[274] After it was released, *Overland* continued its career as a rumrunner.

In between Hen and Chickens Lightship and Brenton Reef off Newport, in the early morning of October 23, 1931, *CG-402*, a new, fast 78-footer, spotted and chased a suspected rumrunner. The commander of *CG-402*, Theodore Losch, including the following in his incident report:

> *Fired 3 blank one-pounders as warning shots and lighted up speedboat with searchlight. Sacks could be plainly seen strewn about the deck of the speedboat. Speedboat increased her speed and laid down a dense smoke screen, zig zagging in a southerly direction. The CG-402 pursued the speedboat for a period of 40 minutes, or until 0140 [1:40 a.m.] when it was lost sight of. During the pursuit 15 pans of machine gun ammunition and 16 one-pounder service ammunition were fired directly at speedboat in an effort to disable her.*
>
> *This speedboat was unquestionably hit badly, for when pursuit started the CG-402 was within 50 yards of her and the sacks on her deck were afire. This speedboat resembled the Overland.[275]*

Overland's experienced commander, Rico de Nadal of Fall River, later informed Fall River authorities of a missing member of his crew, Emile Larchevesque. (Nadal and Larchevesque had both been on board *Yvette June* when it was machine gunned and burst into flames in the Sakonnet River in July 1931). De Nadal said that his vessel had departed Newport in between 8:00 p.m. and 9:00 p.m. on Thursday, October 22, went out about fifty miles (to make contact with an outside vessel, which de Nadal left unsaid) and then headed back in toward Newport. On the return voyage, with all crew members below decks, de Nadal said, Larchevesque declared that he was going on deck for a smoke. Sometime later, crew members noticed that Larchevesque was missing. De Nadal had *Overland* turned around to retrace its course for about fifteen miles, but Larchevesque was not spotted. De Nadal searched the next day too, but no trace of the missing crew member was found. Larchevesque was presumed drowned; he left a wife and a baby born just two weeks earlier.[276]

On October 28, the *Providence Journal* reported that "Coast Guard headquarters at New London admitted that a patrol boat had pursued a speedboat loaded with liquor and resembling the *Overland* last Thursday night but that the supposed rum-runner had escaped despite heavy gunfire." Note that de Nadal, in his explanation, never mentions being chased by a Coast Guard patrol vessel. He likely wanted to avoid confessing to charges of illegal rumrunning and fleeing from a Coast Guard vessel. But the Coast Guard's statement strongly indicates that it was *Overland* at which *CG-402* had let loose perhaps more than seven hundred machine gun bullets, as well as sixteen live one-pounder shells. Was de Nadal hiding that Larchevesque had been hit by the gunfire and knocked off the boat? Or did the crew member accidentally fall of the boat at a time when the boat was not being attacked? Either scenario is possible, but the truth will never be known.

The next incident occurred more than a month later. At about 9:30 p.m. on November 11, a lookout on *CG-813*, commanded by Chief Boatswain's Mate Cecil MacLeod and operating out of Woods Hole, spotted what was a suspected rumrunner heading north for Sakonnet Point. The rumrunner refused to stop when signaled by MacLeod's boat, including tracer machine gun bullets fired across the vessel's bow. MacLeod then ordered his machine gunner to open fire, reportedly using steel-jacketed bullets. According to MacLeod, *CG-813* then fired about forty rounds into the boat, directed at the engine room "in order to disable it." *CG-813* was a speedboat, the former rumrunner *Tramp*. After a short chase, the rumrunner stopped and surrendered about two and a half miles south of Sakonnet Point, close to the Massachusetts–Rhode Island border.

The boat was the motorboat *Je T'Aime*. Customs officials in Providence described the vessel as the "queen" of the rumrunners operating off Block Island and Cape Cod. Its two motors were capable of a total of one thousand horsepower.

Je T'Aime was built at East Greenwich in 1930. It was 76 feet long, 16 feet wide, 8 feet deep and weighed about 25 tons. Customs officials and Prohibition agents thought that a South Providence syndicate and a well-known Boston gang joined together in the venture to bring in a large load for the upcoming Thanksgiving and Christmas holidays.

What was remarkable about this incident was that the crew wore bulletproof vests. They had heard about the trigger-happy Coast Guard gunners and attempted to take at least some precautions. No one was injured by the machine gun fire. Another interesting feature of this incident was that the Coast Guard vessel was easily faster than the rumrunner and yet still employed its machine gun.

Je T'Aime was registered to a Milton Kaufman residing on Gay Street in Providence and captained by Manuel Goulart of East Greenwich and New Bedford. Goulart was probably the brother of John Goulart, one of *Black Duck*'s crew members killed in December 1929.[277] Goulart and six other men (two from Providence and two from New Bedford) were seized as well.

When the boat arrived at Providence the next day, with its crew as prisoners, newspaper reporters could see the holes ripped into the cabin of the motorboat by the Coast Guard's bullets. Customs agents found on board assorted liquors in 1,128 sacks, 24 cases and 37 fifteen-gallon kegs, including William Penn, Gold Label, Walker's Club and other famous liquor brands. The Coast Guard estimated the value of *Je T'Aime* at $50,000 and its cargo at $75,000.

The seven prisoners were taken to the federal courthouse in Providence for arraignment and later pleaded guilty to charges of transporting illegal liquor. On April 15, 1932, *Je T'Aime* was forfeited to the federal government, taken into the service of the Coast Guard as *CG-833* and assigned to Section Base 18.[278]

The Coast Guard had been alerted to the anticipated appearance of *Je T'Aime* by an informer acting on behalf of a rival gang of rumrunners. As a result of the tip that a major landing of liquor was planned for midnight at Briggs Beach at Little Compton, a party of federal Prohibition agents and Rhode Island state troopers hid near the expected drop site. If *Je T'Aime* had

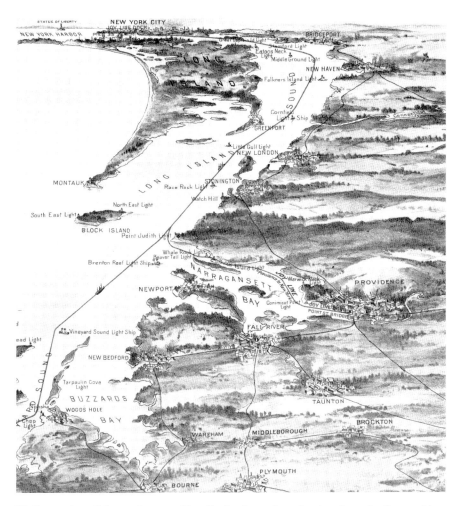

Bird's-eye view of the southeastern New England coastline, showing the path of steamships of the Joy Steamship Company, in 1905. This map also shows a bird's-eye view of, from east to west, Woods Hole, New Bedford, Newport, Fall River, Providence and New London. *Library of Congress, Map Division.*

somehow managed to avoid the picket of Coast Guard boats prowling for it that night and made the planned drop off, the liquor it carried probably would have fallen into the hands of the lawmen waiting on land.

As the agents and troopers lay in hiding on the beach, they spotted four large trucks, a light truck and twenty men, all or most likely all of them local men looking for remunerative part-time work to unload *Je T'Aime* and place its cargo onto the trucks. The light truck was to have been used to take the liquor and haul it to the larger trucks. Some wood planks had been laid down on part of the sandy beach to prevent the light truck, when loaded, from sinking in the sand. But at 2:00 a.m., with *Je T'Aime* already two hours late, the landing party discovered the presence of the Prohibition agents and state troopers and left the scene with their empty trucks.[279]

Unknown investors, perhaps based in Providence, likely concerned about the difficulty of hiring crew members when the Coast Guard was so willing to fire at them with machine guns, made a bold decision. They agreed to fund an innovation—placing steel plates on the deck and around the pilothouse of a new speedboat, which they called *Nola*. The boat's wooden hull was not protected by armor, but it was hoped that the bullets would not penetrate the thick wood into the boat's lower holds. The innovation was expensive and would surely slow the speed of the motor-powered rumrunner, but it was thought worth the try to see if it worked against the Coast Guard's firepower.

Nola was built at Kelley's Shipyard in New Bedford and launched in August 1931. It was 60 feet long and 13 feet wide and powered by three Detroit Aero Marine engines (*Black Duck* had carried two of them). The speedboat had steel plate covering its stern and steel plates from the deck line to the waterline two and a half feet down from the main deck. Steel plate also protected the pilothouse and the engine room.[280]

Arthur Francis ("Frank") Butler of Martha's Vineyard and New Bedford claimed credit for coming up with the idea for the steel plate and designing the steel plate covering for *Nola*. He was also the boat's master. The vessel was registered to Jesse Sylvia of Newport.[281] Butler reportedly bragged about the invulnerability of his boat and that he would never be captured alive.

Nola was not the first armored rumrunner. Others, particularly funded by investors out of New York City, had tried and failed. For example, bullets bounced off the steel turret of the armored *Vee*, but a New York City police speedboat succeeded in capturing the rumrunner in October 1924.[282]

On the night of December 12, 1931, Boatswain Cecil MacLeod, again commanding *CG-813* operating out of Woods Hole, was stationed four miles west of Cuttyhunk Island, waiting for "sea-going Santa Clauses laden with alcoholic cheer" for patrons wanting to enjoy the upcoming holiday season. MacLeod was about to encounter one of the most extraordinary boats ever seen in New England waters during Prohibition.

At about 9:00 p.m., looking through his night glasses, Alfred Phalen of *CG-813* spotted a vessel operating without lights. Within fifty yards of the boat, MacLeod turned on his vessel's searchlight, fired flares into the dark sky and shined the searchlight alternately on the unidentified boat and on his vessel's flag. The boat ignored the signals, swung away from *CG-813*, showing its stern, and put on speed. Phalen could easily read the boat's name on its stern, "Nola of Newport, R.I." Coast Guardsmen had heard about this rumrunner becoming an armored vessel and were ready for it.

MacLeod ordered Phalen, his machine gunner, to fire three bursts of machine gun fire "over and ahead" of the fleeing rumrunner, but the fire made no impression. MacLeod then ordered Phalen to fire at *Nola*'s stern. The bullets bounced off the steel plate, but some bullets directed at *Nola*'s deck struck sacks of liquor piled high, causing a small fire. *CG-813* fired at *Nola* an astounding twenty-one pans of machine gun bullets, almost one thousand of them. So far, the armor was working, and *Nola* began to outdistance the slower *CG-813*.

Other Coast Guard vessels in the area saw the flares and machine gun fire that lit up the night. They joined in the chase, including the picket boat *CG-2297*, operating out of Woods Hole and commanded by Irwin Yost, which drew up alongside *CG-813* on its port side.

CG-405, a 78-footer commanded by Christopher Barrett and operating out of New London, was stationed about six miles south of the Sakonnet Lighthouse when it also saw the action. It joined in the chase at about 9:25 p.m. There was some rivalry between Coast Guardsmen based in New London and those stationed at Woods Hole. Believing that *CG-813* was falling behind and "not making any progress" in stopping the rumrunner, Barrett used his vessel's superior speed to cut in front of *CG-813*. This maneuver annoyed MacLeod, who was forced to cease firing his machine gun for fear of a friendly fire incident. He was also surprised to see *CG-405* so far from its home base of New London. *CG-405* came up alongside of *Nola* and rammed the rumrunner, hoping to force the fleeing vessel to heave to. When that did not work, *CG-405* sheared off and rammed *Nola* again.

Changing tactics, Barret drew *CG-405* abreast of the rumrunner and at a distance of seventy-five feet opened fire with its one-pounder. A second live round was fired. Both projectiles smashed into the rumrunner's wooden hull. The broadsides fired by *CG-405* as it motored parallel to *Nola* resembled a battle of sailing ships during the War of 1812. There were a few differences—in the 1931 incident, *Nola* did not fire back and all the participants were Americans.

After the second one-pounder was fired, *Nola* turned away from *CG-405*, but that maneuver opened a lane for *CG-2297*. Boatswain Yost ordered his machine gunner to fire a pan of bullets into the flailing rumrunner. Finally, "finding it was getting too hot," *Nola* hove to and surrendered, about four miles southeast of the Vineyard Lightship.

As *CG-2297* first drew up alongside the stricken *Nola*, smoke began to rise from a smoldering fire that began to grow rapidly. Yost sent a man aboard, who grabbed a sack of liquor as evidence and threw it onto *CG-2297*. *CG-405* then forced *CG-2297* to shear off. The Coast Guardsmen on the 78-footer found five men aboard and took them prisoner and nabbed another sack of liquor as well. The prisoners, most of them hailing from New Bedford, were brought to New London for arraignment.

Next *CG-813* drew up alongside *Nola* and its crew spotted a member of the rumrunner's crew sprawled on the deck almost unconscious in front of the pilothouse. He was Seraphine Nunes of New Bedford, an immigrant from the Azores who had been on the forecastle in front of the pilothouse for the entire chase, unseen by the Coast Guardsmen. He had been hit with machine gun fire. After Nunes was given some first aid, he was quickly removed and taken aboard *CG-813*.

Meanwhile, the Coast Guard destroyer *Wilkes*, alerted by the gunfire, arrived at the scene at 10:15 p.m. After extinguishing most of the fire on board *Nola*, a Coast Guardsman from *Wilkes* jumped aboard *Nola* and fastened a line to its bow. *Wilkes* began to tow the stricken vessel, intending to

Unknown persons on board the deck of the steel-plated *Nola* before its capture and sinking on December 12, 1931. *National Archives.*

bring it to New London, but afterward an unextinguished fire expanded or another fire broke out on *Nola*, followed by a number of explosions. Within a few minutes, just before 3:00 a.m. on December 19, the rumrunner sank to the bottom on the ocean.[283]

Seraphine Nunes, in critical condition with his life hanging in the balance, was rushed to the U.S. Marine Hospital at Vineyard Haven on Martha's Vineyard. A machine gun bullet had severed an artery in his thigh, and he was bleeding profusely. The *Boston Globe* reported the next day that Nunes's wound was likely fatal. However, because there was no subsequent press report of his death, Nunes likely survived. A man by the same name who would have been eighteen years old in 1931 was listed as a bartender in New Bedford in the 1940 census.[284]

Two other wounded crew members were taken to Section Base 4's sickbay at New London. One of them was *Nola*'s master, Frank Butler. He suffered a wound in his wrist and in his thigh, caused by shrapnel from the second of the one-pounder shells bursting through the pilothouse. Perhaps what hurt him most was the pummeling that the Coast Guard machine guns and one-pound cannon inflicted on his allegedly invulnerable rumrunner. Harry Gleckman of Dorchester, Massachusetts, had a machine gun bullet slice through his hand, and his neck was creased by another. It was apparently his first trip on a rumrunner.

The Coast Guard was fortunate that it did not have another *Black Duck* incident on its hands, with three dead rumrunners.[285] McLeod petulantly complained that *CG-405* had prevented *CG-813* from making the capture. But it seems that *CG-405*'s one-pounder fire led to the surrender of *Nola*. Had it not surrendered, *CG-813* would have continued pummeling *Nola* with machine gun fire, which may have killed or seriously injured other *Nola* crew members.

Chapter 17

1932 AND 1933

THE LAST RUMRUNNERS ARE MACHINE GUNNED IN NARRAGANSETT BAY (*KELBLE* AND *MITZI*)

By 1932, the writing was on the wall: Prohibition was coming to an end. The country was in the grips of a severe economic downturn, with high unemployment, called the Great Depression. The current occupant of the White House, Herbert Hoover, was not viewed as flexible enough to use the powers of the federal government to try to extricate the country from the economic calamity. The Democratic Party candidate for president of the United States, Franklin D. Roosevelt, promised to do more. He was also perceived as an enemy of Prohibition—although not wanting to alienate "dry" voters, he never publicly announced that he intended to work to repeal Prohibition. Roosevelt became the favorite to win the presidential election of November 1932.

The General Assembly enacted a law providing for a statewide vote and a convention to be held to repeal the Eighteenth Amendment. This was the first time in state history that a convention was convened for the purpose of amending the U.S. Constitution. On May 1, 1933, Rhode Island voters voted for convention delegates to repeal the Eighteenth Amendment by a margin of 150,244 to 20,874. The vote in Providence was 66,667 for repeal and 6,628 against. A week later, the thirty-one delegates (twenty-five men and six women) unanimously ratified the Twenty-First Amendment, which was to repeal the Eighteenth Amendment. One delegate who spoke passionately against the Eighteenth Amendment, Walter Sundlun, father of future governor Bruce Sundlun, made the point that the Eighteenth

Amendment had been so unpopular that it had turned good people into lawbreakers: "Men and women who in every other respect are law abiding citizens of our great country have, during the years that prohibition has been in force, gradually adopted a philosophy that to conspire with and aid the bootlegger in his illegal sale of liquors was not contrary to good morals or ethical conduct." But as Rhode Island was only the third state to vote for repeal, its citizens would have to wait for other states to ratify the Twenty-First Amendment before it would become the law of the land.[286]

Admiral Billard died of an illness on May 17, 1932, at the age of fifty-eight. He enjoyed informing the public of the number of lives each year saved by the Coast Guard's heroic efforts, but at his death the *New York Times* led with the headline "Admiral Billard, Rum Row's Foe, Dies." Under Billard's watch, the good name of the Coast Guard became the subject of heated argument.[287]

How often did rumrunners successfully elude the Coast Guard and land their liquor on shore in Rhode Island waters? Charles H. Eden, an assistant federal district attorney who served in Rhode Island during Prohibition, in 1932 estimated that "for every cargo of liquor intercepted fifteen elude capture." Eden said that an attorney who represented rumrunners estimated that the ratio was ten to one, while crew members on rumrunners Eden interviewed (who were in the best position to know but were not always credible) informed him that the ratio was twenty to one.[288]

Despite popular sentiment turning heavily against Prohibition, in 1932 and 1933 machine guns on board Coast Guard vessels saw more action. The Coast Guard continued to insist on enforcing Prohibition and customs laws at sea. In the spring of 1932, the Coast Guard fired its machine guns into three rumrunners operating in Rhode Island waters.

The first shooting incident involved Boatswain Cecil MacLeod, in command of *CG-813*, the former rumrunner *Tramp*, and operating out of Section Base 18 at Woods Hole. MacLeod was called a "liquor ace" by the *Boston Globe* for his seizure or sinking of eight rumrunners in a six-month period.

At about 1:10 a.m. in the morning of March 5, a lookout on *CG-813* spotted a vessel running without lights off Warren Point (frequently misspelled as "Warren's Point") in Little Compton. It was the American gas screw *Kelble*, which was so new that its paint and trimmings still gleamed. It was 63 feet long, had a 13-foot beam and weighed 32 gross tons. It had four Liberty motors and was one of the fastest yachts afloat, able to reach more than thirty knots. It was registered in Boston and its owners hailed from that

The rumrunner *Kelble*, still gleaming from its recent construction and with sacks of liquor on its deck, tied to a wharf at Woods Hole, Massachusetts, probably on March 5, 1932. Next to *Kelble* is the Coast Guard speedboat *CG-813*, the former rumrunner *Tramp*, which had just fired its machine guns at and captured *Kelble*. *National Archives.*

city, but it was traveling off Little Compton, a common location for liquor drop offs for Boston outfits.

CG-813 sent up three flares and fired warning shots from its machine gun, signaling for *Kelble* to heave to. Instead, the motorboat put on speed, zigzagged and threw out a smokescreen. MacLeod gave chase and, despite falling behind, for six minutes peppered *Kelble*'s stern and one side of the fleeing boat with machine gun fire. By its erratic course, the rumrunner left itself exposed to the more than sixty machine gun bullets shot at it. Its captain surrendered his vessel. The machine gun bullets striking the craft caused small fires to break out in the engine room and in some sacks of liquor on the deck. After his crew extinguished the flames, the boatswain drove the captured rumrunner to Section Base 18, running the craft at three-quarters power and reaching twenty-six knots, even with 654 sacks of liquor on board. MacLeod later reported that during the chase, *CG-813* had reached thirty knots.

Four crew members, none of whom was injured, gave their residences as Staten Island, New York City, Baltimore and Philadelphia. There was also Henry Johnson of Providence, who, despite his name, was a Norwegian immigrant. Johnson, an experienced deckhand on rumrunners, had previously been captured on board *Mitzi*. The value of *Kelble* was reported as $75,000, and the value of the cargo of liquor on board was estimated to be $80,000. It was a severe loss for the rumrunning syndicate involved.

MacLeod later testified in a court proceeding that the crew of *Kelble* had thrown out a smokescreen using gas. The boatswain did not claim that anyone on his vessel had become ill from the gas attack.[289]

The Coast Guard went out in a blaze of glory the night of May 31, waking up residents of Aquidneck Island and Jamestown with machine gun fire. Following the incident, Boatswain's Mate W.E. Nickerson of the Brenton Point Coast Guard Station at Newport told newspaper reporters about what he saw and did on May 31. Thus, while not clearly stated in newspaper reports, he was probably in command of picket boat *CG-2343*.

Nickerson said that in the early evening of May 30, he saw the rumrunners *Mitzi* and *Idle Hour* speeding out of Narragansett Bay. Both

The *Good Luck* of Newport had a long career of rumrunning in Narragansett Bay before it was captured. It is shown here in the control of the Coast Guard, probably shortly before it was converted to Coast Guard speedboat *CG-994* on March 24, 1932. *National Archives.*

Mitzi, operated out of Providence, and *Idle Hour*, based at East Greenwich, had been captured several times before. Surmising that they would make contact with an outside vessel and return that night loaded with contraband liquor, he called New London for assistance. Two more patrol boats were assigned to aid him, in addition to his picket boat and one other at the station. Nickerson's picket boat mounted guard at the mouth of Narragansett Bay at Castle Hill, while the three other patrol boats cruised in different parts of the bay.

Rather than spotting the rumrunners, it seems more likely that Nickerson had information about their activities that evening from an informer. The *Newport Mercury* reported, "It was evident that the Coast Guard was acting on information, as two boats from Price's Neck were patrolling from Fort Adams to Beaver Tail Light, while two others from New London were farther up the bay."[290] One of the New London Coast Guard vessels was a speedboat, *CG-822*, under the command of Chief Boatswain's Mate John Lenci. It had been formerly known as the rumrunner *Chickie* and owned by a New York syndicate, but on June 29, 1930, in Block Island Sound, *CG-290*, commanded by Alexander Cornell, captured it with some 350 sacks of liquor on board. On April 7, 1931, *Chickie* became *CG-822* and was assigned to Section Base 4.[291]

Nickerson's vigil paid off. Early in the morning of May 31, he saw two rumrunners near the Brenton Reef Lightship speeding into the East Passage running without lights. Nickerson fired warning shots, but to no avail. He then fired flares to alert the other Coast Guard patrol boats, which soon were pursing the two rumrunners fleeing up Narragansett Bay.

The Coast Guard vessels opened up with their one-pounders and machine guns. The *Providence Journal* stated in that morning's edition, "Hundreds of persons at Jamestown and along the western passage of Narragansett Bay were awakened shortly before 1 o'clock yesterday morning by the roar of the Coast Guard's guns."[292]

Most of the gunfire was targeted at *Mitzi*. *Mitzi* was "riddled," reported the Associated Press, "with hundreds of bullets fired at her by a cordon of four Coast Guard boats." The Associated Press further explained that "*Mitzi* fought her way through the hail of [one pound] shells and [machine gun] bullets fired by three patrol boats, only to be cornered near Warwick Neck by the fourth craft" (meaning *CG-822*).[293]

Finally, after outdistancing the pursuing Coast Guard boats for twelve miles, *Mitzi* was overtaken about one-quarter of a mile off Warwick Point Lighthouse. *CG-822* chased down *Mitzi*, shining its searchlight on it and firing a warning flare. The rumrunner temporarily became grounded on a shoal at Pojac

Point. Before *CG-822* could seize the vessel, however, *Mitzi* freed itself using its powerful motors, threw out more smokescreen and attempted to escape. Lenci ordered live machine gun bullets fired at the fleeing craft. At 1:00 a.m., *Mitzi* was again overtaken about one-quarter mile off Warwick Neck. Three of its crew members escaped by diving overboard and swimming ashore. Two other crewmen were found swimming near their vessel and were hauled in by *CG-822*. The captives gave their names as Ray Simmons of Providence and George Watkins of Fall River. It was Lenci's third capture commanding *CG-822*. *CG-400*, a 78-footer that also participated in the chase, towed *Mitzi* into Providence. A federal assistant district attorney reported that *Mitzi* "had 237 machine gun bullet holes in her hull, the gasoline tanks were like sieves and all the engines and engine room equipment were badly damaged."[294]

The rumrunner *Idle Hour* was also a casualty the morning of May 31. *Idle Hour*, the rumrunner involved in the shooting incident in the summer of 1929 in which *CG-290* reportedly fired bullets into a Tiverton house, was the target of more Coast Guard machine guns. *Idle Hour* was controlled by gang leader Carl Rettich, and its captain was still probably Manuel Goulart, the brother of John Goulart of Fairhaven, one of the *Black Duck* victims.[295]

Arthur B. Gibbs, the commander of the 78-foot cutter *CG-401*, filed a report stating that around 1:00 a.m., while patrolling the West Passage of Narragansett Bay, he sighted in the sky flares from a Coast Guard vessel off the East Passage. Gibbs steamed around the northern tip of Conanicut Island into the East Passage and spotted a speedboat running without lights. Gibbs changed his patrol boat's course and began to pursue the vessel, which released a smokescreen and then grounded itself on the northern coast of Jamestown half a mile north of Fowlers Rocks. Gibbs's men seized the grounded vessel, with contraband liquor on board, but the crew escaped. Gibbs did not report firing any machine gun bullets.[296]

The *Providence Journal* had another take. On the front page of its May 31 edition, it reported, "Several residents of Jamestown…believed at least two craft were involved in the shooting." Providence's *Evening Bulletin* stated, "Inhabitants of Jamestown also were awakened by another battle, which resulted in the capture of the *Idle Hour*."[297] The *New London Day* also reported that after "a short engagement with several coast guard patrol vessels," the *Idle Hour* was "beached by its crew."[298]

However, because no Coast Guard boat is known to have filed a report that it fired at *Idle Hour*, and no report of damage from machine gun bullets is known to exist, it is not counted as an attack by the Coast Guard using a large-caliber weapon.

Boarding *Idle Hour*, Coast Guardsmen found 500 cases of assorted liquors, which were confiscated along with the vessel and taken to Providence. There were also 366 sacks of liquor on *Mitzi*. A report from Providence said that *Mitzi* was damaged by "hundreds of bullets fired at her by the Coast Guard boats."[299]

On occasion, a rumrunner was fired at by a Coast Guard vessel but escaped and could not be identified. This occurred on the night of August 7, 1932, when the speedboat *CG-833* (formerly the rumrunner *Je T'Aime*) saw a vessel running without lights headed for the entrance to the Sakonnet River. The Coast Guard vessel, commanded by Carl Grenager, got within two hundred yards of the rumrunner and then made signals for it to heave to, including firing blank one-pounder shells. The pursued boat responded by laying down a smokescreen and changing its course. Before losing sight of the vessel about half a mile east of Warren Point, *CG-833* fired about twenty-one bullets with its machine gun at the boat's stern.[300]

The only publicized firing of machine guns by the Coast Guard in Rhode Island waters in 1933 occurred in the night of October 16. Fittingly, it was again *Mitzi*, captured by *CG-808*, the former *Black Duck*. The Coast Guard was on the lookout for a rum boat coming up the West Passage, as an informer had relayed that a rumrunner had dropped off a load of contraband liquor near Warwick Neck early in the morning of October 15.

At about 8:10 p.m., while patrolling off Whale Rock Lighthouse at the entrance to the West Passage, near Beavertail Lighthouse at the southern tip of Jamestown, Louis Gavitt, the commander of *CG-808*, spotted *CG-401* chasing a speedboat running without lights heading its way. It was *Mitzi*, which veered away from *CG-808*, running north near the shore of the West Passage. Crew members on the rumrunner began hurling sacks of liquor overboard. Because of the proximity of the rumrunner to the coast, Gavitt decided not to use his machine gun. But when at 9:15 p.m. the speedboat reached Warwick Point Lighthouse, Gavitt had more room and ordered his machine gunner to open fire. More than two hundred machine gun bullets were fired at *Mitzi*, whose captain made a sharp left and ran his boat ashore at Pojac Point in East Greenwich Bay, near the mouth of the Potowomut River. Grounding the rumrunner was a favorite tactic of the speedboat's captain when being chased and machined gunned by Coast Guard patrol boats. It is not clear if any of the shots struck *Mitzi*.

Three members of *Mitzi*'s crew jumped overboard and escaped to the land. One crew member remained aboard. Gavitt had him brought aboard his vessel. *CG-808* then returned to Whale Rock Lighthouse (which would be destroyed

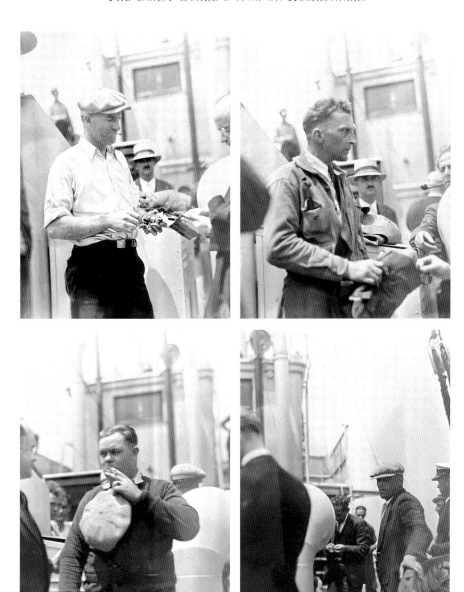

These are crew members of the captured speedboat *Whispering Winds*. *Top left corner*: Andy Moore of Boston, the master of the vessel. *Top right corner*: Robert Wilson of Providence, the chief engineer. *Bottom left corner*: Joseph Cummings of Dorchester, Massachusetts, assistant engineer. *Bottom right corner*: Roy White of Wakefield (or Wyoming), Rhode Island, deckhand. None of the crew members looks like a hardened criminal, whom the Coast Guard claimed operated many rumrunners. Roy White looks a bit rough, but Wakefield and Wyoming were small towns in rural South County, hardly places where hardened criminals were typically made. Fishermen do come from those places. *National Archives*.

by the Hurricane of 1938 and not replaced), where *CG-401* had remained. Both vessels then returned to Pojac Point, attached lines to *Mitzi* and pulled the rumrunner from the sand into the bay. *CG-401* towed *Mitzi* to Providence.[301]

At least the Coast Guardsmen had captured one crew member. Or had they? A large crowd of spectators had arrived at the Customs Service dock in Providence, having heard about *Mitzi*'s capture. But as *CG-401* maneuvered to dock its vessel, the agile captive jumped onto the wharf and escaped into the crowd. The Coast Guard crew decided not to fire at him, given the many spectators who had assembled nearby. Customs officials did confiscate twenty-three bags of liquor and thirty-three kegs of malt left behind on *Mitzi*.[302]

Several other rumrunners based in Rhode Island were machine gunned in 1932 and 1933, but not in Rhode Island waters.

Finally, Congress passed the Twenty-First Amendment to repeal the Eighteenth Amendment, which ultimately became effective on December 5, 1933. Prohibition officially ended. President Roosevelt, on March 22, 1933, had already legalized 3.2 percent beer.

The rumrunning racket dried up. There was no reason now for outside vessels to hover twelve miles offshore and transfer their stocks of liquor to smaller vessels. Instead, cargo ships filled with liquor could sail right into American ports and sell the alcohol above board to wholesalers.

A handful of rumrunners owned by hardcore criminal syndicates continued, in an effort to avoid federal excise tax on liquor, including several owned by Carl Rettich. But most boats ended their careers as rumrunners, with many returning to their more humdrum (and less remunerative) lives as fishing vessels. At least their crew members no longer had to fear Coast Guard vessels firing machine guns and one-pounder cannons at them.

Thus ended a remarkable time in American history when Americans serving the federal government legally and frequently fired machine guns and other large-caliber weapons at fellow Americans who were not hardened criminals. While the firing was mostly not promiscuous, it was often directed at the boats being pursued. Even if not intentional, not surprisingly, this gunfire sometimes led to the deaths or serious maiming of crew members on board the fleeing vessels. It is surprising more deaths and serious injuries did not occur. Those that did occur were the result of policies instituted by the Coast Guard that permitted the firing of large-caliber weapons at fleeing vessels that were suspected of carrying illicit liquor. The aggressive policy had little effect on the investors in rumrunners, whose crews continued to try to bring in illegal liquor to sell to an appreciative public until Prohibition ended in 1933.

COAST GUARD SHOOTINGS OF RUMRUNNERS IN RHODE ISLAND WATERS, 1929–1933

Date of Incident	Vessel Name	CG Vessel (and Type)	Commander of CG Vessel (if known)	Ammunition Fired from Machine Gun (MG) and One-Pounder	Injuries/Damage from MG and One-Pounder Fire
7-27-29	*Idle Hour*	*CG-290* (75-footer)	Cornell	Multiple MG bullets fired.	Hull is riddled with bullet scars and after cabin has two bullet holes; bullet lodges in house in Tiverton.
12-29-29	*Black Duck*	*CG-290* (75-footer)	Cornell	21 MG bullets fired.	Three crew members are killed and one is wounded.
2-24-30	*Monolola*	*CG-234* (75-footer)	Overhauser	260 MG bullets fired.	MG fire dents hull and breaks windows; fresh bloodstains are found on deck, so a crew member must have been wounded.
2-27-30	*Madame X*	*Downes* (destroyer)	Smith	One-pounder shells fired and reportedly MG fired too.	Not reported.

Date of Incident	Vessel Name	CG Vessel (and Type)	Commander of CG Vessel (if known)	Ammunition Fired from Machine Gun (MG) and One-Pounder	Injuries/Damage from MG and One-Pounder Fire
8-26-30	*Mardelle*	*CG-134* (75-footer) *CG-808* (former *Black Duck*)	*** Gavitt	MG bullets fired directly at the craft.	MG bullet lodges in crew member's lung; another pierces his chest and goes through his body.
9-30-30	***	*CG-289* (75-footer)	Losch	376 MG and 7 one-pounder shells fired.	Small fire breaks out.
10-24-30	*Helen*	*CG-290* (75-footer) *CG-289* (75-footer) *CG-134* (75-footer)	Cornell Lenci ***	Estimated that more 500 MG bullets and 40 one-pounder shells fired.	MG fire causes boat to begin to sink, then crew beaches it; pilothouse badly damaged.
10-31-30	*High Strung*	*CG-290* (75-footer)	Cornell	11 one-pounder shells fired.	Several hits are made; tiller is disabled.
2-23-31	*Monolola*	*CG-234* (75-footer) *CG-289* (75-footer)	Overhauser Losch?	More than 200 MG bullets and 12 one-pounder shells fired by *CG-234* alone; *CG-289* also fired MG bullets and its one-pounder.	Several hits are made.
2-24-31	*Alibi II*	*CG-235* (75-footer)	Prentice	2 one-pounder shells and MG bullets fired.	Boat catches fire and explodes; crew might have set boat on fire, but unlikely.

Date of Incident	Vessel Name	CG Vessel (and Type)	Commander of CG Vessel (if known)	Ammunition Fired from Machine Gun (MG) and One-Pounder	Injuries/Damage from MG and One-Pounder Fire
4-11-31	868-G	CG-2343 (picket boat)	Lathan	20 MG bullets fired.	MG fire likely punctured gas line, causing gas to explode. A crew member is blown off boat and drowns. MG fire wounds one other in leg.
May 1931	Follow Me	CG-2343 (picket boat)	Lathan	MG bullets fired.	Some hits on the boat.
5-31-31	Mitzi	CG-822 (former Chickie)	Lenci	Hundreds of MG bullets fired; one-pounder shells also fired.	Not reported but likely hits are made.
		CG-400 (78-footer)	***		
6-13-31	Eaglet	CG-287 (75-footer)	Bartlett	300 MG bullets fired.	Bullets damage hull.
6-18-31	Whispering Winds	CG-401 (78-footer)	Gibbs	One-pounder and MG bullets fired.	Fire scores hits.
7-5-31	Mitzi	CG-2343 (picket boat)	Lathan	About 300 MG bullets fired.	Bullets shatter deck; bullets are dislodged from holds and hull.
7-7-31	Yvette June?	Unknown	***	Estimated 300 bullets fired.	Unknown as boat escapes. Likely some bullets hit boat.
7-14-31	Yvette June	CG-400 (78-footer)	***	MG bullets fired, reportedly hundreds of them.	MG fire sinks vessel; top of pilothouse is almost sheared off.
		CG-284 (75-footer)	***		

Date of Incident	Vessel Name	CG Vessel (and Type)	Commander of CG Vessel (if known)	Ammunition Fired from Machine Gun (MG) and One-Pounder	Injuries/Damage from MG and One-Pounder Fire
8-8-31	*Eaglet*	CG-813 (former *Tramp*)	MacLeod	Almost 500 MG bullets fired.	MG bullet punctures gas tank causing explosion. Boat catches fire and sinks. A crew member's hand is shattered. Two others are slightly injured.
9-1-31	*Mitzi*	CG-2343 (picket boat)	Lathan	350 MG bullets fired.	Bullets fired at stern; civilian complains bullets reached Plum Beach.
10-2-31	*Mitzi?*	CG-290 (75-footer)	Cornell	45 MG bullets and 2 one-pounder shells fired.	Unknown, as vessel escapes, but hits likely made.
10-6-31	*Rhode Island*	CG-2297 (speedboat)	Yost	Many MG bullets fired.	MG fire likely causes boat to sink; bullets fired at hull and once into wheelhouse.
10-23-31	*Overland*	CG-402 (78-footer)	Losch	More than 700 MG bullets and 16 one-pounder shells are fired.	Boat is struck but escapes. One crew member drowns, possibly from the gunfire. Fire is started.
11-12-31	*Je T'Aime*	CG-813 (former *Tramp*)	MacLeod	About 40 MG bullets fired.	MG fire hits engine room and cabin.

Date of Incident	Vessel Name	CG Vessel (and Type)	Commander of CG Vessel (if known)	Ammunition Fired from Machine Gun (MG) and One-Pounder	Injuries/Damage from MG and One-Pounder Fire
12-12-31	*Nola*	*CG-813* (former *Tramp*) *CG-405* (78-footer) *CG-2297* (speedboat)	MacLeod Barrett Yost	More 1,000 MG bullets and 2 one-pounder shells are fired.	MG and one-pounder fire pummels armored vessel. A crew member is severely injured in artery in thigh by MG fire. Two others are slightly wounded. Pilothouse hit.
3-5-32	*Kelble*	*CG-813* (former *Tramp*)	MacLeod	More than 60 MG bullets fired.	MG bullets hit boat's stern and side; small fires break out on deck.
5-31-32	*Mitzi*	*CG-822* (former *Chickie*) *CG-400* One other unidentified	Lenci *** ***	MG bullets fired, reportedly hundreds of them.	MG and one-pounder fire causes considerable damage to boat. 237 MG bullet holes are found in its hull.
8-8-32	***	*CG-833*	Grenager	47 MG bullets fired.	Stern of boat is fired at and is likely hit.
10-16-33	*Mitzi*	*CG-808*	Gavitt	200 MG bullets fired.	Not reported but likely hits are made.

*** = Unidentified

Total Deaths by Machine Gun Fire: 3 or 4 (Weisman, Goulart and Brandt) (possibly a fourth, Larchevesque, on Overland*).*
Total Deaths by Explosions Caused by Machine Gun Fire: 1 (O'Brien).
Total Critically Wounded by Machine Gun Fire: 2 (Munson and Nunes).
Total Others Wounded by Machine Gun Fire: 8 (Travers, Mousseau, Fitzler, Sunderland, McGraw, Butler, Gleckman and unidentified crew member on Monolola*).*

Total Boats Exploded or Caught Fire after Machine Gun and/or One-Pounder Fire: 6.
Total Other Boats Sunk by Machine Gun and/or One-Pounder Fire: 3.
Total Machine Gun and/or One-Pounder Fire Incidents, with Boats Hit or Likely Hit: 29.

Number of known firing incidents in Rhode Island waters Alexander Cornell involved in: 6.
Number of known firing incidents in Rhode Island waters Elsworth Lathan involved in: 5.
Number of known firing incidents in Rhode Island waters Cecil MacLeod involved in: 4.
Number of known firing incidents in Rhode Island waters Theodore Losch involved in: 3.
Number of known firing incidents in Rhode Island waters John Lenci involved in: 3.

NOTES

Introduction

1. "Bullets Riddle Rum Boat," *Providence Journal*, October 25, 1930, 2.
2. "Machine Gun Used Too Freely by Coast Guard to Stop Rum Runners, Federal Judge Asserts," *Cincinnati Enquirer*, March 22, 1932, 12 (AP report); "Coast Guard Use of Machine Gun Hit," *Boston Globe*, March 21, 1932, 9.

Chapter 1

3. Quoted in Okrent, *Last Call*, 172.
4. Much of the background discussed in this and the next several paragraphs is from Lerner, *Dry Manhattan*, chapters 1 and 2.
5. *Journal of the Senate*, State of Rhode Island, 1917–19, Rhode Island State Archives. For a good discussion of how Prohibition came to Rhode Island, see Casey, "Little Rhody's Big Thirst."
6. Okrent, *Last Call*, 105.
7. Conley, *Democracy in Decline*, 374–76.
8. Ibid., 376–77, n115.
9. Sterne, *Ballots and Bibles*, 154.
10. Luconi, *Italian-American Vote in Providence, Rhode Island*, 54.
11. See DeSimone, "Rhode Island's 19th Century Experiments with Prohibition."
12. See Lerner, *Dry Manhattan*, 44–46.

13. New England Historical Society, "How Narragansett Beer Survived Prohibition"; Turley, *Narragansett Brewing Company*, 23–25.
14. "Three States Still Wet," *Ogden (UT) Standard-Examiner*, February 19, 1922.
15. Burbank, "Noble Experiment," H-162 and H-164.
16. "City's Senior Saloon Keeper Honored on 90th Birthday," *Newport Mercury*, October 8, 1971, 2; Burbank, "Noble Experiment," H-164. The violator reportedly was Billy Goode, who operated The Mission, a speakeasy on West Broadway in Newport. After Prohibition, he operated a bar in Newport for decades.
17. *Report of the National Convention of the Woman's National Committee*, 47.
18. Okrent, *Last Call*, 222.

Chapter 2

19. Jacquart, "Running It In," 3 and 42.
20. This article is reprinted in Anthony, *Best News Stories of 1923*, 38–42.
21. "May Use Submarines in Rum Warfare," *St. Louis Globe-Democrat*, Sunday Magazine, June 15, 1924, 3 and 17.
22. Herbert Corey, "Now Ready to Fight Rummers," *Boston Globe*, June 15, 1924, 15. This article was republished in many newspapers nationally.
23. William J. McEvoy, "Admiral Billard Heads Crusade on Rum-Runners," *Pittsburgh Press*, August 14, 1924, 14.
24. "The Dry Navy About Ready for Real Action," *Bangor (ME) Daily News*, August 18, 1924, 1.
25. "New Coast Guard Speed Boat Now in Service Against Rum-runners," *Hartford Courant*, August 25, 1924, 8.
26. Canney, *Rum War*, 7–8.
27. Jacquart, "Running It In," 42.
28. "$100,000 Liquor Cargo Will Be Taken to Federal Building Today," *Bridgeport (CT) Telegram*, June 7, 1924, 1–2; "Yacht Which Cost $200,000 Sold for $900 to Attorney," ibid., September 3, 1924, 1; *Boston Globe*, June 7, 1924, 18; Naval History and Heritage Command, "Sovereign II (SP-170)."
29. *Bridgeport (CT) Telegram*, June 10, 1924, 1.
30. For *Vereign*'s capture, see "3 Are Wounded Aboard Rum Ship," *Brooklyn Daily Eagle*, June 5, 1924, 1; "Cutter Fires on Whiskey Runner," *Evening Times* (Sayre, Pennsylvania), June 5, 1924, 5 (UPI report); "Wounds Will Keep Stack in Hospital for Two Months," *Hartford Courant*, June 7, 1924, 11; "$100,000 Liquor Cargo Will Be Taken to Federal Building Today," *Bridgeport (CT) Telegram*, June 7, 1924,

1–2; "Yacht Which Cost $200,00," *Rutland (VT) Daily Herald*, September 3, 1924 (AP report), 1; Willoughby, *Rum War at Sea*, 53.

31. *Herreshoff*'s capture is based on descriptions in Willoughby, *Rum War at Sea*, 95–96; Allen, *Black Ships*, 244; "Rum Craft Tries to Ram Cutter," *Boston Globe*, November 13, 1923, 14; "Coast Guard Vessel Makes Capture of Considerable Liquor Today," *North Adams (MA) Transcript*, November 12, 1923, 1.

32. See, e.g., newspaper reports cited in note immediately above.

33. *The Herreshoff*, 6 F.2d 414 (First Circuit Court of Appeals, 1925).

34. Quoted in Allen, *Black Ships*, 244.

Chapter 3

35. Quoted in "L.I. Bootleggers Entangle Pursuing Ships in Nets," *Brooklyn Daily Eagle*, May 18, 1925, 1.

36. "Whisky Craft Are Too Fast for Coast Guard Speed Boats," *Atlanta Constitution*, December 27, 1925, 7.

37. "Packard Motors in Speed Boats," *Lancaster (PA) New Era*, August 31, 1929, 7.

38. "Government Mobilizing Its Dry Navy for War," *St. Louis Globe-Democrat*, April 5, 1925, second section, 1.

39. Ibid.

40. Eden, "Wet Goods in the Water States," 14.

41. Quoted in "Uncle Sam Now Marshaling Forces to Wipe Rum Row from the Seas," *Buffalo Courier*, December 14, 1924, 12; Eden, "Wet Goods in the Water States," 23.

42. G.H. Cohen, U.S. Attorney, to U.S. Attorney for Connecticut, September 21, 1932, Coast Guard Records, RG 26, Entry 291, Seized Vessels, Box 56, Monolola File, National Archives, Washington, D.C. The vessel had been valued by the collector of customs at $7,500 and by court-appointed appraisers at $5,500. Ibid. These values likely did not take into account the boat's best use as a rumrunner.

43. Eden, "Wet Goods in the Water States," 23

44. Okrent, *Last Call*, 237.

Chapter 4

45. Summary of Patrol and Picket Boat Activities for the Quarter Ended March 30, 1929, May 1, 1929, Coast Guard Records, RG 26, Entry 82A, Scope of Operations, January–June 1929 to July–December 1930, General, Box 1103, National Archives, Washington, D.C.

46. Information on the Lewis gun is from *Military Factory*, "Famous Lewis Gun"; "Noted Inventor Dies Suddenly," *Charlotte (NC) Observer*, November 10, 1931, 1 (AP report). For a pan containing forty-seven machine gun bullets, see also Testimony of Alexander C. Cornell, December 30, 1929, Board of Investigation transcript, Coast Guard Records, RG 26, Entry 283A, Boards of Inquiry, Box 160, CG-290 File, National Archives, Washington, D.C.; Officer-in-Charge, *CG-9251*, to Commander, Base 18, in ibid., Seized Vessels, Box 56, Monolola File.

47. Quoted in Earl Chapin May, "Outwitting the Rum Runner," *Atlanta Constitution*, February 16, 1930, 67.

48. "In Battle with Rum Runner," *Pottsville (PA) Republican*, July 29, 1924, 5 (AP report); see also "Norfolk Man Taken with a Rum Vessel," *Daily Press* (Newport News, Virginia), July 31, 1924, 2.

49. "Rum Runners Have Field Day," *Nashville Banner*, January 12, 1923, 18.

50. Technical information on the Hotchkiss one-pounder is difficult to find. This information is based in part on the testimony of Admiral Billard in *United States Coast Guard Law Enforcement*, 15–16.

51. "Government Mobilizing Its Dry Navy for War," 1.

52. *Daily News* (Brooklyn, New York), February 1, 1926, 20.

53. "Rum Chasers to Carry Cannon to Help Out Speed," *Oakland Tribune*, September 27, 1924, 9.

54. Quoted in "Government Mobilizing Its Dry Navy for War," second section, 1. The author does not know the identity of the rumrunner.

55. For a version of the incident from the Coast Guard's perspective, see Willoughby, *Rum War at Sea*, 144–45. For the accusations by the Canadian crew, the hearing and the results of the investigation, see "Cutter Crew Cleared in Fatal Rum Chase," *Sacramento (CA) Bee*, January 31, 1931, 8 (AP report); "Accuse Coast Guard Crew," *Los Angeles Evening Express*, January 27, 1931, 1 (UPI report); "Start Probe of Slaying," *Lancaster (PA) New Era*, January 27, 1931, 2 (UPI report); "Official Probe Opens on Death of Rum Runner," *Standard Union* (Brooklyn, New York), January 27, 1931, 1 and 8.

56. Tally's charges were first reported in David Booth, "Says Coast Guard Murdered Skipper," *Daily News* (Brooklyn, New York), August 22, 1931, 3 and 5.

57. Quoted in "Shells for Rum Vessels," *Windsor (CAN) Star*, May 8, 1928, 9.

58. "Opportunity for Rum Spies," *Boston Globe*, May 7, 1925, 23.

59. Memorandum from Superintendent of Construction and Repair, July 6, 1931, Coast Guard Records, RG 26, Entry 283A, Scope of Operations, Box 1226, CG-403 File, National Archives, Washington, D.C.

60. "Whisky Craft Are Too Fast for Coast Guard Speed Boats," 7.

61. "Guards to Chase Bandits in Their Own Speed Boats," *Statesman Journal* (Salem, Oregon), April 19, 1925, 6.

Chapter 5

62. G.A. Youngquist to H. Boss, December 31, 1929, Coast Guard Records, RG 26, Entry 291, Seized Vessels, Box 20, Misc. "C" Vessels File (for C-5677), National Archives, Washington, D.C.

63. Ibid., 2 (citing Act of March 2, 1799, c. 22, 1 Stat. 627, 700, Section 101).

64. Ibid., 3 (citing U.S.C., Title 14, Section 68).

65. Ibid., 3 (citing U.S.C., Title 14, Section 68).

66. Ibid., 3 (citing U.S.C., Title 14, Sections 1 and 66).

67. U.S. Coast Guard, *Instructions, Customs, Navigation, and Motor-Boat Laws*, paragraph 14, 3.

68. Ibid., paragraph 1, 1.

69. Ibid., 3 (citing Section 581 of the Tariff Act of 1922, U.S.C., Title 14, Section 481).

70. See Eskridge, Frickey, Garrett and Brudney, *Cases on Legislation and Regulation*, 1210.

71. U.S. Coast Guard, *Instructions, Customs, Navigation, and Motor-Boat Laws*, 3–4.

72. Commandant to All Units, April 11, 1929, Coast Guard Records, RG 26, Entry 82A, Scope of Operations, 1932 General File, Box 1102, National Archives, Washington, D.C.

73. Ibid.

74. Commandant to All Units, September 7, 1932, in ibid., January–June 1929 to July–December 1930 General File, Box 1103.

Chapter 6

75. Commandant to Commander, Destroyer Force, Section Base 4, Coast Guard Records, RG 26, Entry 283A, Boards of Inquiry, Box 160, CG-291 File, National Archives, Washington, D.C.

76. See official Navy and Coast Guard Service Records of Alexander C. Cornell, Coast Guard Records, National Personnel Records Center, National Archives, St. Louis, Missouri (copy in the John Taft Collection, Newport, Rhode Island). The quotations are from Special Quarterly Report on the Fitness of Temporary Warrant Officers, R.W. Dempwolf, Commander, Section Base 4, August 2, 1928, and from Commander, Section Base 4, to Commander, Destroyer Force, Section Base 4, October 24, 1930, in ibid.

77. For information on *Idle Hour*, see *Ships Documents of Rhode Island*, vol. 2, 41; Report of Violation of Customs, CG-290, October 5, 1929, Coast Guard Records,

RG 26, Entry 291, Seized Vessels, Box 37, Idle Hour File, National Archives, Washington, D.C.; A.C. Cornell to Commander, Section Base 4, July 29, 1929, in ibid., Scope of Operations, Box 1225, CG-290 File. *Idle Hour*'s master by May 1930 (and for some time before, perhaps in the summer of 1929) was Manuel Goulart. Ibid. Manuel Goulart was likely the brother of John Goulart of Fairhaven, Massachusetts, one of *Black Duck*'s crew members who would be machine gunned and killed by a Coast Guard vessel in Narragansett Bay in December 1929. For John and Manuel Goulart as brothers, see www.ancestry.com (search for John Goulart of Fairhaven, Massachusetts, birth date of 1902, and view his entry in Massachusetts, U.S., Birth Records, 1840–1915, for John L. Goulart and his parents' entry in the U.S. Federal Census of 1920, which mentions both John and Manuel Goulart).

78. "Rettich Hearing to Be Formality," *Boston Globe*, May 14, 1935, 1; see also "Jury Expected to Indict," *Providence Journal*, May 14, 1935, 14. Credit goes to John Taft for discovering the connections between Mary Rittenhouse and Carl Rettich, and Manuel and John Goulart.

79. See memorandum from unidentified informant, January 22, 1930, Coast Guard Intelligence Files, John Taft Collection, Newport, Rhode Island.

80. Officer-in-Charge, *CG-290*, to Commander Section, Base 4, July 29, 1929, Coast Guard Records, RG 26, Entry 291, Seized Vessels, Box 37, Idle Hour File, National Archives, Washington, D.C.

81. The information on the chase and capture of *Idle Hour* is from the incident report in prior footnote; Records of Proceedings of a Board of Investigation Convened at Fogland Point, Rhode Island, August 18, 1929, in ibid., Entry 283A, Boards of Inquiry, Box 160, CG-290 File; Allen, *Black Ships*, 161–62; Willoughby, *Rum War at Sea*, 102; "Bullet Holes in Idle Hour," *Boston Globe*, July 31, 1929, 13; "Investigation Awaited," *Newport Mercury*, August 9, 1929, 8.

82. "Two Fines Dismissed," *Providence Journal*, August 23, 1929, 14; "Two Penalties Paid," *Boston Globe*, August 23, 1929, 5.

83. "I Ran Rum," *Evening Bulletin*, August 4, 1934, 20.

84. Senator Metcalf to Rear Admiral Billard, August 13, 1929, Coast Guard Records, RG 26, Entry 283A, Scope of Operations, Box 1225, CG-290 File, National Archives, Washington, D.C.; see also "Investigation Sought," *Newport Mercury*, August 16, 1929, 1.

85. See, e.g., "Senator Metcalf Protests Random Firing Upon Boats," *Providence Journal*, August 14, 1930, 1; "Protest Carelessness of Shooting Officers," *Boston Globe*, August 8, 1929, 8; "Shot Fired in Rum Chase Enters Home," *Hartford Courant*, August 14, 1929, 13 (AP report); "Senator Protests Firing by Dry Boat Into Private Home," *Morning News* (Wilmington, Delaware), August 14, 1929, 12

(AP report); "Metcalf Protests Dry Force Shooting," *New York Times*, August 14, 1929, 2; "Senator Protests Coast Guard Shot," *St. Louis Globe-Democrat*, August 14, 1929 (AP report).

86. Records of Proceedings of a Board of Investigation Convened at Fogland Point, Rhode Island, August 18, 1929, Coast Guard Records, RG 26, Entry 283A, Boards of Inquiry, Box 160, CG-290 File, National Archives, Washington, D.C.

87. Officer-in-Charge, *CG-290*, to Commander, Section Base 4, July 29, 1929, in ibid., Entry 283A, Scope of Operations, Box 1225, CG-290 File.

88. Commandant Billard to Senator Metcalf, August 23, 1929, in ibid. For the "somewhat inadequately" comment, see Commandant Billard to Commander, Section Base 4, August 23, 1929, Coast Guard Records, RG 26, Entry 283A, Scope of Operations, Box 1225, CG-290 File, National Archives, Washington, D.C.

89. "Coast Guard Will Fire with Caution," *Providence Journal*, August 28, 1930, 3.

90. Commandant Billard to Commander, Section Base 4, August 23, 1929, Coast Guard Records, RG 26, Entry 283A, Scope of Operations, Box 1225, CG-290 File, National Archives, Washington, D.C.

91. Commander, Section Base 4, to Commandant Billard, August 30, 1929, in ibid.

Chapter 7

92. Testimony of Lieutenant Robert C. Jewell, January 4, 1930, Board of Investigation transcript, New London, CT, 41, Coast Guard Records, RG 26, Entry 283A, Boards of Inquiry, Box 160, CG-290 File, National Archives, Washington, D.C.

93. Testimony of Alexander C. Cornell, January 3, 1930, in ibid., 33–34; Narrative Report filed by M.H. Low, October 16, 1928, in ibid., Seized Vessels, Box 20, Misc. "C" Vessels File (for C-5677); Violations Report filed by M.H. Low, October 12, 1928, in ibid.

94. "Pilots' Group Charges Guard Imperils Others," *Boston Globe*, January 5, 1930, 22 (AP report). According to John Taft of Newport, the current Bell Buoy #9 is about two hundred yards south where Bell Buoy #1 stood in 1929.

95. Ibid. For more on Travers's background, see www.ancestry.com (search for Charles Travers of Fairhaven, Massachusetts, birth date of 1906; the best sources are his entry in the U.S. Federal Census of 1930, Social Security Information for Charles Travers and his and his parents' entries in the U.S. Federal Censuses of 1910 and 1920). See also Charlie's entry at Find A Grave (the best way to locate is to do the same search as above in www.ancestry.com).

96. "Guardsmen Shoot as 'Black Duck' Fails to Heave To," *Providence Journal*, December 30, 1929, 1.

97. Officer-in-Charge, *CG-290*, to Commander, Section Base 4, December 31, 1929, Coast Guard Records, Seized Vessels, Box 20, Misc. "C" Vessels File (for C-5677), National Archives, Washington, D.C.
98. Intelligence Report, August 17, 1928, in ibid. A separate handwritten note provides, "Black Duck owned by Joe Dressler and Joe Berkleheimer." Ibid.
99. This information was conveyed to me in an e-mail to me from John Taft, based on John's speaking with a great-nephew of Joe Dressler and receiving an e-mail from the same descendant. See e-mail from J. Taft to C. McBurney, October 28, 2022 (author's collection). According to the great-nephew, who spoke with elderly family members, Joe Dressler left the rumrunning business after a cousin was killed in a shootout with government agents (this was probably a reference to Jake Weisman's killing). The family invested its earnings from rumrunning in a legitimate cattle dealing and meat cutting business (which business the family had conducted in eastern Europe before immigrating to the United States). In Rhode Island, the business was operated in Pawtucket for many years as Colfax Shortening and Oils. In Europe, the Dressler family had been Ukrainian Jews from a part of Ukraine then controlled by the Austro-Hungarian Empire. Ibid.
100. For *Symor* being the outside vessel, see Intelligence Report, January 28, 1930, Coast Guard Records, Seized Vessels, Box 20, Misc. "C" Vessels File (for C-5677), National Archives, Washington, D.C.
101. Testimony of Lieutenant Robert C. Jewell, January 4, 1930, Board of Investigation transcript, New London, CT, 41, in ibid., Entry 283A, Boards of Inquiry, Box 160, CG-290 File; "Jury to Convene January 13 to Probe Rum Boat Deaths," *Providence Journal*, January 4, 1930, 4.
102. This revelation appeared in an interview given by a rumrunner late in his life, which was published in a local Maine history book. John Taft of Newport realized that the person was Charlie Travers and showed the excerpt to the author. Quoted in Jackson and Robinson, "Pirate," *Salt Book*, 172.
103. Quoted in Charles Merrill, "Travers Declares Killings 'Brutal,'" *Boston Globe*, December 31, 1929, 1.
104. The distances are based on the Coast Guard's "Sketch of Probable Action in Seizure of C-5677," Coast Guard Records, RG26, Entry 291, Seized Vessels, Box 20, Misc. "C" Vessels File (for C-5677) and Entry 283A, Boards of Inquiry, Box 160, CG-290 File, National Archives, Washington, D.C. (see reproduction at page 93).
105. Except as otherwise noted, the account of the firing at *Black Duck*, its capture and towing to Fort Adams in Newport is based primarily on the following sources: Statement of Alexander C. Cornell to Customs Service, December 30, 1929, in ibid., Entry 283A, Boards of Inquiry, Box 160, CG-290 File; Statement of

Lewis R. Pearson, December 30, 1929, in ibid.; Statement of Risden Bennett, December 30, 1929, in ibid.; Statement of Louis W. Gavitt, December 30, 1929, in ibid.; Testimony of Alexander C. Cornell, Lewis R. Pearson, Robert C. Jewell and others, December 30, 1929–January 6, 1930, Board of Investigation transcript, New London, CT, 1–46, in ibid; Findings of Fact, Opinion and Recommendations of Board of Investigation in the case of capture of motorboat C-5677 (Black Duck), January 6, 1930, 46–53, Board of Investigation, New London, CT, 46–53, in ibid.; "Sketch of Probable Action in Seizure of C-5677" and "Sketch of C-5677," Coast Guard Records, RG26, Entry 291, Seized Vessels, Box 20, Misc. "C" Vessels File (for C-5677) and Entry 283A, Boards of Inquiry, Box 160, CG-290 File, in ibid. (reproduced on pages 89 and 93). Some of the statements by the crew and Board of Investigation testimony are published in Allen, *Black Ships*, 248–57. See also Willoughby, *Rum War at Sea*, 148–50. In a December 30 interview with newspapermen, Travers said that he and Weisman were on the deck of their rumrunner when the shooting occurred and that that was where Weisman had been gunned down. See "Travers Declares Killings 'Brutal,'" 4. Travers's December 30 account is not credible in several places, but he may be accurate here.

106. Testimony of William E. McLellan, Surgeon, U.S. Public Health Service, Section Base 4, New London, January 4, 1930, Board of Investigation, New London, CT, 37, Coast Guard Records, RG 26, Entry 283A, Boards of Inquiry, Box 160, CG-290 File, National Archives, Washington, D.C.

107. Testimony of Arthur Dye, Ship's Cook, Second Class, January 4, 1930, in ibid., 24; "Cousin and Rev Mr Magoun Only Ones to See Travers," *Boston Globe*, December 30, 1929, 6.

108. "Appeal to Walsh," *Boston Globe*, December 30, 1929, 6.

109. Quoted in Allen, *Black Ships*, 249.

110. For the other interview, see Charles Merrill, "Travers Declares Killings 'Brutal,'" *Boston Globe*, December 31, 1929, 1; "Injured Rum Runner Declares Guards Fired without Warning," *Providence Journal*, December 31, 1929, 1–2.

111. "Jury to Convene January 13 to Probe Rum Boat Deaths," *Providence Journal*, January 4, 1930, 6.

112. "Coast Guardsmen Kill Three Men in Rum Craft Chase Off Newport," *Boston Globe*, December 30, 1929, 1 and 9.

113. "Cousin and Rev Mr Magoun Only Ones to See Travers," 6.

114. Statement of Alexander C. Cornell, undated (probably December 29, 1929), in Allen, *Black Ships*, 248.

115. "Three Investigations of Shooting Under Way," *Boston Globe*, December 30, 1929, 6; "Jurisdiction Not Decided in Rum Runners' Deaths," *Boston Globe*, December 30,

1929, 9. The *Boston Globe* article inaccurately treated von Paulsen's investigation and the Coast Guard's Board of Investigation hearing as separate investigations.

116. "Cousin and Rev Mr Magoun Only Ones to See Travers," 6.

117. "Jurisdiction Not Decided in Rum Runners' Deaths."

118. Charles A. Merrill, "Black Duck Skipper Is Released on Bail," *Boston Globe*, January 1, 1930, 14; "Travers Released in $10,000 Bail," *Providence Journal*, January 1, 1930, 1.

119. "Claims Black Duck Fired at from Rear," *Boston Globe*, January 4, 1930, 12.

120. "Customs Guard on Black Duck Goes on Spree," *Providence Journal*, January 6, 1930, 1; "Rum Boat Guard Ousted as Tipsy, Black Duck Watchman Waves Pistol," *Boston Globe*, January 6, 1930, 1 and 22; "Customs Guard on Seized Craft Under Suspension," *Green Bay Press-Gazette*, January 6, 1930, 1 (UPI report).

121. "No Warning Shot Was Fired at Rum-Runner Black Duck," *Boston Globe*, January 4, 1930, 1 and 6.

122. "Grand Jury to Probe Coast Guard Killings," *Providence Journal*, December 31, 1929, 1.

123. "No Indictment in Rum Killings," *Boston Globe*, January 15, 1930, 1 and 32.

Chapter 8

124. Quoted in "Pastor Calls Rum Killings 'Murder,'" December 30, 1929, *Providence Journal*, 1; "Calls Triple Killing 'Downright Murder,'" *Boston Globe*, December 30, 1929, 6.

125. Quoted in Garrett D. Byrnes, "The Way We Were, Prohibition in R.I. Brought Out the Criminal and the Colorful," *Providence Journal*, November 28, 2010, D7.

126. "Sen Walsh Demands All Facts in Killing of Rum-Runners," *Boston Globe*, December 30, 1929, 1.

127. "Billard Says Coast Guard Will Use No Soft Policy," *Boston Globe*, December 30, 1930, 1 (AP report).

128. Quoted in "Walsh Protests Service Inquiry," *Boston Globe*, December 31, 1929, 4.

129. Quoted in "Lowman Defends Guardsmen," *Boston Globe*, January 1, 1930, 14.

130. "'Newport Massacre' Causes Protest in Faneuil Hall," *Boston Globe*, January 2, 1930, 1 and 15.

131. "Would Disarm the Coast Guard," *New York Times*, December 31, 1929, 8.

132. Quoted in "Walsh to Demand Inquiry," *Boston Globe*, January 3, 1930, 25.

133. "Address of Fitzgerald," *Boston Globe*, January 3, 1930, 1 and 25.

134. "Coast Guard Recruiting Signs Are Torn Down on Common," *Boston Globe*, January 3, 1930; "Coast Guard Stops Displaying Posters," *Boston Globe*, January 4, 1930, 6.

135. Untitled article, *Boston Globe*, January 3, 1930, 25 (AP report).

136. Quoted in "Sec Mellon Defends Coast Guard in Killing Three Men," *Boston Globe*, January 3, 1930, 1 and 3.

137. "Gang Attacks Coast Guards," *Boston Globe*, January 4, 1930, 6.

138. Ibid.

139. "Coast Guard's Craft Is Stoned by Gang," *Boston Globe*, January 7, 1930, 7.

140. See handwritten letter addressed to "Mr. Cornell, the Hun," Coast Guard Records, RG 26, Entry 291, Seized Vessels, Box 20, Misc. "C" Vessel File (for C-5677), National Archives, Washington, D.C.

141. "Report Threat Made to Blow Up Black Duck," *Boston Globe*, January 8, 1930, 1 (AP).

142. *Washington Post*, January 5, 1930 (also quoting from the *New York Herald Tribune*), 8.

143. Quoted in *Washington Post*, January 5, 1930.

144. "Detour Ahead and It's All Wet!," *Cincinnati Enquirer*, January 6, 1931, 1.

145. "La Guardia Calls Killings Typical," *Providence Journal*, January 8, 1930, 1; "House Cheers Dry Demanding Support from Coast Guard," *New York Times*, January 8, 1930, 1.

146. "Claims No Signal Given to Black Duck," *Boston Globe*, January 3, 1930, 1 and 25.

147. "Coast Guard Cleared in Black Duck Case," *Providence Journal*, January 15, 1930, 1.

148. See "Upholds Coast Guard in Black Duck Killings," *New York Times*, January 17, 1930, 2; Testimony, Findings of Fact, Opinion and Recommendations of Board of Investigation in the case of capture of motorboat C-5677 (Black Duck), December 30, 1929–January 6, 1930, Board of Investigation, New London, CT, 52, Coast Guard Records, RG 26, Entry 283A, Boards of Inquiry, Box 160, CG-290 File, National Archives, Washington, D.C.

149. Larson, "What Are Homicide and Murder."

150. Commander, Eastern Division to all Units, Eastern Division, February 6, 1930, Coast Guard Records, RG 26, Entry 82A, Circular Letters, Box 86, Circular Letters to General, 1917–32, National Archives, Washington, D.C.

151. Statement of Alexander C. Cornell, undated (probably December 29, 1929), in Allen, *Black Ships*, 248.

152. "Guardsmen Shoot as 'Black Duck' Fails to Heave To," 1.

153. Eden, "Wet Goods in the Water States," 14.

154. Author Everett Allen agrees with this conclusion. See Allen, *Black Ships*, 257–58.

155. Quoted in John J. Donovan, "Searchers at Base Find Part of Liquor," *Boston Globe*, December 31, 1929, 1 and 4.

156. Testimony of Alexander C. Cornell, January 3, 1930, Board of Investigation transcript, New London, CT, 32, Coast Guard Records, RG 26, Entry 283A, Boards of Inquiry, Box 160, CG-290 File, National Archives, Washington, D.C.

157. Findings of Fact, Opinion and Recommendations of Board of Investigation in the case of capture of motorboat C-5677 (Black Duck), January 6, 1930, Board of Investigation, New London, CT, 52, in ibid.

158. "Newport Massacre."

159. "Sen Walsh Demands All Facts in Killing of Rum-Runners," *Boston Globe*, December 30, 1929, 8.

160. Quoted in "Would Disarm the Coast Guard," *New York Times*, December 31, 1929, 8.

161. Quoted in "Walsh Suggests Probe of Need for Rum Killings," *Boston Globe*, January 7, 1930, 32.

162. "Address of Fitzgerald," *Boston Globe*, January 3, 1930, 1 and 25.

163. "Dive for Evidence Against Travers," *Providence Journal*, January 10, 1930, 2.

164. "Coast Guardsmen Kill Three Men in Rum Craft Chase off Newport," *Boston Globe*, December 30, 1929, 1 and 9; "Weisman Under Indictment," *Boston Globe*, December 30, 1929, 9. For more on Weisman's background, see www.ancestry. com (search for Jacob Weisman of Providence, Rhode Island, birth date of 1900, and view his entry in World War I Draft Registration Cards, 1917–1918, his and his parents' entries in the U.S. Federal Censuses of 1910 and 1920 and his parents' entry in the City Directory for Providence, Rhode Island, 1928). See also Jake's entry at Find A Grave (accessed on www.ancestry.com), in which the photograph of his gravestone indicates a birth date of September 16, 1901, and is partly in Yiddish.

165. Quoted in "Heart-Broken Girl Sobs Over Weisman," *Boston Globe*, December 31, 1929, 4.

166. "Weisman Under Indictment," *Boston Globe*, December 30, 1929, 9; Allen, *Black Ships*, 246. For more on Goulart's background, see www.ancestry.com (search for John Goulart of Fairhaven, Massachusetts, birth date of 1902, and view his entry in Massachusetts, U.S., Birth Records, 1840–1915 for John L. Goulart and his parents' entry in the U.S. Federal Census of 1920).

167. Quoted in "Heart-Broken Girl Sobs Over Weisman," 4.

168. "Appeal to Walsh," 6. For more on Brandt's background, see www.ancestry. com (search for Dudley Brandt of Boston, Massachusetts, view his entries related to World War I and search for Dudley A. Brandt of Boston, Massachusetts, birth date of 1906, in each of the U.S. Federal Censuses of 1900, 1910 and 1920).

169. Quoted in Babcock, "'Let Them Have It!," draft manuscript, 6.

170. "No Indictment of Travers," *Boston Globe*, March 4, 1930, 21.

Chapter 9

171. "Coast Guard Cutter Fires on Vessel," *Boston Globe*, February 25, 1930, 16 (AP report).

172. "Rum Runner Captured by Coast Guard," *Newport Mercury*, February 28, 1930, 6.

173. "Security Shrouds Rum Boat Capture," *Providence Journal*, February 26, 1930, 15.

174. C. Dench to Collector of Customs, Providence, March 10, 1930, Coast Guard Records, RG 26, Entry 283A, Scope of Operations, Box 1223, CG-234 File, National Archives, Washington, D.C.

175. "Worker Injured in Ship Explosion," *Providence Journal*, September 1, 1930, 3.

176. "Boat Operated Out of This City," *Newport Mercury*, February 28, 1930, 1.

177. "Guard Confirms Rum Boat Seizure," *Providence Journal*, February 27, 1930, 17.

178. For the capture of *Monolola*, see Officer-in-Charge, *CG-234*, to Commander, Section Base 4, February 25, 1930, Coast Guard Records, RG 26, Entry 283A, Scope of Operations, Box 1225, CG-234 File, National Archives, Washington, D.C.; Statements of F.D. Overhauser and Joseph Lesniak Relative to the Monolola on February 25, 1930, March 10, 1930, in ibid.; "Boat Taken at Fall River Docked in New London," *Boston Globe*, February 26, 1930, 9; "Rum Boat Suspect Caught by Coast Guard," *Hartford Courant*, February 26, 1930, 6; "Security Shrouds Rum Boat Capture," *Providence Journal*, February 26, 1930, 15; "Guard Confirms Rum Boat Seizure," *Providence Journal*, February 28, 1930, 17; "Suspected Liquor Runner Is Held at New London," *Hartford Courant*, February 27, 1930, 2; "Rum Runner Captured by Coast Guard," *Newport Mercury*, February 28, 1930, 6; "Boat Operated Out of This City," *Newport Mercury*, February 28, 1930, 1.

179. "Suspected Liquor Runner Is Held at New London," 2.

180. Commander, Section Base 4, to Collector of Customs, Providence, February 28, 1930, Coast Guard Records, RG 26, Entry 291, Seized Vessels, Box 56, Monolola File, National Archives, Washington, D.C.

181. For information on the capture of *Madame X* in late February 1930, see Lieutenant Commander Edward Smith Narrative Report, February 28, 1930, Coast Guard Records, RG 26, Entry 291, Seized Vessels, *Madame X* File, Box 49, National Archives, Washington, D.C.; Commanding Officer, *Downes*, to Commandant, March 6, 1930, in ibid.; "Coast Guard Captures Two More Boats," *Hartford Courant*, March 2, 1930, 13 (machine gun bullets fired); "Fishing Boat Captured After Running Fight," *Sheboygan (WI) Press*, March 1, 1930, 2 (AP report).

182. For *Madame X* being built at the Casey Boat Building Company, see "Heart-Broken Girl Sobs Over Weisman," 1. The detailed description of the boat in this article fits that of *Madame X*.

183. For information on the capture of *Madame X* on September 30, 1932, see Officer-in-Charge, *CG-2296*, to Commander, Section Base 18, September 30, 1932, Coast Guard Records, RG 26, Entry 291, Seized Vessels, *Madame X*, Box 49, National Archives, Washington, D.C.; Statement of Alfred Phalen to Intelligence Officers in Connection with the Seizure of Madame X of Newport, R.I., September 30, 1932, ibid; "Held in Bail for Federal Grand Jury," *Newport Mercury*, October 28, 1932, 10.

Chapter 10

184. See *Crowninshield Shipbuilding Co. v. United States*, 54 F.2d 879 (First Circuit Court of Appeals, 1932). This case involved an attempt by Crowninshield to collect about $8,000 from the sale proceeds of *Mardelle* to pay amounts allegedly due to Crowninshield for constructing and repairing the *Mardelle*. Judge Letts rejected the claim and found that a Crowninshield official had committed perjury while testifying. It appears that the Crowninshield official and the owners of the *Mardelle* hoped to split the expected $8,000 award. The Court of the Appeals for the First Circuit in Boston upheld the perjury verdict. Ibid; see also "Appeals Court Upholds Mardelle Case Decision," *Providence Journal*, January 9, 1932, 19.

185. "Fall River Man Critically Wounded," *Providence Journal*, August 27, 1930, 1.

186. Officer-in-Charge, *CG-808*, to Commander, Section Base 4, August 26, 1930, Coast Guard Records, RG 26, Entry 283A, Scope of Operations, Box 1226, CG-808 File, National Archives, Washington, D.C.

187. For the capture of *Mardelle*, see ibid; "Coast Guard Shoots Rum Runner in Bay," *Providence Journal*, August 27, 1930, 1; "Liquor Boat Trio Released in Bail," ibid., August 28, 1930, 1 and 12; "One of the Crew Wounded When Coast Guard Opens Fire on Craft," *North Adams (MA) Transcript*, August 26, 1930, 1 (AP report); "Coast Guard Bullet Wounds Rum-Runner," *Boston Globe*, August 27, 1930, 9; "Rum-Runner's Crew All Bay State Men," *Boston Globe*, August 28, 1930, 8; "Man Badly Wounded," *Newport Mercury*, August 29, 1930, 1.

188. "Liquor Boat Trio Released in Bail," *Providence Journal*, August 28, 1930, 12.

189. Photo Caption of *Mardelle* in *Daily News* (Brooklyn, New York), August 28, 1930, 217.

190. "Fifth Man Sought in *Mardelle* Case," *Boston Globe*, August 29, 1930, 21.

191. "Coast Guard Uses Noted Rum Runner as Pursuer," *Providence Journal*, August 29, 1930, 18; see also Seized Boats Assigned to the Coast Guard, 1925–35, 605, Coast Guard Records, RG 26, Entry 283A, History of Seized Boats (1925–35), Box 396, History of Seized Vessels File, National Archives, Washington, D.C.

192. "*Black Duck* Turned Over to Coast Guard," *Berkshire Eagle* (Pittsfield, Massachusetts), March 7, 1930, 28 (AP report).

193. "*Black Duck* Was Used by Coast Guardsmen," *Newport Mercury*, September 5, 1930, 8.

194. Ibid.; "Fifth Man Sought in *Mardelle* Case," 21.

195. Seized Boats Assigned to the Coast Guard, 1925–35, 619, Coast Guard Records, RG 26, Entry 283A, History of Seized Boats (1925–35), Box 396, History of Seized Vessels File, National Archives, Washington, D.C.

Chapter 11

196. Scott McKay and Jody McPhillips, "The Rhode Island Century: 1920–1930 in the Roaring Twenties the Question Here Was: What Prohibition," *Providence Journal*, April 25, 1999, A1.

197. M.E. Hennessy, "Metcalf and Gerry Running Close Race," *Boston Globe*, October 27, 1930, 13. Gerry had already voted against the Eighteenth Amendment and also announced that he would vote for its repeal. Ibid.

198. Commandant to A.C. Cornell, March 6, 1930, Coast Guard Records, RG 26, Entry 283A, Scope of Operations, Box 1225, CG-290 File, National Archives, Washington, D.C.

199. "Claims Houses Struck by Rum Fight Bullets," *Boston Globe*, October 24, 1930, 13 (AP report).

200. For the capture of *Helen*, see Officer-in-Charge, *CG-290*, to Commander, Section Base 4, October 24, 1930, Coast Guard Records, RG 26, Entry 291, Seized Vessels, "H" Misc. File, Box 33, National Archives, Washington, D.C.; Officer-in-Charge, *CG-241*, to Commander, Section Base 4, October 30, 1930, in ibid.; Report of Violations, October 24, 1930, filed by A.C. Cornell, and filed by John Lenci, October 24, 1930, in ibid.; "Bullets Riddle Rum Boat," 1 and 5; "Rum Runner Crew Held for Hearing," *Providence Journal*, October 26, 1930, 3; "Rum Boats Raked with Gunfire in $100,000 Seizure," *Times Union* (Brooklyn, New York), October 24, 1930, 44 (UPI report); "Claims Houses Struck by Rum Fight Bullets," *Boston Globe*, October 24, 1930, 13 (AP report); "Guardsmen Sink One Ship, Take Another," *Evening Sun* (Baltimore, Maryland), October 24, 1930 (AP report); "Speed Boat Helen Regarded as Total Loss," *Newport Mercury*, November 7, 1930, 5; Willoughby, *Rum War at Sea*, 92.

201. "Coast Guard Bullets Halt Speed Boats," *Hartford Courant*, October 25, 1925, 22 (AP report).

202. "Bullets Riddle Rum Boat," 1 and 5.

203. Ibid., 5.

204. "Claims Houses Struck by Rum Fight Bullets," *Boston Globe*, October 24, 1930, 13.

205. For the dimensions and weight of the boat, see *Ships Documents of Rhode Island*, vol. 2, 134. This source also spelled the registered owner's name as Jacob Teitelbaum "of East Greenwich, R.I." as of September 1933.

206. For information on the capture of *High Strung*, see "Coast Guard Captures Rum Boat After Chase," *Hartford Courant*, November 16, 1930, 32; "Double Blows Cut New York' Liquor," *Evening Star* (District of Columbia), November 16, 1930, 1 (AP report); "Three Rum Ships Seized in Drive on Holiday Flow," *Times Union* (Brooklyn, New York), November 16, 1930, 1; "Libels Filed Against Speed Boat High Strung," *Boston Globe*, December 9, 1930, 21 (AP report); "Dry Agents Smash Huge Liquor Ring," *Providence Journal*, November 16, 1930, 1 (UPI report); "Libel Is Filed Against Teitelbaum's Vessel," *Providence Journal*, December 10, 1930, 26; Officer-in-Charge, *CG-290*, to Commander, Section Base 4, November 15, 1930, Coast Guard Records, RG 26, Entry 283A, Scope of Operations, Box 1225, CG-290 File, National Archives, Washington, D.C.

207. Officer-in-Charge, *CG-290*, to Commander, Section Base 4, November 15, 1930, Coast Guard Records, RG 26, Entry 283A, Scope of Operations, Box 1225, CG-290 File, National Archives, Washington, D.C. Malcolm F. Willoughby, in his official history of the Coast Guard's war against rumrunners, repeated the story of the attempted ramming. Willoughby, *Rum War at Sea*, 93.

208. "Coast Guard Captures Rum Boat After Chase," *Hartford Courant*, November 16, 1930, 32.

209. Officer-in-Charge, *CG-289*, to Commander, Section Base 4, September 30, 1930, Coast Guard Records, RG 26, Entry 283A, Scope of Operations, Box 1225, CG-289 File, National Archives, Washington, D.C.

Chapter 12

210. For the chase of *Monolola*, see Officer-in-Charge, *CG-234*, to Commander, Section Base 4, February 25, 1931, Coast Guard Records, RG 26, Entry 291, Seized Vessels, Box 56, Monolola File, National Archives, Washington, D.C.; "Rum Boat, Fleeing Coast Guard, Sunk," *Providence Journal*, February 24, 1931, 1; "Rum War Flares Again Off Coast," *Boston Globe*, February 24, 1931, 1 and 12; "Rum Ship Evades Coast Guard in Fast Chase," *Reno Gazette-Journal*, February 23, 1931, 1 (AP report); "Coast Guard Bombards Three Alleged Rum Boats Off Coast," *The News* (Patterson, New Jersey), November 23, 1931, 15 (UPI report).

211. "The Alibi II, Rum-Runner, Is No More," *Newport Mercury*, February 27, 1931, 3. The *Boston Globe* reported, "People in Newport and along the adjacent coast were awakened during the night by the rat-tat-tat of machine guns, and the roar of one-pounders." "Rum War Flares Again Off Coast," 1 and 12.

212. Ibid.; "Alibi II, Rum-Runner, Is No More," 3.

213. "Rum Boat, Fleeing Coast Guard, Sunk," 1; "Rum War Flares Again Off Coast," 1 and 12; "Worker Injured in Ship Explosion," 3.

214. "R.I. Speedboat Men Held in New London," *Providence Journal*, January 13, 1932, 2. The most reliable account of this incident is Officer-in-Charge, *CG-405*, to Commander, Section Base 4, January 17, 1932, Coast Guard Records, RG 26, Entry 291, Seized Vessels, Box 56, Monolola File, National Archives, Washington, D.C. Two Newport men, including its captain, were arrested on board *Monolola* when it was again machine gunned and stopped by a Coast Guard patrol boat off Gay Head light in May 1933. Officer-in-Charge, *CG-402*, to Commander, Section Base 4, May 17, 1933, in ibid; "Rum Runner Monolola Taken to New London," *Providence Journal*, May 18, 1933, 11.

215. See *Ships Documents of Rhode Island*, vol. 2, 6.

216. "Rum Boat, Fleeing Coast Guard, Sunk," 1.

217. "Alibi II, Rum-Runner, Is No More," 3; see also "Rum Boat, Fleeing Coast Guard, Sunk," 2. The *Providence Journal* article reported that a third vessel was shot at in Narragansett Bay, an outside vessel called *Accuracy*, and "escaped under a fusillade of machine-gun bullets and one-pounders." But the Coast Guard later stated that *Accuracy* was not spotted inside the twelve-mile limit of the U.S. shore. "Boat, Fired on, Sighted Outside 12-Mile Limit," *Boston Globe*, February 24, 1931, 12. Reporters must have confused this gunfire with the fusillade directed by *CG-289* against *Monolola*.

218. For the running down and sinking of *Alibi II*, see articles in note 212 and "Rum War Flares Again Off Coast," 1 and 12.

219. "Alibi II, Rum-Runner, Is No More," 3.

220. "Rum Boat, Fleeing Coast Guard, Sunk," 2.

221. "Liquor Runners and Coast Guard Stage Sea Fight," *Ithaca Journal*, February 23, 1931, 1 (AP report).

Chapter 13

222. "Provides State System of Liquor Control," *Newport Mercury*, March 20, 1931, 5.

223. For the capture of *868-G* and its destruction by explosion, see "An Alleged Rum Runner Is Sunk," *Newport Mercury*, April 17, 1931, 1; "Rum Runner Shot in R.I.

Battle," *Boston Globe*, April 11, 1931, 1; "Rum Boat Blown Up," *Cincinnati Enquirer*, April 12, 1931, 56 (AP report); "Letts Condemns Coast Guardsmen," *Providence Journal*, October 16, 1931, 16; "No Bullet Wounds on O'Brien's Body," *Newport Mercury*, April 17, 1931, 6. Walter Mosher's last name is sometimes misspelled as Mosker.

224. "No Bullet Wounds on O'Brien's Body," 6.

225. Ibid.

226. See chapters 12 (*Alibi II*) and 14 (*Eaglet*) of this book; see also "U.S. Cutter Disables and Sinks Rum Ship," *Long Beach Telegram and the Long Beach Daily News* (Long Beach, California), June 28, 1924, 1 ("The speed boat was disabled by a shot from the one-pounder gun on the *Arcata*, her gasoline tank blew up and she sank").

227. Officer-in-Charge, *CG-808*, to Commander, Section Base 4, August 26, 1930, Coast Guard Records, RG 26, Entry 283A, Scope of Operations, Box 1226, CG-808 File, National Archives, Washington, D.C.

228. "Letts Condemns Coast Guardsmen," 16.

229. "I Ran Rum," Installment XIX, *Evening Bulletin* (Providence, Rhode Island), August 10, 1934, 16.

230. For the capture of *Whispering Winds*, see Officer-in-Charge, *CG-401*, June 18, 1931, to Commander, Base 4, Coast Guard Records, RG 26, Entry 291, Seized Vessels, Box 83, Whispering Winds File, National Archives, Washington, D.C.; "Liquor Yacht Captured," *Charleston (WV) Daily Mail*, June 18, 1931, 1 (AP report); Paul S. Walcott, "Rum Row, Now Just a Memory, Flourished 25 Years Ago," *Evening Day* (New London, Connecticut), July 13, 1954, 11; Willoughby, *Rum War at Sea*, 95.

231. Seized Boats Assigned to the Coast Guard, 1925–35, 662-E, Coast Guard Records, RG 26, Entry 283A, History of Seized Boats (1925–35), Box 396, History of Seized Vessels File, National Archives, Washington, D.C.

232. "Local Sea Scouts Guests for Day of Coast Guard Black Duck," *Hartford Courant*, January 5, 1934, 2.

Chapter 14

233. For the chase and sinking of *Yvette June*, see "Sunken Rum Boat Had Escaped Under Gunfire," *Boston Globe*, July 14, 1931, 1; "Coast Guard Guns Sink Rum-Runner," *New York Times*, July 15, 1931, 15; "Rum Vessel Sunk by Coast Guards," *Providence Journal*, July 15, 1931, 1 and 6; "Fired Rum Boat Sinks," *Detroit Free Press*, July 15, 1931, 8 (AP report); "Crew of Sunken Rum Boat Held in Bail at

Providence," *Boston Globe*, July 15, 1931, 36 (AP report); *Daily News* (Brooklyn, New York), July 15, 1931, 264; Report of the *Yvette June*, Coast Guard Service Record of Alexander C. Cornell, Coast Guard Records, National Personnel Records Center, National Archives, St. Louis, Missouri (copy in John Taft Collection, Newport, Rhode Island).

234. "Cutter Rams and Sinks Rum-Runner," *St. Albans (VT) Daily Messenger*, July 14, 1931, 1 (AP report).

235. See, for example, "Judge Letts Dismisses Lebel on Yvette June," *Providence Journal*, April 6, 1932, 21.

236. Commander, Section Base 4, to Commander, Destroyer Force, September 24, 1931, Coast Guard Records, RG26, Entry 283A, Boards of Inquiry, Box 161, CG-400 File, National Archives, Washington, D.C.

237. "Divers at Work on Rum Runner and Cargo," *Boston Globe*, July 15, 1931, 13; "Coast Guard Try to Raise Rum Ship," *Providence Journal*, July 16, 1931, 1. The *Boston Globe* and *Providence Journal* accounts initially stated that 800 sacks of liquor worth $40,000 were salvaged. But later reports said 538 sacks of liquor worth $29,500 were salvaged. See, e.g., "Rum Boat Seized; Seven Men Held," *Providence Journal*, November 12, 1931, 3.

238. For the attempts to float *Yvette June* and the court case over it, see "Divers at Work on Rum Runner and Cargo," 13; "Effort to Raise the Yvette June Fails," *Newport Mercury*, July 17, 1931, 2; "Rum Yacht Yvette June Raised at Common Fence," *Providence Journal*, August 16, 1931, 10; "Sunken Boat Raised," *Boston Globe*, September 15, 1931, 9; "Legal Fight Looms Over Salvaged Craft," *Boston Globe*, September 16, 1931, 3; "Shipbuilding Concern Claims Ownership," *Newport Mercury*, September 18, 1931, 1; "Yvette June Seized to Answer Old Charge," *Newport Mercury*, September 18, 1931, 2.

239. "Judge Letts Dismisses Libel on Yvette June," *Providence Journal*, April 6, 1932, 21; "Judge Letts Decides Against Government," *Providence Journal*, January 18, 1933, 22 (on rehearing).

240. "Shipbuilding Concern Claims Ownership," 1.

241. "Rum Boat Escapes by Smoke Use," *Evening News* (Harrisburg, Pennsylvania), July 7, 1931, 9 (AP report).

242. For information on this machine gunning of *Yvette June*, see "Coast Guards Take Rum Ship," *North Adams (MA) Transcript*, April 4, 1932, 1 (AP report); "Grounded Speedboat Nets $40,000 Cargo," *Boston Globe*, April 5, 1932, 27; "Rum Patrol Captures Newport Speed Boat," *Newport Mercury*, April 8, 1932, 6.

243. Seized Boats Assigned to the Coast Guard, 1925–35, 662, Coast Guard Records, RG 26, Entry 283A, History of Seized Boats (1925–35), Box 396, National Archives, Washington, D.C.

244. The background information on *Eaglet* is from "Two of Eaglet's Seamen Wounded," *Providence Journal*, August 10, 1931, 1; Fred Edgecomb to Commander, Section Base 4, September 25, 1930, Coast Guard Records, RG 26, Entry 283A, Scope of Operations, Box 1225, CG-283 File, National Archives, Washington, D.C.

245. Quoted in Allen, *Black Ships*, 165–66.

246. Memoranda for Intelligence Files, August 17, 1928, Coast Guard Records, RG 26, Entry 291, Seized Vessels, Box 23, Eaglet File, National Archives, Washington, D.C.; Memorandum to Commander, Destroyer Force and Commander Dench, Section Base 4, June 4, 1929, Coast Guard Intelligence Files, John Taft Collection, Newport, Rhode Island.

247. See various Memoranda dated June 13, 1931, Coast Guard Records, RG 26, Entry 291, Seized Vessels, Box 23, Eaglet File, National Archives, Washington, D.C..

248. For *Tramp*'s conversion to a Coast Guard vessel, see Seized Boats Assigned to the Coast Guard, 1925–35, 628, Coast Guard Records, RG 26, Entry 283A, History of Seized Boats (1925–35), Box 396, History of Seized Vessels File, National Archives, Washington, D.C.

249. Memorandum from Charles E. Rucker Jr. to Commander, Section Base 18, August 9, 1931, in ibid., Entry 291, Seized Vessels, Box 23, Eaglet File.

250. Memorandum from Cecil MacLeod to Commander, Section Base 18, August 9, 1931, in ibid.

251. "Rum Boat Burns," *Boston Globe*, August 10, 1931, 3.

252. "Two of Eaglet's Seamen Wounded," 1. The *Providence Journal* also reported that the explosion had blown three men overboard. The newspaper added, "They were picked up by the Coast Guardsmen, who boarded the flaming hulk and removed the other four men later, while a steamer stood by ready to lend aid." No other newspaper reported that three men were blown off the boat.

253. Coast Guard telegram, August 8, 1931, Coast Guard Records, RG 26, Entry 291, Seized Vessels, Box 23, Eaglet file, National Archives, Washington, D.C.

254. "Two in Rum Boat Crew Are Jailed," *Providence Journal*, March 25, 1932, 22.

255. "Two of Eaglet's Seamen Wounded," 1.

256. For information on the chase and sinking of *Eaglet*, see various reports and memoranda, dated August 8–10, 1931, Coast Guard Records, RG 26, Entry 291, Seized Vessels, Box 23, Eaglet File, National Archives, Washington, D.C.; "Rum Boat Eaglet Sunk in Flames," *Providence Journal*, August 9, 1931, 1; "Two of Eaglet's Seamen Wounded," 1; "Rum Boat Burns," 1 and 3; "Crew of Eaglet Held," *Boston Globe*, August 11, 1931, 28; "Men Jailed in Lieu of Total Bail," *Newport Mercury*, August 14, 1932, 6; *United States v. Davidson*, 63 F.2d 9 (First Circuit Court of Appeals, 1933).

257. "Men Jailed in Lieu of Total Bail," 6; "Liberty Granted 7 Men Under Bail of $25,000 in Rum Yacht Sinking," *Brooklyn (NY) Citizen*, August 10, 1931, 1 (UPI report).

258. *United States v. Davison*, 50 F.2d 517 (First Circuit Court of Appeals, 1931).

259. "Bond of Sunk Rum Boat Eaglet Ordered Paid at Providence," *Boston Globe*, November 5, 1931, 2.

260. See "Seven Convicted as Rum-Runners," *Providence Journal*, March 22, 1932, 26; "Machine Gun Used Too Freely by Coast Guard to Stop Rum Runners, Federal Judge Asserts," *Cincinnati Enquirer*, March 22, 1932, 12 (AP report); "Coast Guard Use of Machine Gun Hit," *Boston Globe*, March 21, 1932, 9.

Chapter 15

261. See *Ships Documents of Rhode Island*, vol. 2, 125. Gaul was also reported as owning the vessel in June 1932, ibid. See also "Nola's, Mitzi Crews Are Given Hearings," *Providence Journal*, December 20, 1932, 7.

262. Officer-in-Charge, *CG-2343*, to Commander, Third District, July 5, 1931, Coast Guard Records, RG 26, Entry 291, Seized Vessels, Box 56, Mitzi File, National Archives, Washington, D.C.; *Gaul v. U.S.*, 62 F.2d 559 (First Circuit Court of Appeals, 1933).

263. E-mail from Irving Sheldon to Christian McBurney, August 28, 2017 (author's collection).

264. Officer-in-Charge, *CG-2343*, to Commander, Third District, September 3, 1931, Coast Guard Records, RG 26, Entry 291, Seized Vessels, Box 56, Mitzi File, National Archives, Washington, D.C.

265. Commandant Billard to Senator Felix Hebert, October 24, 1931, in ibid.

266. "Talcott Attacks Billard's Story," *Evening Bulletin* (Providence, Rhode Island), October 28, 1931, 12; see also "Talcott Charges Denied by Billard," *Evening Bulletin* (Providence, Rhode Island), October 28, 1931.

267. B.M. Griswell, Acting Commandant, to Brenton Point Station, undated [sometime in October 1931], Coast Guard Records, RG 26, Entry 291, Seized Vessels, Box 56, Mitzi File, National Archives, Washington, D.C. The first page of this memorandum is missing from the files.

268. Commandant to Commander, Third District, October 26, 1931, in ibid.

269. A.G. Ramstad to Commander, Section Base 4, October 7, 1931, in ibid., Entry 283A, Scope of Operations, Box 1225, CG-290 File.

Chapter 16

270. Report of Violations, February 15, 1925, Coast Guard Records, RG 26, Entry 291, Seized Vessels, Box 69, Rhode Island File, National Archives, Washington, D.C.

271. Intelligence Memorandum, October 29, 1927, in ibid.

272. For information on the capture of *Rhode Island*, see Coast Guard telegram from Commander, Section Base 18, October 7, 1931, ibid, Seized Vessels, Box 69, Rhode Island File, in ibid.; "Liquor-Laden Speed Boat Sunk," *Boston Globe*, October 7, 1931, 4; "Five Rescued as Rum Ship Sinks," *Evening News* (Harrisburg, Pennsylvania), October 7, 1931, 10 (International News Service report); "Rum-Runners Sink Vessel Under Fire," *Rutland (VT) Daily Herald*, October 8, 1931, 2 (AP report); "Rum Craft Is Sunk," *Boston Globe*, October 8, 1931, 9.

273. "Rum Craft Is Sunk," 9.

274. For information on *Overland* and its January 1931 capture, see *Ships Documents of Rhode Island*, vol. 2, 140; *United States v. Corriveau*, 56 F.2d 361 (1st Cir. Ct. App. February 25, 1932); "Preliminary Trial Set for February 10," *Newport Mercury*, January 30, 1931, 1; "Power Boat Captured off Seaconnett Dock, R.I.," *Lancaster (PA) New Era*, January 27, 1931, 2 (UPI report).

275. Officer-in-Charge, *CG-402*, to Commander, Section Base 4, October 23, 1931, Coast Guard Records, RG 26, Entry 283A, Scope of Operations, Box 1226, CG-402 File, National Archives, Washington, D.C.

276. "Vanishes from Boat," *Boston Globe*, October 27, 1931, 3; "Coast Guard Fired on Fleeing Boat," *Providence Journal*, October 28, 1931, 2.

277. For Manuel and John Goulart likely being brothers, see note 77.

278. Seized Boats Assigned to the Coast Guard, 1925–35, 616, Coast Guard Records, RG 26, Entry 283A, History of Seized Boats (1925–35), Box 396, History of Seized Vessels File, National Archives, Washington, D.C.; "Rum Ship Forfeiture Libels Arc Filed," *Providence Journal*, February 16, 1932, 6.

279. For the chase and capture of *Je T'Aime*, see Memorandum, Commander, Section Base 18, to Commander, Eastern Division, November 12, 1931, Coast Guard Records, RG 26, Entry 291, Seized Vessels, Box 39, *Je T'Aime* File, National Archives, Washington, D.C.; "Rum Boat Seized, Seven Men Held," *Providence Journal*, November 13, 1931, 3; "Machine-Gun Fire Halts Rum Runner," *Boston Globe*, November 12, 1931, 10; "Capture Rum Vessel," *North Adams (MA) Transcript*, November 12, 1931, 31 (AP report).

280. Memorandum from Commander, Eastern Division, to All Units, Eastern Division, August 12, 1931, Coast Guard Records, RG 26, Entry 291, Seized Vessels, Nola File, National Archives, Washington, D.C.

281. Report of Violations, December 18, 1931, in ibid.; Currier, "Let's Raise a Glass to Prohibition."

282. Caption for photograph, *Evening News* (District of Columbia), October 7, 1924, 22; see also "Armored Rum Runner Is Caught by Coast Guard," *Altoona (PA) Tribune*, September 19, 1925, 2 (boat's four occupants escaped injury from machine gun fire by huddling in the pilothouse protected by bulletproof glass) (AP report); "Piracy and Murder in Rum-Running," *Boston Globe*, December 13, 1926, 12 (Canadian officials testify that U.S. rumrunners in Puget Sound are using high-speed vessels that have steel armor-plated sides).

283. The description of the taking of *Nola* is primarily from various incident reports, dated December 19, 1931, by the commanders and other crew members of *CG-813*, *CG-405* and *CG-2297*, Coast Guard Records, RG 26, Entry 291, Seized Vessels, Box 59, Nola File, National Archives, Washington, D.C.; see also transcript of Investigation of Special Agent G.W. O'Keefe, Customs Service, in connection with the Seizure of the Speed Boat "Nola," December 19, 1931, in ibid., Entry 283A, Scope of Operations, Box 1226, CG-813 File.

284. See www.ancestry.com (search 1940 census for Seraphine Nunes of New Bedford, Massachusetts).

285. For information on *Nola* and its capture from newspapers, see "Coast Guard Guns Sink Rum-Runner," *Boston Globe*, December 19, 1931, 1; "Crews of Rum-Runners Held at New London," *Boston Globe*, December 19, 1931, 16 (AP report); "Capture Armed Rum Speedboat," *Burlington (VT) Daily News*, December 19, 1931, 1 (AP report); "Four Coast Guard Ships Sink Liquor Boat After Chase," *News Journal* (Wilmington, Delaware), December 19, 1931, 17; "Coast Guard Guns Fell 3 of Crew," *Baltimore Sun*, December 20, 1931, 2.

Chapter 17

286. "Rhode Island Convention to Vote Repeal Monday," *Boston Globe*, May 3, 1933, 14; "All Rhode Island Votes for Repeal," *Boston Globe*, May 9, 1933, 20; *Proceedings of the Constitutional Convention*, 19.

287. "Admiral Billard, Rum Row's Foe, Dies," *New York Times*, May 18, 1932, 21.

288. Eden, "Wet Goods in the Water States," 9

289. For information on the seizure of *Kelble*, see various memoranda from C. MacLeod and other crew members of *CG-813*, March 5, 1932, Coast Guard Records, RG 26, Entry 291, Seized Vessels, Box 44, Kelble File, National Archives, Washington, D.C.; Memorandum, Commander, Section Base 18, to Commandant, March 7, 1932, in ibid.; "New $75,000 Yacht and Liquor Seized," *Boston Globe*, March 5, 1932, 1; "Rum

Boat Crew Held in $13,500," *Providence Journal*, Mary 6, 1932, 17; "Coast Guards Clash with Rum Runners Early Today," *Daily Times* (New Philadelphia, Ohio), March 5, 1932, 3 (UPI report); "Rum Boat Seized After Battle of Gas and Bullets," *Chicago Tribune*, March 6, 1932, 7. After *Kelble* was released on a bond, a Coast Guard crew from the Brenton Point Coast Guard Station in Newport found *Kelble* stranded on a reef at Bonnett Shores in Narragansett. The Coast Guard found no liquor on board, and *Kelble*'s crew refused any assistance. "Suspected Rum Runner of Boston Runs Aground," *Boston Globe*, April 25, 1932, 4. Harry Johnson's true name was likely Lief Nelson (probably originally Nielson) of 24 Balcom Street of Providence. He was sentenced to jail, along with the boat's master and another crew member. "Three of Rum Vessel's Crew Jailed and Fined," *Providence Journal*, May 12, 1932, 24.

290. "Two Rum Runners are Taken in Bay," *Newport Mercury*, June 3, 1932, 6.

291. A.C. Cornell to Commander, Section Base 4, June 29, 1930, Coast Guard Records, RG 26, Entry 283A, Scope of Operations, Box 1225, CG-290 File, National Archives, Washington, D.C.; see also Seized Boats Assigned to the Coast Guard, 1925–35, 605, in ibid., Entry 283A, History of Seized Boats (1925–35), Box 396, History of Seized Vessels File.

292. "Two Rum Craft Captured in Bay," *Providence Journal*, June 1, 1932, 12. The article on the shooting incident was covered several days later by the *Newport* Mercury; its coverage mirrored that of the *Providence Journal* and the Associated Press report. See "Two Rum Runners are Taken in Bay," 6.

293. "Four Guard Boats Capture Rum Craft," *Lewiston (ME) Evening Journal*, May 31, 1932, 1 (AP report).

294. For information on the captures of *Idle Hour* and *Mitzi*, see Officer-in-Charge, *CG-822*, to Commander, Section Base 4, May 31, 1932, Coast Guard Records, RG 26, Entry 291, Seized Vessels, Box 56, Mitzi File, National Archives, Washington, D.C.; "Two Rum Boats Taken After Chase," *Boston Globe*, May 31, 1932, 2; "Two Rum Runners Are Taken in Bay," 6; "Shots Riddle Liquor Craft," *Fitchburg (MA) Sentinel*, May 31, 1932, 1 (AP report); "Three Rum Runners Captured," *New London Day*, May 31, 1932, 1; Eden, "Wet Goods in the Water States," 32 (237 bullets).

295. Manuel Goulart was reported as the captain of *Idle Hour* both in May 1930 and May 1933. Mary Rittenhouse was reported as its owner in May 1928 and May 1930. After the rumrunner's capture, by May 1933, ownership had been transferred to Mandel Schechter of Providence. See *Ships Documents of Rhode Island*, vol. 2, 41. For Manuel and John Goulart likely being brothers, see note 77, and for Rittenhouse being the wife of gang leader Carl Rettich, see main text accompanying note 78.

296. Memorandum from Arthur B. Gibbs, May 31, 1932, Coast Guard Records, RG 26, Entry 291, Seized Vessels, Box 37, Idle Hour File, National Archives, Washington, D.C.

297. "Speedy Rum Boat Captured After Spectacular Race," *Evening Bulletin* (Providence), May 31, 1932, 1; "Machine Gun Fire Heard Along the Bay," *Providence Journal*, May 31, 1932, 1; "Two Rum Craft Captured in Bay," June 1, 1932, *Providence Journal*, 12.

298. *New London Day* article, undated, Coast Guard Records, RG 26, Entry 291, Seized Vessels, Box 56, Mitzi File, National Archives, Washington, D.C.

299. "Two Liquor Boats Captured After Exchange of Fire," *St. Louis Post-Dispatch*, May 31, 1932, 12.

300. Officer-in-Charge, *CG-833*, to Commander, Section Base 18, August 8, 1932, Coast Guard Records, RG 26, Entry 283A, Scope of Operations, Box 1226, CG-833 File, National Archives, Washington, D.C.

301. For the chase and capture of *Mitzi*, see Officer-in-Charge, *CG-808*, to Commander, Base 4, October 18, 1933, in ibid., Entry 291, Seized Vessels, Box 56, Mitzi File; "Notorious Rum Runner Captured in Spectacular Gun Fight in Bay," *Providence Journal*, October 17, 1933, 1.

302. Commander, Base 4, to Commandant, November 3, 1933, Coast Guard Records, RG 26, Entry 291, Seized Vessels, Box 56, Mitzi File, National Archives, Washington, D.C.

BIBLIOGRAPHY

Original Sources

Christian McBurney Collection, Kensington, MD
    Eden, Charles H. "Wet Goods in the Water States." Unpublished manuscript and undated (text indicates manuscript was written in the summer of 1932).
John Taft Collection, Newport, RI
    Various copies of Coast Guard Records from the National Archives
National Archives, Building 1, Washington, D.C.
    Records of the U.S. Coast Guard, RG 26
        General Correspondence, 1910–41
            Correspondence, 1920–35
                Boards of Inquiry—Units Only, Entry 283A
                Scope of Operations, Entry 283A
                Scope of Operations, Entry 82A
                Seized Vessels Case Files, 1926–35, Entry 291* (entry numbers are those on current boxes, although they are scheduled to be changed soon)
National Archives, Building 2, Silver Spring, MD
    Photography Division
Rhode Island State Archives, Providence, RI
    Journal of the Senate, State of Rhode Island, 1917–19

Newspapers

Boston Globe
Brooklyn Daily Eagle
Daily News (Brooklyn, NY)
Evening Bulletin (Providence, RI)
Hartford Courant
Newport Mercury
New London Day
New York Times
North Adams (MA) Transcript
Providence Journal
St. Louis Globe-Democrat
Times Union (Brooklyn, NY)
Washington Post

Also including numerous other newspapers nationwide, primarily used to obtain Associated Press (AP) and United Press International (UPI) reports.

Original Sources, Published

Anthony, Joseph. *The Best News Stories of 1923*. Boston, MA: Small, Maynard & Company, 1924.

Proceedings of the Constitutional Convention of the State of Rhode Island Held on the Eighth Day of May, A.D. 1933, as Provided for in Chapter 2014 of the Public Laws of Rhode Island. Providence, RI: Oxford Press, 1933. Copy in the Rhode Island State Archives.

Register of the Commissioned and Warrant Officers and Cadets, and Ships and Stations of the United States Coast Guard, January 1, 1929. Washington, D.C.: U.S. Government Printing Office, 1929.

Register of the Commissioned and Warrant Officers and Cadets, and Ships and Stations of the United States Coast Guard, February 1, 1933. Washington, D.C.: U.S. Government Printing Office, 1933.

The Report of the National Convention of the Woman's National Committee for Law Enforcement, Held in Hotel Washington, April 10–11, 1924. Boston, MA: Woman's National Committee for Law Enforcement, 1924.

Ships Documents of Rhode Island. Vol. 2. Providence, RI: Work Projects Administration, 1941.

U.S. Coast Guard. *Instructions, Customs, Navigation, and Motor-Boat Laws and Duties of Boarding Officers, 1923.* Washington, D.C.: Government Printing Office, 1924.

United States Coast Guard Law Enforcement: Hearings Before the Committee on Interstate and Foreign Commerce, House of Representatives, Sixty-Eighth Congress, First Session, on H.R. 6815, a Bill of Authorize a Temporary Increase of the Coast Guard for Law Enforcement. Washington, D.C.: Government Printing Office, 1924.

Federal Court Cases

The following cases are in *Federal Reporter*, Second Series, vols. 1–999. St. Paul, MN: West Publishing, 1924–93.

Crowninshield Shipbuilding Co. v. United States, 54 F.2d 879 (First Circuit Court of Appeals, 1932).

Gaul v. U.S., 62 F.2d 559 (First Circuit Court of Appeals, 1933).

The Herreshoff, 6 F.2d 414 (First Circuit Court of Appeals, 1925).

United States v. Davidson, 63 F.2d 9 (First Circuit Court of Appeals, 1933).

Secondary Sources

Allen, Everett S. *Black Ships: Rumrunners of Prohibition.* Boston, MA: Little, Brown & Company, 1965.

Burbank, Calef M. "The Noble Experiment." *Rhode Island Magazine* (1969): H-162-H-164.

Canney, Donald. *Rum War: The U.S. Coast Guard and Prohibition.* Washington, D.C.: U.S. Coast Guard, 1990.

Conley, Patrick T. *Democracy in Decline: Rhode Island's Constitutional Development, 1776–1841.* East Providence: Rhode Island Publications Society, 2019.

Eskridge, William N., Jr., Phillip P. Frickey, Elizabeth Garrett and James J. Brudney. *Cases on Legislation and Regulation: Statues and the Creation of Public Policy.* 5th ed. St. Paul, MN: West Academic Publishing, 2014.

Jackson, Paul, and Clint Robinson. "Pirate." In *The Salt Book: Lobstering, Sea Moss Pudding, Stone Walls, Rum Running, Maple Syrup, Snowshoes, and Other Yankee Doings.* Edited by Pamela Wood. Garden City, NJ: Anchor Press, 1977.

Jacquart, Rolland R. "Running It In: A True Story of the U.S. Coast Guard." *Our Navy* 20, no. 7 (August 1, 1926): 3–42.

Lerner, Michael A. *Dry Manhattan: Prohibition in New York City.* Cambridge, MA: Harvard University Press, 2007.

Luconi, Stefano. *The Italian-American Vote in Providence, Rhode Island, 1916–1948.* Madison, NJ: Fairleigh Dickinson University Press, 2004.

Okrent, Daniel. *Last Call: The Rise and Fall of Prohibition*. New York: Scribner, 2010.

Sterne, Evelyn. *Ballots and Bibles: Ethnic Politics and the Catholic Church in Providence*. Ithaca, NY: Cornell University Press, 2004.

Turley, Hazel B. *Narragansett Brewing Company*. Images of America series. Charleston, SC: Arcadia Publishing, 2007.

Willoughby, Malcolm F. *Rum War at Sea*. Washington, D.C.: Government Printing Office, 1964.

Unpublished Secondary Sources

Ancestry.com. Various entries.

Babcock, Judith A. "Let Them Have It!" Draft manuscript and undated (appears to be around 2000). In Christian McBurney Collection, Kensington, MD.

Casey, Eric. "Little Rhody's Big Thirst: Rhode Island and Alcohol Prohibition, 1919–1934." Undergraduate paper for Professor Mather, University of Rhode Island, April 17, 2014, available online at https://www.scribd.com/document/224360711/Little-Rhody-s-Big-Thirst-Alcohol-Prohibition-in-Rhode-Island-1919-1934.

Currier, Geoff. "Let's Raise a Glass to Prohibition, It's the 100th Anniversary of the Great Experiment and the Vineyard Was Right in the Thick of It." *MV Times*, October 8, 2020. Accessed at www.mvtimes.com/2020/10/08/lets-raise-a-glass-prohibition.

DeSimone, Russell J. "Rhode Island's 19th Century Experiments with Prohibition." Online Review of Rhode Island History. smallstatebighistory.com/rhode-islands-19th-century-experiments-with-prohibition.

Find A Grave. Various entries.

Larson, Aaron. "What Are Homicide and Murder." Expert Law. https://www.expertlaw.com/library/criminal-law/what-are-homicide-and-murder.

Military Factory. "The Famous Lewis Gun Was Used in All Manner of Ways throughout World War 1 and World War 2." July 31, 2019. https://www.militaryfactory.com/smallarms/detail.php?smallarms_id=765#:~:text=At%20its%20core%2C%20the%20Lewis,German%207.92x57mm%20Mauser%20round.

Naval History and Heritage Command. "Sovereign II (SP-170)." https://www.history.navy.mil/content/history/nhhc/research/histories/ship-histories/danfs/s/sovereign-ii.html.

New England Historical Society. "How Narragansett Beer Survived Prohibition (But Still Couldn't Escape the Government)." www.newenglandhistoricalsociety.com/how-narragansett-beer-survived-prohibition-but-still-couldnt-escape-the-government.

INDEX

ABOUT THE AUTHOR

After growing up in Kingston, Rhode Island, and attending Brown University, Christian became an attorney in Washington, D.C., and raised a family in Kensington, Maryland. Christian and his wife have a second home in West Kingston. He is the author of four books on Rhode Island and the American Revolution, most recently *Dark Voyage: An American Privateer's War on Britain's African Slave Trade* (Westholme, 2022). Earlier books include *The Rhode Island Campaign: The First French and American Operation of the Revolutionary War* (Westholme, 2011), *Kidnapping the Enemy: The Special Operations to Capture Generals Charles Lee & Richard Prescott* (Westholme, 2014) and *Spies in Revolutionary Rhode Island* (The History Press, 2014). He was also the lead coauthor of *World War II Rhode Island* (The History Press, 2017) and *Untold Stories from World War II Rhode Island* (The History Press, 2019); these two books cover the incredible story of what happened in the state during the war. To learn more about his books, visit www.christianmcburney.com. Christian is also the founder, publisher and chief editor of a leading Rhode Island history blog at www.smallstatebighistory.com.